Demographic and Socioeconomic Outcomes Across the Indigenous Australian Lifecourse

Evidence from the 2006 Census

Demographic and Socioeconomic Outcomes Across the Indigenous Australian Lifecourse

Evidence from the 2006 Census

Nicholas Biddle and Mandy Yap

ANU
THE AUSTRALIAN NATIONAL UNIVERSITY
E PRESS

Centre for Aboriginal Economic Policy Research
College of Arts and Social Sciences
The Australian National University, Canberra

Research Monograph No. 31
2010

ANU
E PRESS

Published by ANU E Press
The Australian National University
Canberra ACT 0200, Australia
Email: anuepress@anu.edu.au
This title is also available online at: http://epress.anu.edu.au/c31_citation.html

National Library of Australia
Cataloguing-in-Publication entry

Author: Biddle, Nicholas.

Title: Demographic and socioeconomic outcomes across the indigenous
          Australian lifecourse : evidence from the 2006 census /
          Nicholas Biddle and Mandy Yap.

ISBN: 9781921862021 (pbk.) 9781921862038 (ebook)

Notes: Includes bibliographical references.

Subjects: Aboriginal Australians--Social conditions.
          Aboriginal Australians--Economic conditions.
          Economic forecasting--Australia.
          Social prediction--Australia.

Other Authors/Contributors:
          Yap, Mandy.
          Dewey Number: 362.849915

Cover design by ANU E Press.

Contents

List of Tables

List of Figures

Foreword

Across almost all standard indicators, the Indigenous population has worse outcomes than the non-Indigenous population. Despite the abundance of statistics and a plethora of government reports on Indigenous outcomes, there is very little information on how Indigenous disadvantage accumulates or is mitigated through time at the individual level. The limited research that is available seems to point to two conclusions. Firstly, that Indigenous disadvantage starts from a very early age and widens over time. Secondly, that the timing of key life events including education attendance, marriage, childbirth and retirement occur on average at different ages for the Indigenous compared to the non-Indigenous population. To target policy interventions that will contribute to meeting the Council of Australian Governments' (COAG) Closing the Gap targets, it is important to better understand and acknowledge these differences between the Indigenous and non-Indigenous lifecourse, as well as the factors that lead to variation within the Indigenous population.

This research is part of the CAEPR Indigenous Population Project, sponsored by the Ministerial Council for Aboriginal and Torres Strait Islander Affairs (MCATSIA). The core aim of the project is to further explore the dynamics and regional geography of Indigenous population and socioeconomic change. The research program recognises that there is a strong interaction between demography and socioeconomic change. A number of research outputs from the Population Project have demonstrated a relationship between lifecourse patterns and regional change. This monograph extends this work by looking at a much greater range of individual variables using a new source of quantitative data, the 5 per cent Census Sample File from the 2006 Census of Population and Housing.

The topics covered involve complex social issues facing Indigenous Australians and the authors allude to some of these within the limitations set by available data. The material presented is unapologetically technical in nature as it forms a part of CAEPR's long term commitment to robust evaluation and analysis of data collections. In this endeavour we have maintained a productive and collaborative relationship with the Australian Bureau of Statistics (ABS) and we recognise their dedication to improving future statistical collections. A key finding is the need for a new structure for Indigenous data collection on order to track individual outcomes through time. The authors argue for a new National Closing the Gaps Survey (NCGS) that will not only allow yearly progress towards government targets to be assessed, but also a greater understanding of the timing and determinants of key life events.

John Taylor
Director, CAEPR

Abbreviations and acronyms

ABS	Australian Bureau of Statistics
AIHW	Australian Institute of Health and Welfare
ANZSCO	Australian and New Zealand Standard Classification of Occupations
ATSIC	Aboriginal and Torres Strait Islander Commission
CDEP	Community Development Employment Projects (Program)
COAG	Council of Australian Governments
CSF	Census Sample File
DEEWR	Department of Education, Employment and Workplace Relations
ERP	estimated resident population
FaHCSIA	Department of Families, Housing, Community Services and Indigenous Affairs
HILDA	Household Income and Labour Dynamics in Australia (survey)
HREOC	Human Rights and Equal Opportunity Commission
NATSIHS	National Aboriginal and Torres Strait Islander Health Survey
NATSISS	National Aboriginal and Torres Strait Islander Social Survey
NCGS	National Closing the Gap Survey
SCRGSP	Steering Committee for the Review of Government Service Provision
VET	vocational education and training

Acknowledgements

The research reported in this monograph was conducted with financial support from the Ministerial Council for Aboriginal and Torres Strait Islander Affairs (MCATSIA) through the Indigenous Population Project based at the Centre for Aboriginal Economic Policy Research, in the College of Arts and Social Sciences, at The Australian National University. The results of part of this research project were presented at a seminar at the University of Canberra and we thank the participants at the seminar for their constructive feedback; we are also grateful to MCATSIA and its various State and Federal stakeholders for useful comments on this research. We are especially indebted to Gillian Cosgrove for preparation of the graphics, layout and final document and Hilary Bek for expert editorial advice. Last but not least, we would like to thank the two external referees for this volume, Dr Anne Daly from the University of Canberra and Dr Martin Cooke from the University of Waterloo, for their generous time in providing constructive feedback.

1. The Indigenous lifecourse: Introduction and overview

Introduction

Across almost all standard indicators including employment, education, housing, income and health, the Indigenous population has worse outcomes than the non-Indigenous population (Steering Committee for the Review of Government Service Provision (SCRGSP) 2009). In his apology to the stolen generations in early 2008, Australia's then Prime Minister Kevin Rudd outlined a 'new partnership on closing the gap'. The focus of this partnership, from the government's point of view, was a number of explicit targets aimed at eliminating or at least substantially reducing these disparities between Indigenous and non-Indigenous Australians.

The statistics on Indigenous disadvantage are well-known by both researchers and policy-makers. Furthermore, keen attention is paid to how the relevant outcomes are trending through time with a major report to parliament every two years on 'Overcoming Indigenous Disadvantage' (SCRGSP 2009) as well as a smaller report every year that documents progress made against the six Closing the Gap targets (Department of Families, Housing, Community Services and Indigenous Affairs (FaHCSIA) 2009). Despite the abundance of statistics and a plethora of government reports on the degree of disadvantage faced by Indigenous Australians, there is very little information on how Indigenous disadvantage accumulates or is mitigated through time at the individual level. Particular outcomes for the Indigenous population as a whole may be getting better or worse through time, but whether this represents substantial change for individual Indigenous Australians is not known. Furthermore, research on other population groups would suggest a correlation between disadvantaged circumstances as a child and poor outcomes as an adult. However, the extent to which this holds for the Indigenous population is unclear. It is perhaps not surprising that there is a dearth of research on these issues, as the longitudinal data sets that are increasingly being mined for such information on the total population do not contain a sufficient sample for detailed analysis of the Indigenous population. The Household Income and Labour Dynamics in Australia (HILDA) survey and the Longitudinal Study of Australian Children both have small Indigenous samples.[1] The Longitudinal Study of Indigenous Children has the potential to provide some information on the developmental pathways of two cohorts of children aged 6–18 months and $3\frac{1}{2}$–$4\frac{1}{2}$ years respectively. However this study is only in its infancy, with the most relevant longitudinal information still a number of years away.

Although a relative lack of longitudinal information on the Indigenous population precludes answering a number of key research questions, there is much that can still be learned from a detailed analysis of single or repeated cross-sections. In particular, by focusing on the current age distribution of outcomes, it is possible to gain insight into the timing of key life stages and the extent to which they differ for the Indigenous compared to the non-Indigenous population. Furthermore, by looking at the demographic and socioeconomic correlates of these outcomes and whether they vary by age and/or Indigenous status, it may be possible to identify key points of policy intervention across the Indigenous lifecourse.

Analysis of the lifecourse

In all human societies, individuals occupy a multitude of interlinked but chronologically overlapping roles. Defining the lifecourse as 'a sequence of socially defined events and roles that the individual enacts over time' (Giele and Elder 1998: 22), there are a number of common pathways that a person might take. Within the economic sphere in a modern Western society, an individual might start off as a dependent child, enter preschool, complete infants or primary then secondary school, undertake some post-compulsory training or study, enter the workforce, and eventually retire. Parallel to their economic life, the same person might get married, have children, then become grandparents. While this description may seem typical, it is far from universal, with the details and timing of major life events and roles varying substantially. In terms of education, some people will have minimal interaction with post-compulsory schooling, where others will spend their late teens and early twenties undertaking university study. Another group will engage with formal education as a mature-age student only. The different permutations with regards to marriage, fertility decisions and child-rearing are greater still.

There are a number of factors that impact on the specifics of a person's lifecourse. The most obvious source of variation is gender. While there has been considerable convergence in terms of lifetime employment over the last few decades (Daly 2000), the impact of childbirth and family formation is still

---

1 For more information on these surveys go to http://www.melbourneinstitute.com/hilda/ and http://www.aifs.gov.au/growingup/ respectively.

much stronger on average for females compared to males. More females leave the labour force after becoming parents and a greater proportion undertake part-time work on their return (Baxter 2005). Another source of variation in the lifecourse is socioeconomic background or social class. By definition, those from lower socioeconomic backgrounds start off their lives in households with access to fewer resources and poorer employment opportunities. However, when those children themselves grow up, they are more likely to have children at a relatively young age, are less likely to undertake and complete post-compulsory education, and have more precarious employment and income (Caldas 1993). Clearly, there is no single lifecourse. Rather, there are multiple events and experiences that, when combined, define the particular path that each individual's life takes. A lifecourse framework thus provides a perspective for looking at individual experiences, how different factors influence variation in these experiences, as well as the institutional and policy frameworks that shape a person's constraints and opportunities.

The idea of cumulative advantage and disadvantage makes the life course a useful framework for helping to determine the influence of earlier life events on later life and the interconnectedness of the various stages (O'Rand 1996). Some of these variations across individuals such as socioeconomic status prevail over the life time. There are four key insights from lifecourse analysis that are of particular relevance for this study – history, linked lives, institutions and human agency. While they may seem obvious, they are often overlooked when analysing Indigenous disadvantage and setting Indigenous policy.

Firstly, people's lives are shaped by the social and environment conditions in which they are born and exposed to (Elder 1994). It is clear that the circumstances of a person's childhood matters for the options and constraints that they face in adolescence and adulthood. Even at birth, an Indigenous infant already faces different circumstances. They are more likely to have low birth weight and face higher risks of mortality (Australian Institute of Health and Welfare (AIHW) 2008). They are also less likely to participate in early childhood education (Biddle 2010). These factors combined are likely to have long-term impacts over the lifecourse. The individual life course reflects the times in which the individuals live. The most obvious example is the labeling of birth cohorts such as baby boomers or generation Y to reflect the sort of labour market, social norms and lifestyles individuals in the respective birth cohorts are born into. Another example is the changing gender roles in society and the workplace.

Secondly, lifecourse analysis reinforces the fact that individual lives and the subdomains within their lives are inexplicably linked. This is most obvious when one considers the influence of a parent's lifecourse on that of their children, but it is also true when it comes to siblings, peers and neighbours (Edwards 2005). Putting these two together, it is not surprising that Hérault and Kalb (2009) find a significant correlation between parental and child employment in Australia (especially for males), even after controlling for the intergenerational education correlation. The 'linked lives' perspective is one that is particularly pertinent to the Indigenous population, given the social structures and kinship networks within Indigenous societies which provide an important source of support and care giving. The interconnectedness between the domains of work and education, family formation and health at the individual level is also reflected in the life course concept. The timing and ordering of the transitions between these domains produce differences in life pathways for the individual within a birth cohort. Early parenthood for Indigenous mothers for instance inevitably alters the course of education to work transition as well as their later life status

The third insight from lifecourse analysis is that institutions and policies can shape trajectories. A particularly relevant example of this for the Indigenous population is the forcible removal of children from their parents – known as the Stolen Generation in Australia (Human Rights and Equal Opportunity Commission (HREOC) 1997).[2] These policies have been shown to have long-lasting negative effects on the outcomes of those who were impacted directly, as well as their families. On the other hand, the provision of high quality public preschooling has been shown to have enduring, positive effects on the behavioural outcomes of those who attend (Schweinhart et al. 2005). More recently, the policy of increasing minimum school-leaving age in several jurisdictions could potentially alter education and work patterns.

The final insight from lifecourse analysis is the continued importance of human agency. While acknowledging the impact of early childhood, family and institutions, individuals continue to make decisions that have long-lasting impacts. Fertility, education and migration decisions can all shape a person's lifecourse (Elder 1999), as evidenced by falling fertility rates over the last two decades alongside increases in women's participation in education.

An Indigenous lifecourse?

While the implications of an ageing population have been researched widely, very little is known about the experiences of the Indigenous lifecourse. Research devoted to the lifecourse of Indigenous Australians is particularly important not only because of the public policy focus on this population but also because of its relatively young age profile compared to the rest of the population. This is

---

2   Cooke and McWhirter (2008) observe that Residential Schools in North America was a similar situation for the Canadian First Nations population.

demonstrated in Fig. 1.1, which gives the percentage of the Indigenous and non-Indigenous population by sex in each five-year age group (with all those 65 years and over grouped together).

Fig. 1.1 Age distribution of Indigenous and non-Indigenous Australians, 2006

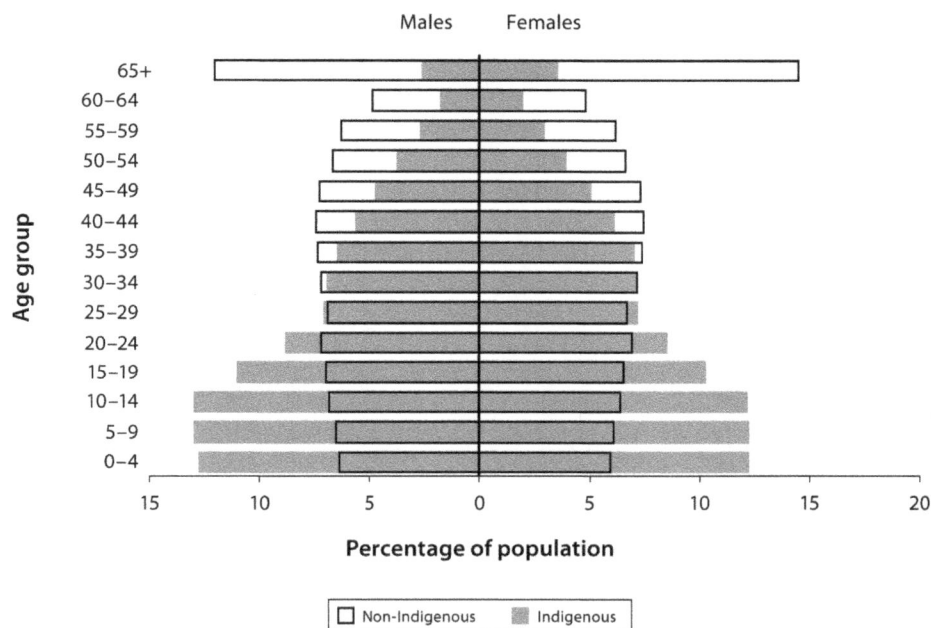

Source: Australian Bureau of Statistics (ABS) 2008b

For both males and females, each of the first four age groups contain 10 per cent or more of the Indigenous population. Putting these groups together with those aged 20–24 years, 56.9 per cent of the Indigenous population in 2006 is aged under 25 years. On the other hand, only 11.6 per cent of the Indigenous population is aged 50 years and over. Compared to this, the non-Indigenous population of Australia is highly skewed towards the upper end of the age distribution. Only 32.9 per cent of the population is aged under 25 years, compared to 31 per cent of the population aged 50 years and over.

The age distributions summarised in Fig. 1.1 highlight a potential gap in the focus and purpose of social and economic policy between the Indigenous and non-Indigenous populations. For the non-Indigenous population, policy is increasingly concerned with the effects and implications of ageing and retirement funding, as outlined in detail in the most recent Intergenerational Report (Commonwealth Treasury 2010). For Indigenous Australians on the other hand, the focus of social and economic policy remains fixed on the provision of education, training and entry into employment (SCRGSP 2009). Ultimately, the extent to which the outcomes of the young Indigenous population are brought into line with that of the non-Indigenous population will determine to a large degree the need for more expensive policy interventions and catch-up into the future. Those looking for work and raising children in 15–25 years time will be those in preschool, primary and secondary school now. This is made abundantly clear when one considers the population projections provided in Biddle and Taylor (2009). These are summarised in Fig. 1.2, which shows the Indigenous population in 2006, the projected population in 2031 and, in Fig. 1.3, the percentage of the total population that are projected to identify as being Indigenous in those two years. Results are presented separately for five policy-relevant age groups.

Fig. 1.2 Indigenous population, 2006 and 2031 (projection)

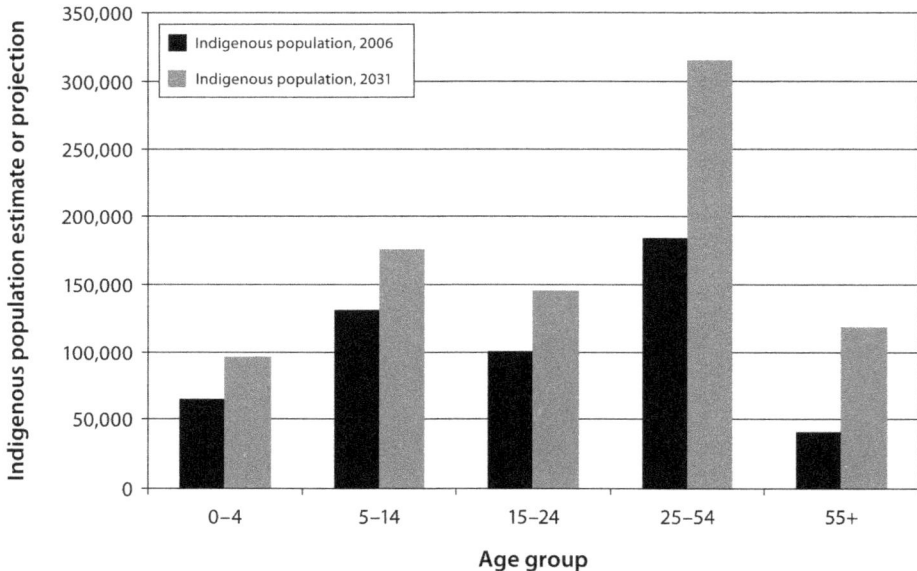

Source: Biddle and Taylor (2009)

Within a total projected increase for the Indigenous population as a whole from around 517 000 in 2006 to around 848 000 in 2031, Biddle and Taylor (2009) project large increases in the Indigenous population for all age groups. In raw terms and as a percentage of the total population, the entire Indigenous population is projected to grow rapidly over the period. However, particular age groups are projected to grow at a faster rate than others. The population of prime working age (25–54 years old) is projected to increase from around 183 000 in 2006 to around 315 000 in 2031. The population that are around retirement age or older (55 years and above) is projected to grow even faster still, almost tripling from around 40 000 in 2006 to around 118 000 in 2031.

Fig. 1.3 Share of total population who identify as being Indigenous, 2006 and 2031 (projection)

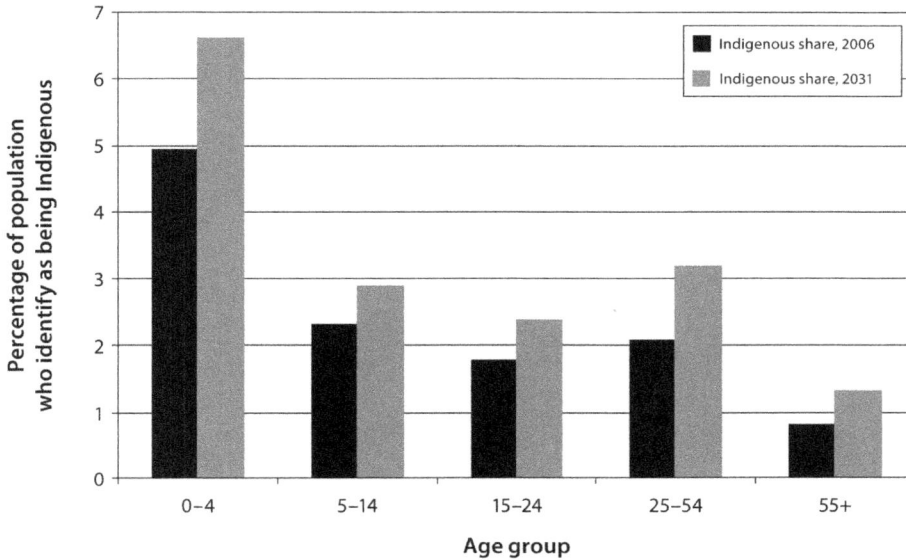

Source: Biddle and Taylor (2009)

While there is substantial diversity within the Indigenous population (as shown throughout this volume), it is clear that for most standard socioeconomic measures, the Indigenous population has worse outcomes than the non-Indigenous population (SCRGSP 2009). The question posed in this study is whether there are particular characteristics of the lifecourse that explain or are explained by this disadvantage. We know, for example, that Indigenous Australians are less likely to attend and complete education: the question is whether those who do undertake education do so at different stages in their lives. Similarly, we know that Indigenous Australians are less likely to be employed than the non-Indigenous population: the question is whether this difference is greater or smaller at particular life stages.

One key difference historically between Indigenous and non-Indigenous Australians is the importance placed on chronological age as a social marker. While birth year locates a person in time, social age locates roles within the social structure (Elder and Rockwell 1979). For the Indigenous population, lifecourse stages are events and transitions in life through which cultural obligations are met and rituals carried out. For example, at a period in life where Western education expects attendance at school and training to progress from primary through secondary, Aboriginal boys progress in stages to manhood with potentially quite different priorities and expectations (Taylor 2009: 122).

In addition, it is not uncommon for young Aboriginal females to experience motherhood during their teenage years, which means that their transition from school to work is often interrupted.

Another difference between the Australian Indigenous and non-Indigenous population is the particular familial and kinship structures. While the nuclear family of two parents and their children is cemented in Western European history and current government policy, a more fluid and contingent system continues to prevail in Indigenous culture and society (Morphy 2006). Indigenous households tend to consist of multiple generations and are compositionally complex in terms of who is considered kin (Finlayson, Daly and Smith 2000). Extended kin relations provide significant social support in childcare arrangements, providing care for their children as well as children of families within the network. Parallel to that, being a part of an extensive network means there are obligations and expectations of sharing of resources, both economic and social which underpin Aboriginal families and communities (Schwab and Liddle 1997).

There is diversity in which the Indigenous lifecourse is experienced. Human agency or the right to pursue the life which the individual desires plays an important role in the trajectories which the individual faces. While the individual is an active agent in the process shaping their lifecourse, cultural norms and expectations often bound the processes. Morphy (2007) gives the example of a youth who has to fulfil obligations expected of him as ritual expert and yet aspires to gain further Western educational qualifications. This is evidence of a constant conflict between cultural obligations and individual aspirations as Indigenous people move along their life pathways.

Geography also shapes the kind of lifecourse an individual faces. In Canada, findings suggest that the transition experiences of First Nations youth living on-reserve are markedly different to those living off-reserve (Taylor and Steinhauer 2008). Like in Canada, the majority of the Australia Indigenous population lives in cities and other large urban centres (Biddle 2009a). However, compared to the non-Indigenous population, Indigenous Australians are much more likely to reside in remote Australia. This is demonstrated in Fig. 1.4, which shows the percentage of the population across Australia who identify as being Indigenous (through the shading on the map) as well as the percentage of the total Indigenous population who live in that region (in brackets after the region name). Results are given for 37 Indigenous Regions, the least disaggregated level in the Australian Bureau of Statistics (ABS) Australian Indigenous Geographic Classification (ABS 2008a) based loosely on the earlier Aboriginal and Torres Strait Islander Commission (ATSIC) Regions.[3]

Fig. 1.4 Percentage of Indigenous Region population who identify as being Indigenous (shading) and percentage of total Indigenous population who live in that region (numbers), 2006

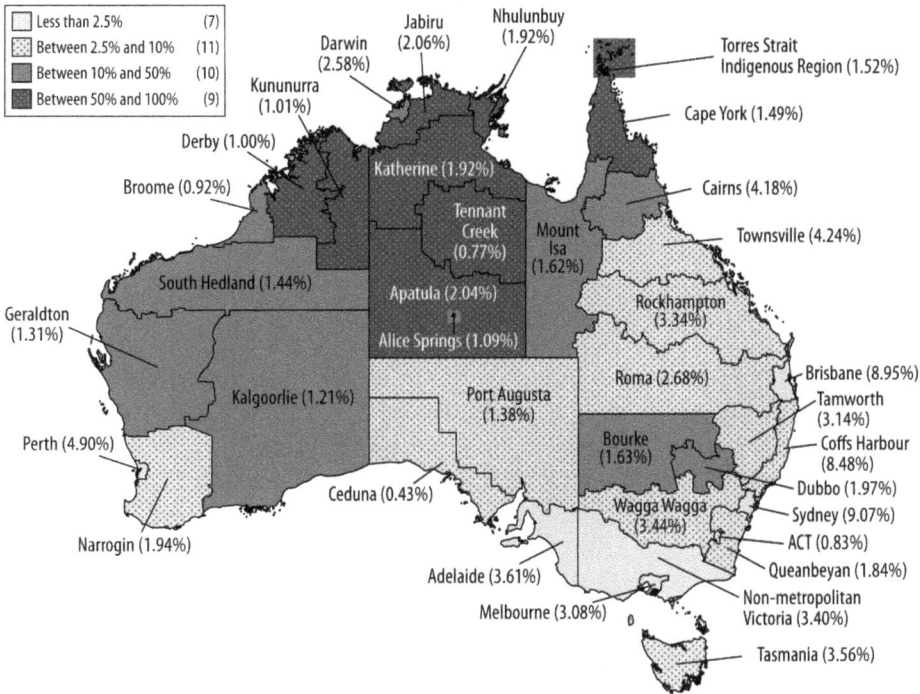

Source: Customised figure derived from the ABS 2006 Census of Population and Housing

One might expect that Indigenous people living in remote parts of Australia would have very different lifecourse patterns to Indigenous people living in major cities or regional centres, especially in terms of access to the more formal sectors of education and employment. An important element which is not necessarily unique to Indigenous Australians but forms a large part of Indigenous life is movement – both temporary and permanent – for ceremonial purposes, for accessing services and for maintaining the relationships which form part of the familial and kinship structures (Prout 2008). Just as it would be an oversimplification to say that there is a typical Australian lifecourse, a

---

3 ATSIC was established by the Australian Government in March 1990 a group of elected individuals with representation divided into regions; it was a key element of the Indigenous affairs administration and representation for 14 years. ATSIC was abolished in 2004.

homogeneous Indigenous lifecourse is also unrealistic. As this paper will show, there is significant variation within the Indigenous population, just as there is between Indigenous and non-Indigenous Australians. Nonetheless, this paper will also show that there are a number of policy-relevant patterns that are common for a number of Indigenous Australians.

A similar lifecourse approach has been used to look at Indigenous populations in Canada. Cooke and McWhirter (2008) investigated the applicability and usefulness of the lifecourse as a research framework for understanding Aboriginal inequality in Canada. Their findings suggest that Aboriginal peoples experience different events, with different timing and sequences from those experienced by the general Canadian population. They observed a pattern of increasing disadvantage over the lifecourse for Aboriginal Canadians, in particular in health status and the probability of having low income. This was largely attributed to the low levels of accumulation of human, social and financial resources. In Australia, the idea of using a lifecourse approach to analyse Indigenous inequality has not been explored to the extent it has been in Canada. However, the policies and frameworks which have been developed to reduce Indigenous disadvantage recognise at least implicitly the impact of cumulative disadvantage and the importance of key life stages and transitions. The Council of Australian Governments (COAG) Closing the Gap agenda, for example, has policies ranging from early childhood education and student participation to transition to employment and life expectancy. The Productivity Commission's Overcoming Indigenous Disadvantage Framework (SCRGSP 2009) more explicitly utilises a lifecourse perspective by considering outcomes from birth to adulthood across a range of indicators. All this in essence points to the usefulness of looking at the development of Indigenous lives using a lifecourse framework.

Longitudinal data allows the researcher to follow the processes in which individuals live their lives. Cross sectional data, on the other hand, can only point to age specific probabilities within a domain or set of domains. So, while the monograph highlights difference between a 30–34 year old and a 50–54 year old in 2006 (for example), how the characteristics of an individual Indigenous Australian changed over a 20-year period is not known. While the research is limited in that aspect, we make recommendations on how the current data collection mechanisms could be extended to allow the experience of various similar age cohorts to be compared over time. Nonetheless, the life course framework provides a useful starting point for connecting together the various stages in the life span with the view that advantage and disadvantage is cumulative and that earlier life events affect later life outcomes. In this monograph, analysis of cross section data across the age groups therefore serves as an initial framework of examining the timing of life events and how they differ across age, gender and ethnicity.

Overview

The aim of this monograph is to analyse the timing of key stages and events across the Indigenous lifecourse. The analysis utilises data from the ABS 2006 5% Census Sample File (CSF), hereafter referred to as the '5% CSF'. As outlined in the following chapter, this dataset allows for analysis of the individual outcomes of 22 437 Indigenous Australians and 913 262 non-Indigenous Australians – a much larger sample size than any dataset previously available to researchers outside the ABS.

Chapter 2 also outlines a methodological approach that consists of identifying a number of dependent variables across seven broad topics. By utilising a regression-style approach using individual data, it is possible to answer the following specific research questions for each of the dependent variables:

- How does the probability of having that dependent variable vary across the lifecourse?
- Does this probability vary by sex?
- Is there any difference between Indigenous and non-Indigenous Australians in the probability after controlling for age and sex?
- Is there still variation across the lifecourse after controlling for geography and other socioeconomic outcomes?
- Is there still a significant difference between the Indigenous and non-Indigenous population after controlling for these characteristics in addition to variation across the lifecourse?
- Do the patterns across the lifecourse and associations with the other demographic, geographic and socioeconomic characteristics hold for the Indigenous population in isolation?

Chapters 3–9 of the monograph look at one or more dependent variables from each of the topics outlined below.

In Chapter 3 we examine two major events that occur across a number of people's lifecourse – getting married and/or having children. We begin with an analysis of the probability of being in a registered or de facto marriage, and then move on to consider the factors associated with the number of children that a female has ever given birth to, as well as whether or not a person provided unpaid child care. Chapter 4 deals with migration and mobility. There is a widely held view that Indigenous Australians are highly mobile. In this chapter we consider the factors associated with residential and temporary mobility. While on average more Indigenous Australians changed usual residence in the years that preceded the census or were away from their place of usual residence on census night, there is also substantial variation across the lifecourse for both the Indigenous and non-Indigenous population in terms of residential and temporary mobility.

Chapter 5 is concerned with participation in education. For many people, formal education is a defining feature of their lifecourse. Those who complete secondary school have generally undertaken 12–13 years of schooling, with post-school education adding a number of additional years of study for a sizeable proportion of the population. Furthermore, those who complete additional years of education tend to have better outcomes across a range of areas including employment, income and health. There are a number of important aspects of education that are not observable on the census including attendance, grades, and literacy and numeracy outcomes. However, it is possible to observe whether or not a person is a student at the time of the census, and in this chapter we consider the factors associated with education participation across adulthood, as well as the education sector in which Indigenous and non-Indigenous school students typically participate.

Chapter 6 recognises that across much of Australia, employment remains one of the key protective factors against poverty and social exclusion. However, even during the most recent period of rapid economic growth (when the last census was undertaken) many individuals were still struggling to find and maintain stable, well-paid employment. On the other hand, there are a number of times across the lifecourse when mainstream employment, and full-time employment in particular, is not the preferred option. This includes during full-time study, during times of childbearing and rearing, after retirement and, especially for the Indigenous population, whilst participating in activities in the customary economy. In this chapter we consider the factors associated with employment, part-time as opposed to full-time employment, and occupational status. Furthermore, we present for the first time results that analyse participation in voluntary work and unpaid domestic work across the lifecourse for both Indigenous and non-Indigenous Australians separately.

One of the most disruptive influences on a person being able to lead the lives that they desire is a lack of access to adequate shelter and housing. Dwellings that are overcrowded are likely to contribute to poor health and also make it difficult for children living there to undertake education. However, the ability of individuals to take control of their own housing situation is determined by their current tenure situation. In Chapter 7 we consider two aspects of housing across the lifecourse – tenure type (including owner occupied, private rental and community or government rental), and household overcrowding. One of the most common measures of the average lifecourse is life expectancy, although it is not always thought of that way. Estimates of life expectancy are generally constructed as the number of years that a child born today would expect to live based on the current age distribution of deaths. In other words, how long their lifecourse might expect to be. Although life expectancy estimates are not based on census data only, one of the key features of the Indigenous lifecourse is a shorter than average duration, and in Chapter 8 we consider how survival probabilities vary across the lifecourse for the Indigenous compared to the non-Indigenous population. Although the measure is far from perfect, we also consider the factors associated with an individual in the census reporting a need for assistance in undertaking a 'core activity'.

In the final section of results presented in the monograph, Chapter 9 returns to the analysis of the typical Indigenous childhood. In particular, we focus on three potential aspects of the childhood experience that have been shown to have an effect on long-term outcomes. These are living in a single-parent family, living in a 'low education' household and living in a 'jobless' household. We consider these aspects of childhood in isolation, as well as the intersection and interaction between them. Chapter 10 summarises the main results from this analysis and draws out a number of policy implications. The final section of Chapter 10 outlines a research agenda on the Indigenous lifecourse, based on either international comparisons or new data that will progressively become available.

2. Data and methods

Data

The analysis presented in this paper is based on data from the 2006 Census of Population and Housing. The census is designed to collect information on every person in Australia with the main aim of obtaining a count of the number of people at a given point in time. This count is then used to allocate the number of seats in Federal and State parliaments, as well as financial grants to various levels of government. At the same time, a large amount of information is collected on the characteristics of those counted in the census which is used for both administrative and research purposes. There were 19 855 288 individuals counted in the 2006 Census, of which 455 030 were identified as being Indigenous. Because information is collected on such large numbers of people, it is possible to obtain information on very specific population subgroups when analysing the census. That is, it is not only possible to analyse differences between the Indigenous and non-Indigenous population, but also to analyse variation within the Indigenous population.

To look at the socioeconomic correlates of particular life events, it is necessary to be able to control for variation in characteristics across individuals. To facilitate such types of analysis, the ABS provides a 5% CSF of occupied private dwellings and individuals in non-private dwellings which can be interrogated online via the Remote Access Data Laboratory. This CSF has information on 1 002 793 respondents, of which 22 437 were identified as being Indigenous; 913 262 were identified as being non-Indigenous; 56 935 did not have their Indigenous status stated; and 10,159 were overseas visitors. The latter two groups were excluded from the remainder of the analysis. Although the 5% CSF available for analysis is ostensibly a random sample, there are a number of reasons why results from the analysis may not reflect the true population values. Firstly, it may be the case that through chance the sample has different characteristics to the total population. Although this sampling error is controlled for, to a certain extent, through the use of standard errors and hypothesis tests (as outlined in the next section), the issue cannot be discounted entirely. The second set of reasons, non-sampling error, is more difficult to control for and can arise because of the way the census itself is collected and processed, or if the selection of the 5% CSF is non-random. We discuss each of these possibilities below.

Although the aim of the census is to collect accurate information on every person in Australia, in reality this aim is not achieved. A number of people are missed, and others are counted twice. The ABS adjusts for the net undercount (the difference between those who were missed and those who were counted twice), as well as Australians who were temporarily overseas, by creating an estimated resident population (ERP). In doing so, the 19 855 288 individuals counted in the 2006 Census were adjusted upwards to create a population estimate of 20 701 448 as of 30 June 2006 (ABS 2008b).

The ABS also calculates a separate ERP for the Indigenous population, with the 455 030 people who identified as being Indigenous according to the 2006 Census count increased to an Indigenous ERP of 517 174 (ABS 2008b). The implied adjustment factor of 13.7 per cent is much higher than the adjustment factor for the total population (4.2 per cent). This is due in part to the fact that some of those who did not have their Indigenous status stated on the census were allocated to the Indigenous ERP. However, the main reason that the Indigenous population estimates were adjusted by a greater percentage than for the total population is that a higher proportion of Indigenous Australians were missed from the census altogether (ABS 2008b). That is, if those collected on the census are viewed as a sample from the true population, then unfortunately this sample is not random. If the only non-random aspect of census undercount was a person's Indigenous status, then it would be possible to adjust the estimates from the census accordingly. However, as noted by a number of authors in Morphy (2007), there are certain characteristics within the Indigenous population that make individuals more or less likely to be missed from the count than other Indigenous Australians. Specifically, individuals who live in remote Australia and in particular those who are highly mobile are more likely to be missed from the census than individuals in non-remote Australia.

Leaving aside the issue of census undercoverage, there is also the possibility that there are systematic aspects of the way in which the 5% CSF is chosen that might lead to further non-sampling error. For example, the number of people in occupied private dwellings that was included in the census was restricted to eight usual residents. Extra persons in households with more than eight usual residents were randomly removed from the sample. While this only resulted in a total of 1 283 person records being removed, it is likely that those removed were disproportionately Indigenous, due to the fact that Indigenous Australians are much more likely to live in large households (Biddle 2008). In aggregate, the size of the Indigenous sample is not substantially lower than would be expected. Indigenous Australians made up 2.5 per cent of the total ERP and 2.4 per cent of the 5% CSF. However, Figures 2.1 and 2.2 show that there is an uneven sample loss across the age distribution. Fig. 2.1 replicates the previous age pyramid, with the distribution of the Indigenous ERP in the grey bars and the distribution of the Indigenous component of the 5% CSF in the hollow bars. Fig. 2.2 has a similar figure for the non-Indigenous population.

Fig. 2.1 Age distribution of the Indigenous ERP and the Indigenous component of the 5% CSF

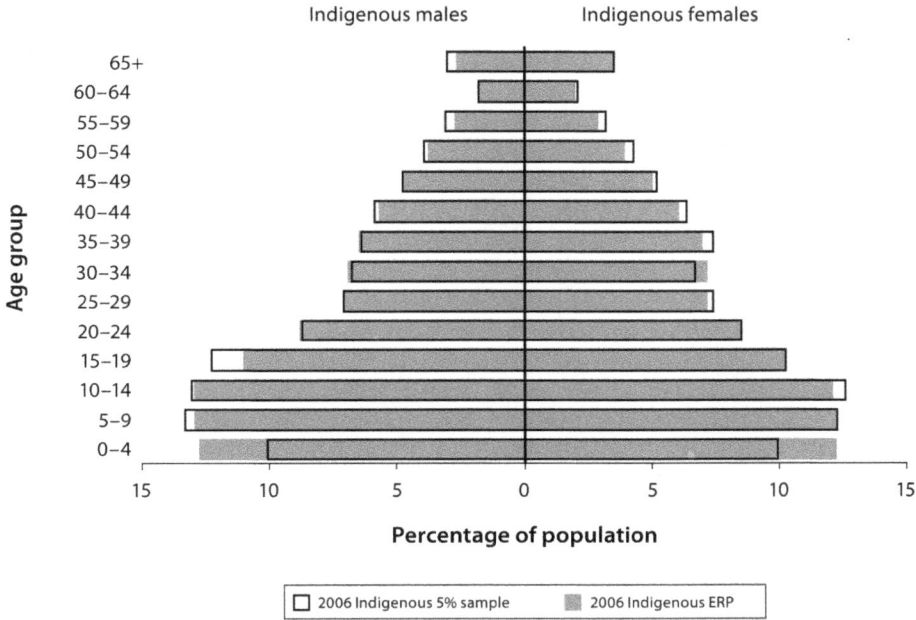

Source: Customised calculations using the 2006 5% CSF, ABS Census of Population and Housing

The percentage of the Indigenous and non-Indigenous samples that are in the majority of the age groups match up reasonably well with the equivalent percentage of the ERP. There were, however, a few exceptions, with a smaller percentage of the sample aged 0–4 years the most notable. This was particularly the case for the Indigenous population, with 10.0 per cent of the Indigenous component of the 5% CSF aged 0–4 years compared to 12.5 per cent of the Indigenous ERP. Counterbalancing the underrepresentation of 0–4 year-olds in the sample, there were slightly more Indigenous males aged 15–19 years and non-Indigenous males and females aged 65 years and over.

Ultimately, the effect of non-sampling error is mitigated to a certain extent by controlling for a number of the observable characteristics that impact on census capture in the model. However, there may still be a residual bias from unobservable characteristics that needs to be kept in mind when interpreting the results.

Fig. 2.2 Age distribution of the non-Indigenous ERP and the non-Indigenous component of the 5% CSF

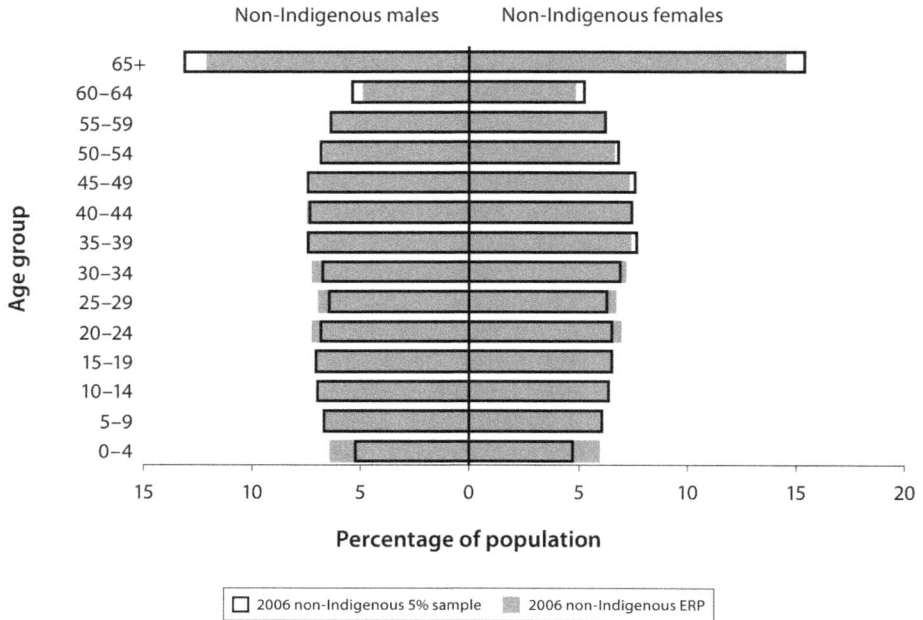

Source: Customised calculations using the 2006 5% CSF, ABS Census of Population and Housing

Model specification

The analysis presented in this paper is structured around a number of thematic topics. Within each of these topics, a number of key dependent variables are chosen and the demographic and socioeconomic factors that are associated with them estimated. Table 2.1 outlines the topics and respective dependent variables. All but one of these dependent variables are binary in that they indicate whether or not a person has that particular characteristic. The exception, the number of children ever born (for females), is a count variable capped at eight children.

A separate set of explanatory variables is used for each of the dependent variables. These are chosen based on a review of the available literature whilst taking into account the limitations that arise from using census data. These specifications are outlined at the start of the relevant sections. However, reflecting our focus on the Indigenous lifecourse, there is a common structure for each of the dependent variables, including a flexible age structure, the use of a number of model specifications, and the inclusion of a separate estimation for the Indigenous population.

Table 2.1 Topics and dependent variables analysed

Topic	Dependent variable
Fertility and family formation	In a registered or de facto marriage
	In a registered marriage (for those in a registered or de facto marriage)
	Number of children ever born (for females)
	Provided unpaid child care
Migration and mobility	Changed place of usual residence between 2001 and 2006
	Away from place of usual residence on census night
Education participation	Participating in education
	Attending a non-government school (for infants, primary and secondary school students)
Employment	Employed
	Employed part-time (for those employed)
	Employed as a Manager or Professional (for those employed)
	Undertook voluntary work for an organisation or group in the last 12 months
	Undertook at least 5 hours of unpaid domestic work in the last week
Housing	Lives in a dwelling that is owned or being purchased
	Lives in a community rental dwelling (those in a rented dwelling)
	Lives in a dwelling with more than one person per bedroom
Health	Has a 'core activity' need for assistance
Childhood outcomes	Lives in a single-parent family
	Lives in a household without anyone employed
	Lives in a household where no-one has completed Year 12

For each dependent variable, a minimum of three specifications is used. In general, the first specification includes a dummy variable for whether or not the person is Indigenous; a dummy variable for whether or not the person is female; and a set of dummy variables that indicates whether the person is in a particular five-year age cohort ranging from 0–4 years to 50–54 years, with the final age cohort aged 55 years and over. The final set of variables in Model 1 is the same age dummies for females only. The purpose of this model is to test whether there is any difference between Indigenous and non-Indigenous Australians in the probability of a person having the particular characteristic after controlling for age and sex.

The second specification adds a number of additional geographic, demographic and socioeconomic characteristics to the explanatory variables in Model 1. All the dependent variables contain a dummy variable indicating that the person's usual residence is in a major city,[1] as well as a set of dummy variables indicating

---

1 Unfortunately, the standard Accessibility/Remoteness Index of Australia is not available for analysis using the 5% CSF. An approximation is used, with the following cities or regions included: Sydney, Newcastle/

whether the person lives in one of the seven States or Territories other than New South Wales. The remaining explanatory variables included in Model 2 vary by dependent variable and are outlined at the start of the relevant section.

The specification for Model 2 is outlined in the following equation, with Model 1 found by setting β_5, β_6 and β_7 to zero:

$$P(y_i = 1) = f\left(\begin{array}{l} \beta_0 + \beta_1 Indig_i + \beta_2 Fem_i + \beta_3 Age_i + \beta_4 Age_i Fem_i + \\ \beta_5 Majcit_i + \beta_6 State_i + \beta_7 X_i \end{array} \right)$$

In the above equation, $Indig_i$, Fem_i and $Majcit_i$ are binary variables indicating the Indigenous status, sex and location of usual residence of individual i, whereas Age_i, $State_i$ and X_i are vectors of characteristics. The coefficients β_1, β_2 and β_5 as well as the vectors of coefficients β_3, β_4, β_6 and β_7 indicate the size and direction of the association between the dependent and explanatory variables. The constant term (β_0) determines the probability of the *base case* individual having that particular characteristic. Apart from being male, non-Indigenous and living outside a major city, this base case is different for different dependent variables and defined in the relevant sections.

There are two ultimate purposes of Model 2. Firstly, to test whether there is still variation across the lifecourse in the probability of having that particular characteristic after controlling for geography and other socioeconomic outcomes. Secondly, to test whether there is still a significant difference between the Indigenous and non-Indigenous population after controlling for these characteristics in addition to variation across the lifecourse.

The third specification that is estimated for all dependent variables is designed to identify whether the patterns across the lifecourse hold for the Indigenous population in isolation. Model 3 is therefore estimated on the Indigenous sample only and has β_1 set to zero.

A fourth specification (Model 4) is also estimated for a number of the dependent variables. This specification is estimated for the Indigenous population only and includes an additional variable for whether or not the individual lives in a mixed Indigenous and non-Indigenous household. This variable is not included in Model 3, as it would make it more difficult to compare the estimated marginal effects with results from Model 2, and it is necessary to restrict the sample to those who live in private dwellings only. For this reason, certain dependent variables that can only take on one particular value for those in a non-private dwelling (for example temporary mobility) do not have a Model 4 estimated for

---

Hunter, Wollongong/Illawarra, Melbourne, Brisbane, Gold Coast, Sunshine Coast, Adelaide, Perth, and the Australian Capital Territory. It was not possible to separately identify Hobart from the rest of Tasmania or Darwin from the rest of the Northern Territory.

them. The following table summarises the four estimated models. There is some variation depending on the particular dependent variable. This is discussed further in the relevant chapter in this volume.

Table 2.2 Summary of estimated models

Model	Population	Included variables
Model 1	Indigenous and non-Indigenous	Indigenous status, sex, five-year age group, sex interacted with five-year age group
Model 2	Indigenous and non-Indigenous	Same as Model 1, plus individual socioeconomic variables
Model 3	Indigenous population only	Same as Model 2, but without Indigenous status
Model 4	Indigenous population living in a private dwelling	Same as Model 3, plus whether or not the household includes non-Indigenous usual residents

Because the majority of the dependent variables are binary (that is you either do or do not have the characteristic), the assumed functional form of the majority of the models is the standard probit. The parameters of the models, that is the β coefficients and their standard errors, are estimated using the maximum likelihood estimation procedure. The only exception to this is the analysis of the number of children ever born. As this dependent variable is constructed using count data, the Poisson model is used (after testing for and rejecting over-dispersion).

It is worth pointing out at this stage the limitations of the analysis presented in this monograph and what it is not trying to achieve. Firstly, in the absence of longitudinal data, it is not possible to analyse how the outcomes of individual Indigenous Australians have changed through time. Rather, comparisons are restricted to the average outcomes of Indigenous or non-Indigenous Australians aged 30–34 years in 2006 with those aged 35–39 years (for example), after controlling for other observed characteristics. A further limitation of using cross-sectional data is that it is not possible to identify causal relationships between the explanatory and dependent variables. That is, it is possible to identify whether or not living in a major city is associated with a higher or lower probability of being married (for example), but not possible to show whether geographic location has a direct impact. It may be a situation of reverse causality, with those who are married being more or less likely to live in a particular area. Alternatively, there may be a third unobserved variable that influences them both.

Because of these limitations, no attempt is made in the analysis to model the dependent variables as a system of equations. It would not be possible with cross-sectional census data to identify instrumental variables that are correlated with the endogenous explanatory variables but not with the dependent variable. Rather, each model is estimated as a single equation, with the potential bias in the estimated standard errors kept in mind when interpreting the robustness of the results. Furthermore, although theoretical justifications are used for each of the model specifications, variables that were used as a dependent variable in a particular estimation are still considered as explanatory variables in other equations.

3. Fertility and family formation

One of the biggest events that occurs across many people's lifecourse is marriage. According to the 2006 Census, 49.6 per cent of Australians aged 15 years and over were in a registered marriage, with a further 17.2 per cent previously married at some point in time (that is, they were currently separated, divorced or widowed). By the 35–44 year age group, 77.3 per cent of the population were married or had been married at a particular point in time, rising to 94.5 per cent for Australians aged 55 years and over.

In addition to Australians who are in a registered marriage, there is also a high proportion of the population identified as being in a de facto marriage that, from a legal point of view, has most of the same rights and obligations as a registered marriage. According to the 2006 Census once again, 59.2 per cent of the population aged 15 years and over are in either a registered or de facto marriage. There are a number of reasons or motivations for two people voluntarily entering into a registered or de facto marriage. The role of joint production and joint consumption as a motivation for getting married is relatively prominent in the field of economics (Weiss 1997). The demographic literature, on the other hand, emphasises the production and rearing of children as a key motivation, or at least a key outcome of marriage (Parker and Alexander 2004). Sociology and anthropology have different focuses still. Whatever the focus, all these motivations are likely to be present to quite varying degrees at different points across the lifecourse.

One of the factors that influences or is influenced by the decision to marry is having and raising children. On the one hand, a significant minority of marriages occur because of pre-existing children in the relationship. On the other hand, individual males and females are more likely to become parents if they are in a registered or de facto marriage (Parker and Alexander 2004). While marriage and fertility decisions are in no way prerequisites for each other, it is clear that there is significant correlation between the two across individuals. According to the 2006 Census, 68.1 per cent of females aged 15 years and over reported having had at least one child. This rises to 83.1 per cent for Australians who are in a registered or de facto marriage, but falls to 47.8 per cent for those who were not married. At a population level, the most obvious impact of fertility decisions is population growth and regeneration. However, there are also a number of impacts on individual parents and other household members. Some of these effects have financial implications, whereas others are more directly related to individual wellbeing and/or other demographic characteristics (Kohler, Behrman and Skytthe 2005).

The analysis in this chapter focuses on four dependent variables. The first of these is whether or not a person is currently married. This can include a registered or a de facto marriage. The second dependent variable focuses on Australians who are married and captures whether they are in a registered as opposed to de facto marriage. The third variable is a count of the number of children that a female has ever given birth to. As this variable is applicable to females only and does not give any indication of the current age of the children (and hence the effect those children have on a person's current responsibilities), the final variable included in the analysis is whether a person provided unpaid child care in the two weeks preceding the census. This is the first time that analysis of such a variable has been undertaken for the Indigenous and non-Indigenous population simultaneously.

Recognising the relationship between marriage and fertility decisions discussed earlier, a person's marital status is not only used as a dependent variable in the first part of the section, it is also used as an explanatory variable when estimating the factors associated with the number of children ever born and providing unpaid child care.

Residential marital status

The probability of being in a registered or de facto marriage[1] across the lifecourse is presented for Indigenous and non-Indigenous males and females aged over 15 years in Fig. 3.1. The probability for the Indigenous population is in black, with Indigenous males represented by the solid line and Indigenous females the broken line. Non-Indigenous Australians are similarly represented in grey.

For both the Indigenous and non-Indigenous population, the probability of being in a registered or de facto marriage rises reasonably quickly across the lifecourse until a person reaches their mid-thirties. The probability then stays reasonably consistent, as those who enter into marriage are balanced by those who are no longer married (because of separation, divorce or widowhood). For females, there is a slight drop-off for Australians aged 55 years and over. This represents to a large extent the higher rate of mortality for males in general and Indigenous males in particular (as discussed in Chapter 8 of this monograph), leading to a significant number of widows. For the first two age groups in Fig. 3.1, the probability of being in a registered or de facto marriage is higher for the Indigenous population compared to the non-Indigenous population. From the 25–29 year age group onwards for males and the 30–34 year age group

---

1 Same-sex marriages were classified as de facto marriages in the 2006 Census.

onwards for females, however, the Indigenous population has a consistently lower probability. In other words, marriage appears to be delayed for longer for the non-Indigenous population, but is eventually more likely to occur.

Fig. 3.1 Probability of being in a registered or de facto marriage, 2006

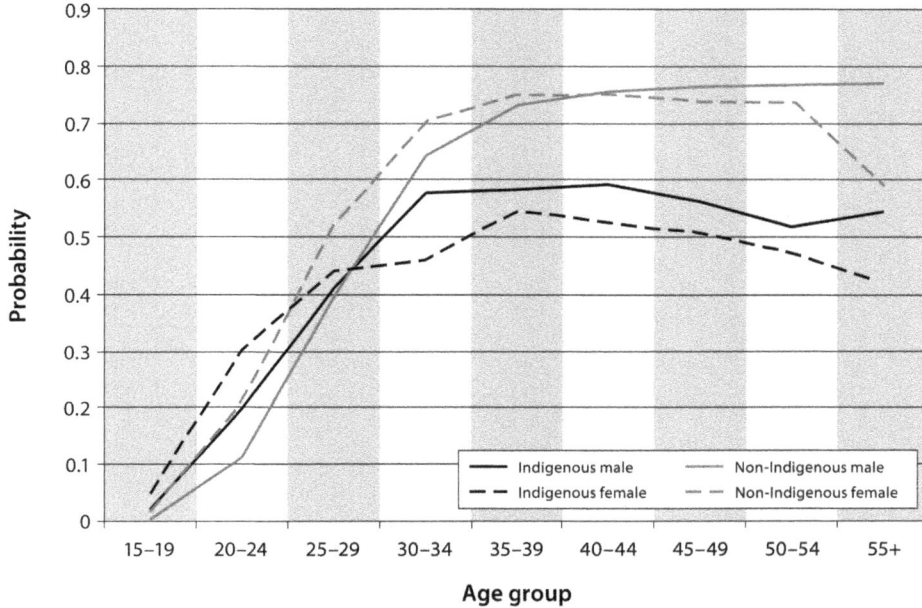

Source: Customised calculations using the 2006 5% CSF, ABS Census of Population and Housing

On average, across the lifecourse Indigenous Australians are less likely to be married than non-Indigenous Australians (39.9 compared to 59.8 per cent respectively). However, this difference is much greater when one considers registered marriages only, as in Fig. 3.2. Of those who are married, 60.3 per cent of Indigenous Australians are in a registered as opposed to de facto marriage, compared to 85.4 per cent of the respective non-Indigenous population. As shown in Fig. 3.2, this difference is relatively large from the early-thirties onwards.

Fig. 3.2 Probability of being in a registered as opposed to de facto marriage, 2006

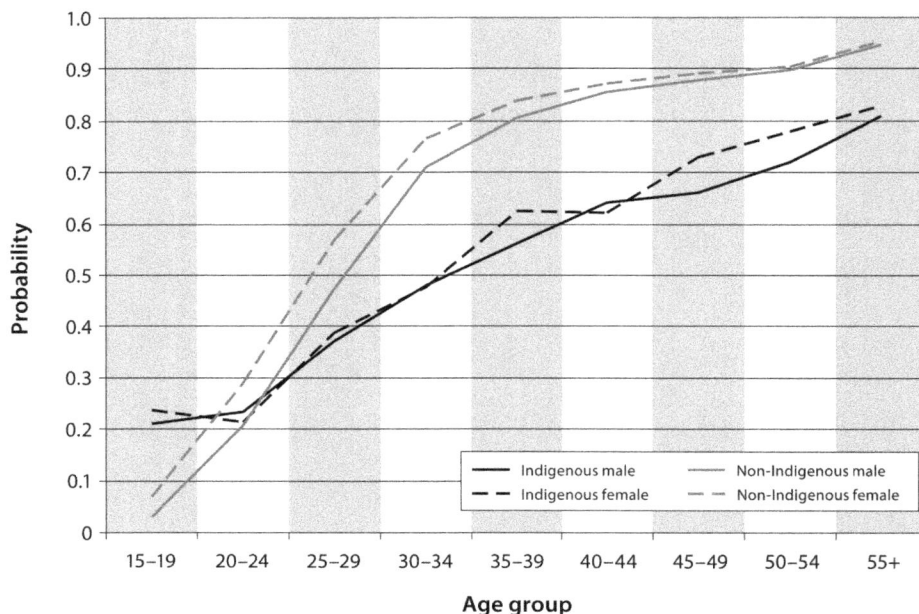

Source: Customised calculations using the 2006 5% CSF, ABS Census of Population and Housing

Modelling marital status across the lifecourse

The dependent variable for the results presented in Table 3.1 is the probability of being in a registered or de facto marriage. Due to the fact that marital decisions are likely to have been made at a point potentially a long time in the past, employment, child care and other household characteristics are more likely to be determined by a person's marital status rather than the other way around. For this reason, a reduced set of explanatory variables are included in Models 2 and 3 with information on State or Territory, geographic area, education completion and English proficiency only.

Table 3.1 Factors associated with the probability of being in a registered or de facto marriage, 2006

	Total population		Indigenous population
Explanatory variables[a]	Model 1	Model 2	Model 3
Indigenous	−0.198	−0.107	
Female	0.082	0.051	−0.089

Aged 15–19	−0.453	−0.691	−0.584
Aged 20–24	−0.427	−0.544	−0.385
Aged 25–29	−0.261	−0.238	−0.156
Aged 35–39	0.132	0.082	n.s.
Aged 40–44	0.185	0.103	n.s.
Aged 45–49	0.211	0.110	n.s.
Aged 50–54	0.232	0.116	n.s.
Aged 55 +	0.273	0.133	n.s.
Aged 15–19, female	n.s.	0.096	0.174
Aged 20–24, female	0.080	0.081	0.186
Aged 25–29, female	0.054	0.051	0.116
Aged 35–39, female	−0.041	−0.037	n.s.
Aged 40–44, female	−0.066	−0.065	n.s.
Aged 45–49, female	−0.086	−0.085	n.s.
Aged 50–54, female	−0.095	−0.089	n.s.
Aged 55 +, female	−0.239	−0.241	n.s.
Victoria		−0.006	n.s.
Queensland		0.023	n.s.
South Australia		0.005	n.s.
Western Australia		0.024	n.s.
Tasmania		−0.020	0.066
Northern Territory		−0.013*	0.063
Australian Capital Territory		0.011	n.s.
Major city		−0.048	−0.021*
Completed Year 9 or less		−0.060	−0.059
Completed Year 10 or 11		0.009	n.s.
Does not have any qualifications		−0.059	−0.060
Has a Diploma or Certificate only		n.s.	n.s.
Speaks another language and English well		0.018	n.s.
Speaks another language and English not well or not at all		0.042	−0.136
Probability of the base case[b]	0.454	0.701	0.622
Pseudo R-Squared	0.1858	0.1940	0.1318
Number of observations	698 847	617 012	9 852

[a.] n.s. = Those variables that were not significant at the 10% level of significance.
 * = Those variables that were significant at the 10% level of significance but not the 5% level.

[b.] The base case for the total population is non-Indigenous. For all estimates, the base case is male and aged 30–34 years and in addition, for Models 2–3 and for the Indigenous estimates, the base case lives in New South Wales, outside a major city, has completed Year 12, has a university degree, and speaks English only.

Source: Customised calculations using the 2006 5% CSF, ABS Census of Population and Housing

The results presented in Model 1 confirm that, after controlling for differences across the lifecourse by age and sex, Indigenous Australians are less likely to be in a registered or de facto marriage than non-Indigenous Australians. An estimated marginal effect of −0.198 relative to the predicted probability of the base case of 0.454 suggests that these differences are quite large. After controlling for a limited number of other demographic, geographic and socioeconomic characteristics, the results from Model 2 show that Indigenous Australians are still less likely to be in a registered or de facto marriage. However, the magnitude of the difference (represented by the marginal effect) is almost half that of the results presented in Model 1. That is, Indigenous Australians are less likely to be in a registered or de facto marriage in part because of their other characteristics.

There are two major differences between the results from Model 2 (estimated on the total sample) and results from Model 3 (estimated on the Indigenous sample only). Firstly, there is no significant difference between those in the last five age cohorts and the base case (those aged 30–34 years). Secondly, those Indigenous Australians who speak a language other than English, and English not well or not at all, are less likely to be in a registered or de facto marriage compared to those who speak English only. For the total population, relatively poor English ability is associated with a higher probability of being in a registered marriage. Those non-Indigenous Australians from a non-English speaking background are likely to be relatively recent arrivals to Australia. For the Indigenous population, on the other hand, those who speak a language other than English at home are likely to be those who have maintained a traditional Indigenous lifestyle. Clearly, there is a significant degree of heterogeneity amongst those from a non-English speaking background which should be recognised in policy delivery.

While there are few legal differences between registered and de facto marriages, research suggests that registered marriages are still less likely to dissolve and more likely to result in children (Dempsey and de Vaus 2004). This in no way implies that children should be seen to be a more legitimate reason for marriage than any other reason and that registered marriages are hence in any way superior. Rather, it signals potentially different motivations for and outcomes from the two types of marriage. The analysis presented in Table 3.2 focuses on the 39.9 per cent of Indigenous Australians and 59.8 per cent of non-Indigenous Australians in any type of marriage and considers the factors associated with the probability of being in a registered as opposed to de facto marriage. Similar to the previous table, three models are used with results presented as the difference in the predicted probability from the base case.

Table 3.2 Factors associated with the probability of being in a registered as opposed to de facto marriage, population aged 15 years and over

Explanatory variables[a]	Total population		Indigenous population
	Model 1	Model 2	Model 3
Indigenous	−0.232	−0.200	
Female	0.057	0.052	n.s.
Aged 15–19	−0.636	−0.628	−0.303
Aged 20–24	−0.493	−0.484	−0.326
Aged 25–29	−0.231	−0.227	−0.096
Aged 35–39	0.097	0.100	n.s.
Aged 40–44	0.145	0.146	0.159
Aged 45–49	0.168	0.169	0.192
Aged 50–54	0.189	0.191	0.246
Aged 55 +	0.238	0.237	0.313
Aged 15–19, female	n.s.	n.s.	n.s.
Aged 20–24, female	0.023	n.s.	n.s.
Aged 25–29, female	0.019	0.014*	n.s.
Aged 35–39, female	−0.021	−0.018	0.100*
Aged 40–44, female	−0.036	−0.031	n.s.
Aged 45–49, female	−0.038	−0.031	n.s.
Aged 50–54, female	−0.050	−0.044	n.s.
Aged 55 +, female	−0.039	−0.028	n.s.
Victoria		n.s.	0.058*
Queensland		−0.016	−0.037*
South Australia		−0.008	0.068*
Western Australia		−0.025	n.s.
Tasmania		−0.035	0.131
Northern Territory		−0.076	0.293
Australian Capital Territory		−0.041	n.s.
Major city		−0.005	0.075
Secondary school student		n.s.	n.s.
Tertiary student		−0.074	n.s.
Part-time student		0.043	n.s.
Completed Year 9 or less		−0.029	n.s.
Completed Year 10 or 11		−0.017	n.s.
Does not have any qualifications		−0.028	−0.118
Has a Diploma or Certificate only		−0.006	−0.072*
Speaks another language and English well		0.163	0.143
Speaks another language and English not well or not at all		0.211	n.s.

Probability of the base case[b]	0.709	0.715	0.531
Pseudo R-Squared	0.1526	0.1732	0.1466
Number of observations	415 779	372 067	4 142

[a.] n.s. = Those variables that were not significant at the 10% level of significance.

  * = Those variables that were significant at the 10% level of significance but not the 5% level.

[b.] The base case for the total population is non-Indigenous. For all estimates, the base case is male and aged 30–34 years and in addition, for Models 2–3 and for the Indigenous estimates, the base case lives in New South Wales, outside a major city, has completed Year 12, has a university degree, and speaks English only.

Source: Customised calculations using the 2006 5% CSF, ABS Census of Population and Housing

Results presented in Model 1 confirm the summary given in Fig. 3.2 which show that Indigenous Australians who are married are less likely to be in a registered as opposed to de facto marriage compared to a married non-Indigenous Australian. Specifically, the model predicts that the probability of a married non-Indigenous male aged 30–34 years being in a registered marriage is 0.709. The probability for a married Indigenous male of the same age is estimated to be 0.477. After controlling for a range of other characteristics, the difference between the Indigenous and non-Indigenous population is still significant, albeit with a slightly smaller marginal effect. Other variables of significance are education participation and attainment (those with higher levels of education are more likely to be in a registered marriage), as well as speaking a language other than English which is associated with a higher probability.

The most interesting difference between the estimates for the total population (Model 2) and for the non-Indigenous population (Model 3) is the association with living in a major city. For the total population, the coefficient is negative and significant, albeit with a very small marginal effect. Essentially, there is no real difference between Australians who live in a major city compared to those that do not. Compared to this, married Indigenous Australians who live in a major city are significantly more likely to be in a registered as opposed to de facto marriage. This is likely to reflect in part the greater access to the formal mechanisms required for a registered marriage for Indigenous Australians in major urban areas and the greater access to marriage rites under customary law in non-urban and (especially) remote Australia. Whatever the reason, it would appear that there are fewer differences between Indigenous and non-Indigenous Australians in a major city than there are between an Indigenous Australian living in a major city and one in the rest of Australia.

Fertility and the number of children ever born

There is clear epidemiological evidence that the age at which a female has a child has significant implications for her health as well as that of her child. The risk of foetal and perinatal complications is higher for teenage mothers and mothers aged 35 years and over (AIHW 2008; Laws, Grayson and Sullivan 2006). In addition to the impacts on health, teenage pregnancies can also significantly alter a female's likely lifecourse trajectory. Females who have children when they are young are less likely to complete high school and post-school qualifications (de Vaus 2002). They also have lower levels of employment participation throughout their lives and lower incomes (Caldas 1993).

Clearly though, children bring substantial benefits to their parents and families that need to be traded off against the costs. For example, Nomaguchi and Milkie (2003: 362) show a higher level of 'social integration with relatives, friends and neighbours' for new parents compared to those who are childless. However, a number of surveys show that females with children report lower levels of subjective wellbeing, even after controlling for other characteristics (Shields and Wooden 2003). The important point in terms of this study though, is that the costs and benefits of children vary substantially across the lifecourse. Fig. 3.3 plots the predicted number of children ever born for Indigenous females and non-Indigenous females by the same five-year age cohorts already presented. It should be noted that these numbers are cumulative and are for the number of children that a female has ever given birth to, not births over a recent period of time. This indicates substantial differences between Indigenous and non-Indigenous females across the lifecourse in terms of the number of children ever born.

According to administrative data (AIHW 2008), Indigenous mothers who gave birth over the 2001–04 period were on average younger than non-Indigenous mothers (median age of 25 years compared to 30 years). This relatively young age profile is confirmed using census data. By the 25–29 age group, for example, Indigenous females were predicted to have had around 1.5 children on average compared to less than 0.5 children for the non-Indigenous population. While there is some convergence through time, the non-Indigenous figure never comes close to reaching the Indigenous figure.

Fig. 3.3 Number of children ever born (up until current age), Indigenous and non-Indigenous females, 2006

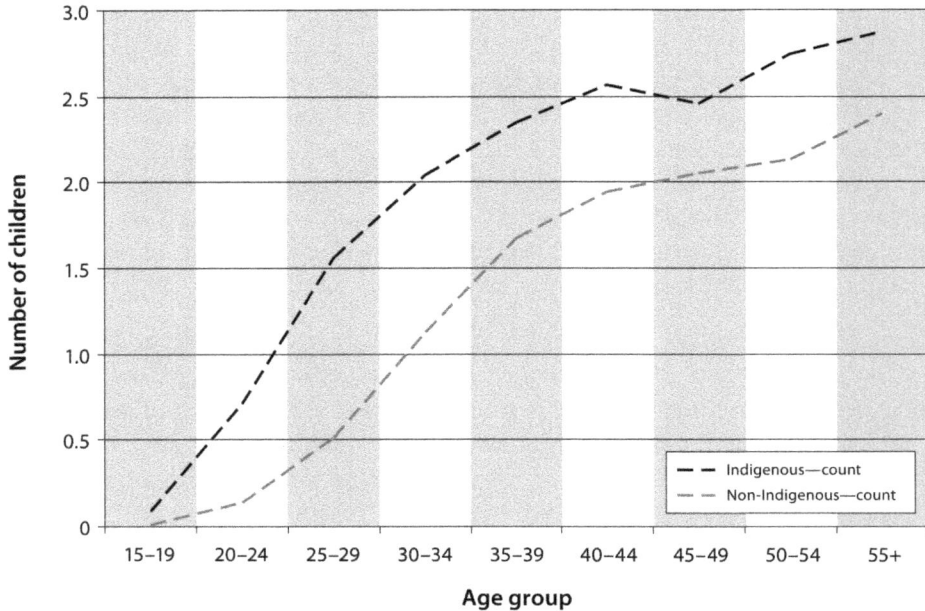

Source: Customised calculations using the 2006 5% CSF, ABS Census of Population and Housing

Modelling the number of children ever born across the lifecourse

Unlike the previous set of estimates (and estimates in the remainder of the monograph), the dependent variable for this part of the analysis is not a simple binary outcome. Rather, the dependent variable is a count of the number of children ever born. While the methodological assumptions are slightly different – for example, the Poisson as opposed to the Probit model is assumed – the results presented in Table 3.3 should be interpreted in a very similar way. The third-last line of the table gives the predicted number of children ever born for the base case (described under the table) and the values for the explanatory variables give the predicted difference in the number of children ever born after changing that category only and holding all else constant.

Four models are given in Table 3.3. The first model includes age, sex and Indigenous status controls only, whereas Model 2 includes a greater range of explanatory variables. Model 3 includes the same explanatory variables as Model 2, but is estimated for the Indigenous population only, whereas Model 4 includes a variable indicating whether or not there are non-Indigenous adults living in the household. The prevalence of mixed households has been shown to vary substantially by geography (Heard, Birrell and Khoo 2009). However, there has been surprisingly little quantitative work on how outcomes vary. The results presented for Model 1 in Table 3.3 confirm that Indigenous females have had a greater number of children ever born after controlling for their age. At the base case age of 30–34 years, the difference is 0.532 children, an almost 50 per cent increase on the 1.129 children predicted for a non-Indigenous female of that age.

Table 3.3 Factors associated with the number of children ever born, females, 2006

Explanatory variables[a]	Total population		Indigenous population	
	Model 1	Model 2	Model 3	Model 4
Indigenous	0.532	0.800		
Aged 15–19	−1.114	−1.342	−1.632	−1.824
Aged 20–24	−0.972	−1.030	−1.109	−1.223
Aged 25–29	−0.599	−0.539	−0.423	−0.456
Aged 35–39	0.547	0.403	n.s.	0.146*
Aged 40–44	0.812	0.532	0.192	0.230
Aged 45–49	0.915	0.543	n.s.	n.s.
Aged 50–54	0.998	0.551	0.206	0.242
Aged 55 +	1.264	0.633	0.184	0.213
Victoria		−0.022	n.s.	n.s.
Queensland		0.028	0.108	0.110
South Australia		n.s.	n.s.	n.s.
Western Australia		0.046	0.203	0.175
Tasmania		−0.068	−0.187	n.s.
Northern Territory		−0.102	−0.159	−0.225
Australian Capital Territory		0.045	n.s.	n.s.
Major city		−0.139	−0.238	−0.240
Secondary school student		−0.990	−1.145	−1.283
Tertiary student		−0.378	−0.363	−0.376
Part-time student		0.411	0.428	0.430
Completed Year 9 or less		0.312	0.686	0.720
Completed Year 10 or 11		0.204	0.534	0.567
Does not have any qualifications		0.270	0.377	0.420
Has a Diploma or Certificate only		0.184	0.181*	0.209*
Speaks another language and English well		−0.075	n.s.	−0.150
Speaks another language and English not well or not at all		n.s.	−0.293	−0.450

Never married		−0.912	−0.372	−0.487
Divorced, separated or widowed		−0.049	0.083	n.s.
Lives in a mixed Indigenous and non-Indigenous household				−0.314
Number of children for the base case[b]	1.129	1.410	1.747	1.953
Pseudo R-Squared	0.1766	0.2242	0.1976	0.2000
Number of observations	374 399	330 181	5 491	5 307

[a.] n.s. = Those variables that were not significant at the 10% level of significance.
[*] = Those variables that were significant at the 10% level of significance but not the 5% level.

[b.] The base case for the total population is non-Indigenous. For all estimates, the base case is aged 30–34 years and in addition, for Models 2–4 (for the total population and for the Indigenous estimates), the base case lives in New South Wales, outside a major city, is not a student, has completed Year 12, has a university degree, speaks English only, and is married. For Model 4, an additional characteristic of the base case is that they are living in an Indigenous-only household.

Source: Customised calculations using the 2006 5% CSF, ABS Census of Population and Housing

After controlling for geography, education attainment, language spoken and marital status, the difference between Indigenous and non-Indigenous females in terms of the predicted number of children ever born actually increases. This is a little surprising as Indigenous Australians have a number of the characteristics associated with higher fertility rates like lower levels of education, living outside a major city, and not attending education. However, the larger marginal effect appears to be driven by the fact that, as shown in the previous section, Indigenous Australians are significantly less likely to be married than non-Indigenous Australians. Once the fact that females who are not married are significantly less likely to have had a child has been controlled for, the difference between Indigenous and non-Indigenous females widens.

It is also interesting that speaking a language other than English is associated with a lower predicted number of children ever born (especially for those who speak English not well or not at all). This is in one sense similar to the results presented in Hunter and Daly (2008), who found using the 2002 National Aboriginal and Torres Strait Islander Social Survey (NATSISS) that individuals who had difficulty speaking English were less likely to have had at least one child. However, their result was reversed when a zero-inflated negative binomial model was used with the number of children ever born as the dependent variable. This different interaction between having had at least one child and the number of children ever born is an interesting avenue of future research.

The marginal effects for the education coefficients in Model 2 are reasonably large. A female (aged 30–34 years) who completes Year 12 and has a degree is predicted to have had 1.410 children. If, however, she completes Year 9 only and has no qualifications, she is predicted to have had 1.992 children. As mentioned, having children when relatively young is likely to make it difficult to continue on at school and/or university (de Vaus 2002). However, females who complete Year 12 or who have a degree are likely to have higher incomes, making the opportunity cost of having children significantly higher. That is, there is likely to be substantial reverse causality with this relationship.

What is perhaps most relevant from Table 3.3 from a policy point of view is that when Model 2 and Model 3 are compared, the size of the marginal effect for the education variables is much larger for the Indigenous population compared to the total population. What this means is that there is less difference in terms of the number of children ever born between an Indigenous and non-Indigenous female who completes Year 12 and has a degree (1.747 compared to 1.410 children respectively), as opposed to an Indigenous and non-Indigenous female without any qualifications who completes Year 9 or less (2.810 compared to 1.992 children). If at least some of this relationship is causal, then improving the levels of education for Indigenous females (for example through meeting COAG's Closing the Gap targets) is likely to have a substantial effect on Indigenous fertility rates.

The final Model 4 in Table 3.3 includes a dummy variable for whether the woman lives in a mixed Indigenous and non-Indigenous household. Compared to Indigenous females who live in an Indigenous-only household, Indigenous females in a mixed household are predicted to have had significantly fewer children. This difference is likely to have been driven in part by high Indigenous paternity, with Indigenous males in the data set having a greater number of children than non-Indigenous males.

Unpaid child care

The preceding analysis shows that Indigenous females have had more children on average than their non-Indigenous counterparts, and have those children at a much younger age. While there are a number of benefits of having children (both for the parents and for society as a whole), there is no doubt that children place constraints on undertaking other activities. This is not only in terms of leisure time, but also activities that generate income in the short term (employment) as well as the long term (education).

Unfortunately, the children ever born variable does not give a good indication of the current time constraints imposed by high levels of fertility, nor is it applicable for males. For example, a woman aged 40 years who has had two children is going to have a very different capacity to undertake paid work if she had those children in her early twenties as opposed to her late thirties. To obtain a more complete understanding, therefore, the analysis in this section looks at variation in, and the factors associated with, providing unpaid child care in the two weeks preceding the census. To reflect the possibility of multi-generational child care, or care for the children of friends and relatives, the analysis includes those who provided care for their own children, as well as other people's children.

The probability of providing unpaid child care across the lifecourse is summarised in Fig. 3.4. The reporting period for providing child care is the two weeks preceding the census, and those who provided child care to one's own and other children are both included. The provision of child care follows a clear pattern, with rates rising throughout a person's twenties, reaching a peak in their thirties, and then declining throughout their forties and fifties. However, the most obvious finding from Fig. 3.4 is that both Indigenous and non-Indigenous females are more likely to provide unpaid child care than their male counterparts. While there is some convergence amongst those in their late forties and onwards (especially for non-Indigenous Australians), there are consistently large gaps up until then. For example, 42.5 per cent of Indigenous females aged 20–24 years were predicted to be providing unpaid child care, compared to only 17.9 per cent of their male counterparts. This represents a substantial constraint on the time available for education and labour market participation of Indigenous females of that age.

Fig. 3.4 Probability of providing unpaid child care, 2006

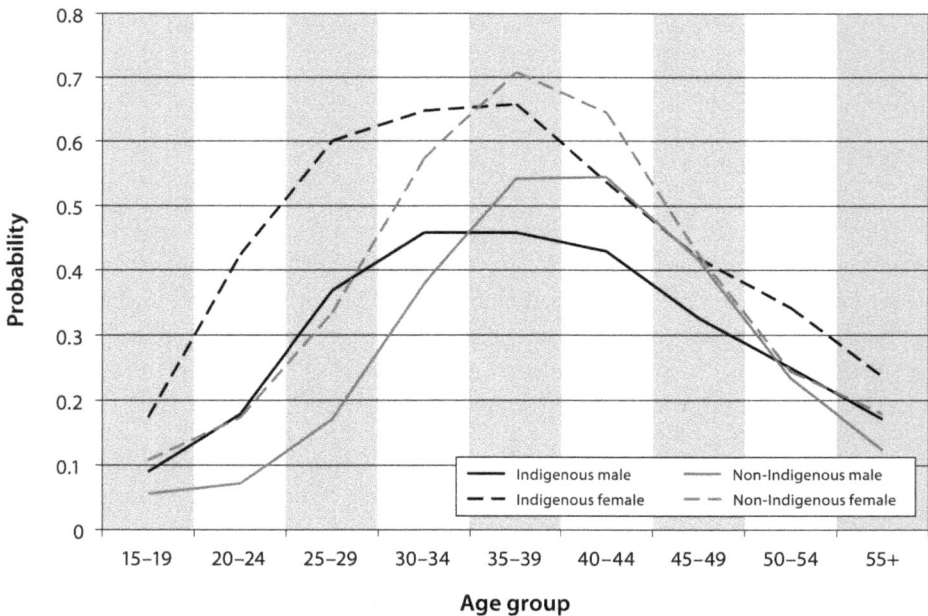

Source: Customised calculations using the 2006 5% CSF, ABS Census of Population and Housing

The provision of child care follows a clear pattern, with rates rising throughout a person's twenties, reaching a peak in their thirties, and then declining throughout their forties and fifties. However, the most obvious finding from Fig. 3.4 is that both Indigenous and non-Indigenous females are more likely to provide unpaid child care than their male counterparts. While there is some convergence amongst those in their late forties and onwards (especially for non-Indigenous Australians), there are consistently large gaps up until then. For example, 42.5 per cent of Indigenous females aged 20–24 years were predicted to be providing unpaid child care, compared to only 17.9 per cent of their male counterparts. This represents a substantial constraint on the time available for education and labour market participation of Indigenous females of that age.

The differences by Indigenous status in Fig. 3.4 are not as clear as the differences by gender. Indigenous males and females aged 15–29 were estimated to be more likely to have provided unpaid child care in the previous two weeks than their non-Indigenous counterparts. This situation is reversed for the population aged in their mid-thirties to late-forties, with Indigenous females in particular having a higher rate from then on. Clearly, the finding from the previous section that Indigenous females have children at a younger age than non-Indigenous females means that their child care responsibilities also occur at a young age. However, the relatively high rate of child care provision for Indigenous females aged 50 years and over is also an indication of a greater rate of multi-generational care amongst Indigenous Australians.

Modelling unpaid child care across the lifecourse

The dependent variable in the following analysis is the probability of providing unpaid child care. Four models are once again estimated, with the last two estimated on the Indigenous population only. Although the results presented in Fig. 3.4 showed that the size and the direction of the differences were not consistent across the lifecourse, the results presented in Table 3.4 show that, at least on average, Indigenous Australians were more likely to have provided unpaid child care in the two weeks preceding the census than non-Indigenous Australians. Furthermore, the marginal effect increases from Model 1 to Model 2, implying that once other characteristics had been controlled for there was a greater difference between the Indigenous and non-Indigenous population.

Table 3.4 Factors associated with unpaid child care provision, females, 2006

Explanatory variables[a]	Total population		Indigenous population	
	Model 1	Model 2	Model 3	Model 4
Indigenous	0.076	0.125		
Female	0.193	0.166	0.188	0.203
Aged 15–19	−0.324	−0.243	−0.319	−0.306
Aged 20–24	−0.307	−0.248	−0.258	−0.255
Aged 25–29	−0.205	−0.148	−0.057*	−0.056*
Aged 35–39	0.160	0.108	n.s.	n.s.
Aged 40–44	0.162	0.078	−0.052*	n.s.
Aged 45–49	0.033	−0.079	−0.192	−0.189
Aged 50–54	−0.146	−0.290	−0.287	−0.278
Aged 55+	−0.255	−0.419	−0.390	−0.360
Aged 15–19, female	−0.048	−0.024	n.s.	n.s.
Aged 20–24, female	0.018	0.029	0.079	0.090
Aged 25–29, female	0.011*	n.s.	n.s.	n.s.
Aged 35–39, female	−0.018	−0.010*	n.s.	n.s.
Aged 40–44, female	−0.084	−0.084	−0.114	−0.121
Aged 45–49, female	−0.159	−0.174	−0.104	−0.103
Aged 50–54, female	−0.155	−0.164	−0.109	−0.106
Aged 55+, female	−0.091	−0.056	−0.086	−0.083*
Victoria		n.s.	n.s.	n.s.
Queensland		0.007	n.s.	n.s.
South Australia		0.017	n.s.	n.s.
Western Australia		0.006	n.s.	n.s.
Tasmania		n.s.	n.s.	n.s.
Northern Territory		n.s.	n.s.	n.s.
Australian Capital Territory		0.011	n.s.	n.s.
Major city		−0.015	−0.035	−0.037
Secondary school student		−0.091	−0.176	−0.165
Tertiary student		−0.099	−0.109	−0.094
Part-time student		0.088	0.090	0.072*
Completed Year 9 or less		−0.014	n.s.	n.s.
Completed Year 10 or 11		0.022	0.030	0.036
Does not have any qualifications		n.s.	n.s.	n.s.
Has a Diploma or Certificate only		0.030	n.s.	n.s.
Speaks another language and English well		−0.068	0.042	0.049
Speaks another language and English not well or not at all		−0.042	n.s.	n.s.

Never married		−0.358	−0.211	−0.202
Divorced, separated or widowed		−0.126	−0.081	−0.076
Lives in a mixed Indigenous and non-Indigenous household				n.s.
Probability of base case[b]	0.1488	0.567	0.608	0.517
Pseudo R-Squared	0.380	0.1959	0.1297	0.1273
Number of observations	714 579	641 491	10 421	10 016

a. n.s. = Those variables that were not significant at the 10% level of significance.
 * = Those variables that were significant at the 10% level of significance but not the 5% level.

b. The base case for the total population is non-Indigenous. For all estimates, the base case is male, aged 30–34 years and in addition, for Models 2–4 (for the total population and for the Indigenous estimates), the base case lives in New South Wales, outside a major city, is not a student, has completed Year 12, has a university degree, speaks English only, and is married. For Model 4, an additional characteristic of the base case is that they are living in an Indigenous-only household.

Source: Customised calculations using the 2006 5% CSF, ABS Census of Population and Housing

Apart from being female, there are two other characteristics strongly associated with providing child care. Firstly, even after controlling for age, students in general and secondary students in particular were significantly less likely to be providing unpaid child care than non-students. It is likely this reflects the time constraints that come from both studying and providing unpaid child care. Secondly, those who have never been married and (to a lesser extent) who were divorced, separated or widowed are less likely to be providing unpaid child care. This once again demonstrates the link between marital status and child rearing.

Fertility and family formation across the Indigenous lifecourse

While the popular saying 'demography is destiny' may be an exaggeration, it is certainly the case that there is a strong association between major demographic outcomes across the lifecourse and many of the standard measures of wellbeing. This is shown a number of times throughout this monograph, and the literature on the effects of key demographic variables is almost limitless.

Two of the major demographic events that can shape a person's lifecourse are marriage and having children. The analysis presented in this chapter shows that Indigenous Australians are less likely to be married than non-Indigenous Australians and, for those who were married, less likely to be in a registered as opposed to de facto marriage. Especially outside of major cities, it would appear that Indigenous males and females are less likely to participate in this most traditional Western institution. This likely reflects a relative preference amongst Indigenous Australians for other forms of marriage and the difficulty of the census to capture the diversity of Indigenous familial relationships (Morphy 2007). However, given the differences between Indigenous and non-Indigenous Australians in major cities are relatively small, it is also likely to reflect a lack of access to the types of institutions and services that facilitate marriage.

While having children should in no way be seen as the sole aim of a marriage, results presented in this chapter confirm that those females who are in a registered marriage have had significantly more children than those who had never been married and, for both sexes, are more likely to provide unpaid child care. Although the marginal effect was smaller, this was also the case for the Indigenous population when analysed separately. An interesting implication of this is that once marriage has been controlled for, the difference between Indigenous and non-Indigenous females in terms of the number of children ever born actually increases.

One of the most important findings from the analysis presented in this section on fertility is the interaction with education. Indigenous females who have completed higher levels of education are estimated to have significantly fewer children than those who left school before completion or who do not have post-school qualifications. This result holds after controlling for age. Furthermore, those who are undertaking full-time education have also had fewer children than those who are not studying. Moreover, education attendance has a large and significant negative association with providing unpaid child care for both Indigenous males and females. The direction of causality between education and fertility is very difficult to disentangle. Childbirth is likely to both impact on and be impacted by education decisions, and there may be additional variables like labour market experience that are associated with both. Although the results cannot shed light on the direction of causality, they nonetheless suggest potentially positive policy interactions, with increases in Indigenous education likely to lead to reductions in fertility.

4. Migration and mobility

Population mobility is the spatial movement of people either locally or internationally. In the census, population movement is measured using data based on the place of usual residence. At first glance, census-based analysis on Indigenous population movement suggests much higher rates of migration and mobility relative to the non-Indigenous population. Between 2001 and 2006, 46.5 per cent of the Indigenous population changed their place of usual residence, compared to 43.1 per cent for the non-Indigenous population as reported in Biddle (2009b). Furthermore, Biddle and Prout (2009) identified a much higher percentage of Indigenous Australians being away from their place of usual residence on the night of the census (6.8 per cent) compared to non-Indigenous Australians (4.3 per cent).

While these percentage comparisons paint an initial picture of a relatively mobile Indigenous population, more detailed analysis by geography and across the lifecourse shows a more complex set of patterns that is obscured by a single summary figure. Both populations exhibit a similar pattern of migration and mobility across the lifecourse, with rates starting off high, declining throughout the school years, reaching a peak in a person's mid- to late-twenties, and then declining slowly across a person's thirties, forties and fifties. However, the size and the duration of the different peaks and troughs are often quite different for Indigenous and non-Indigenous Australians.

At a macro level, using previous censuses Taylor (2006) showed that rates of migration for the Indigenous population converged quite dramatically when the age distributions of the two population were controlled for. It is not so much that the Indigenous population is more likely to change usual residence than the non-Indigenous population, but rather that there are more Indigenous Australians who are of the age where migration is at its highest.

At a micro or community level, migration of Indigenous Australians is one of the main drivers of population change. Biddle (2009b) identified the types of areas that Indigenous Australians were moving from or to and also showed that those who do move have a different age profile to those who do not. However, there has been no recent analysis of the characteristics of the people who do move relative to those who do not nor has it been established if this variation across the lifecourse in migration and mobility holds once other characteristics have been controlled for. Furthermore, the relationship between migration or mobility and other socioeconomic characteristics is also important, as these characteristics are likely to determine the level and types of services that people who have moved might require. Understanding the patterns of migration and mobility across the Indigenous lifecourse as well as the composition of those who do move has important implications for service delivery.

Mobility that is of a temporary nature and does not result in a permanent change of usual residence can also have significant implications for the delivery of services at the local level (Prout 2008). However, the exact type of services that are likely to be called upon depends heavily on the age and characteristics of people who are in an area on a temporary basis. If it is school age students that are highly mobile, then education services are likely to feel the greatest pressure. Movement amongst the elderly or those with poor health is likely to place greater demands on health services.

The analysis in this section focuses on two dependent variables – the probability of a person changing usual residence in the five years preceding the 2006 Census (permanent migration or residential mobility), and the probability of a person being away from their place of usual residence on the night of the census (temporary mobility).[1]

Permanent migration and residential mobility

People change usual residence for a number of reasons, with the literature (summarised in Greenwood 1997) identifying a number of push and pull factors that make the decision more or less likely. Push factors, or factors related to the person's source area, include local housing or employment market characteristics, political conditions, climatology and the presence or absence of social networks. If on balance the characteristics of potential destination areas (pull factors) are more favourable, then a person is more likely to make the decision to move. However there are significant financial and psychological costs associated with migration that need to be weighed up against the benefits before a potential move is considered worthwhile. Furthermore, the decision to migrate is often made at the family or household level with the gains or losses for one member of the family or household needing to be traded against the gains or losses for other members.

The costs and benefits of migrating are likely to vary substantially across the lifecourse. At a very young age, migration decisions are likely to be based on the employment opportunities or social networks of one's parents. Attendance at school imposes a substantial cost on migrating, with graduation or leaving

---

1   The census is limited in capturing mobility in that while it is able to tell whether a person has moved between two points in time, it says nothing about how many times that person has moved within that time frame.

school often providing a catalyst for a change of residence. As an individual moves towards adulthood, full-time work gives the means to move, with family formation often providing the motivation. As a person and/or their spouse settle into a stable job and their children reach school age, home ownership and firm specific human capital add a substantial cost to be weighed up against the diminishing benefits of moving. This variation across the lifecourse is summarised in Fig. 4.1, which shows the percentage of Indigenous and non-Indigenous males and females who changed their place of usual residence between 2001 and 2006 by five-year age cohorts defined at the end of the migration period.[2]

Fig. 4.1 Probability of changing place of usual residence, 2001–06

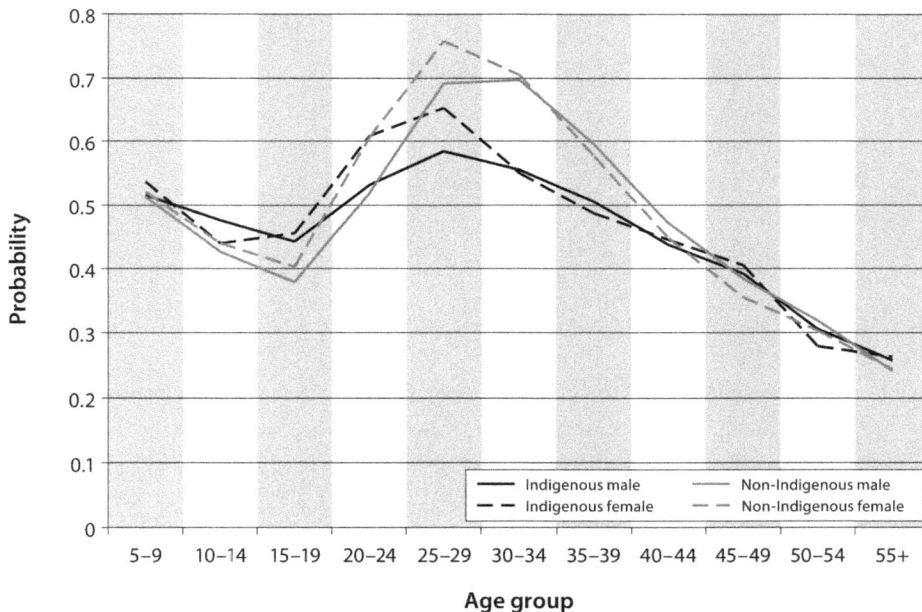

Source: Customised calculations using the 2006 5% CSF, ABS Census of Population and Housing

In general, a similar pattern of migration across the lifecourse is followed by all four demographic groups as shown in Fig. 4.1. Propensity to have moved starts off reasonably high (for those aged 5–9 years) and then declines steadily throughout compulsory schooling age. Beyond the age of 15, however, the

2   In the population literature, a distinction is made between migration and residential mobility (Greenwood 1997). The latter refers to any change in a person's place of usual residence, whereas the former refers to a move from one area to another. Unfortunately, the 5% CSF does not have sufficient geographic detail to separately identify the two.

propensity to change usual residence increases substantially, reaching a peak in a person's mid- to late-twenties. There is then a gradual decline, with people aged 55 years and over having the lowest propensity of all four groups.

The two major differences between the Indigenous and non-Indigenous plots in Fig. 4.1 point to key differences in the cause and effect of long-term migration. The rate of migration for the Indigenous population stays relatively high for people aged 5–20 years. This is likely to both be a reflection of, and potentially an influence on, a relative lack of engagement with formal education. However, the non-Indigenous population in their mid- to late-twenties reach a much higher peak than their Indigenous counterparts. For example, around three-quarters of non-Indigenous females aged 25–29 years changed their place of usual residence in the five years that preceded the most recent census. Biddle and Hunter (2006) speculate that this is partly due to lower rates of employment-driven mobility for the Indigenous population.

One of the interesting points to note from Fig. 4.1 is that there are very few ages where the probability of changing usual residence is higher for the Indigenous population compared to the non-Indigenous population. These generally higher age-specific rates of migration are confirmed in the modelling results presented below.

Modelling residential mobility

The dependent variable for the analysis presented in Table 4.1 is the probability that a person aged 15 years and over changed their place of usual residence between 2001 and 2006. All the explanatory variables are defined based on information from the 2006 Census and hence reflect a person's characteristics after the decision on whether or not to change usual residence has been made. Results are once again presented for four separate models, split across two tables for ease of presentation. A separate set of estimates is given in Table 4.2 for the probability of a person aged 5–14 years having changed their place of usual residence.

Table 4.1 Factors associated with the probability of changing place of usual residence, population aged 15 years and over, 2001–06

Part A: Demographic and geographic variables

Explanatory variablesa	Total population		Indigenous population	
	Model 1	Model 2	Model 3	Model 4
Indigenous	−0.023	−0.034		
Female	0.008	0.017	n.s.	n.s.
Aged 15–19	−0.314	−0.214	−0.090	−0.106
Aged 20–24	−0.175	−0.130	n.s.	n.s.
Aged 25–29	n.s.	0.011	n.s.	n.s.
Aged 35–39	−0.103	−0.106	n.s.	−0.063*
Aged 40–44	−0.224	−0.234	−0.160	−0.160
Aged 45–49	−0.311	−0.326	−0.219	−0.242
Aged 50–54	−0.378	−0.400	−0.305	−0.322
Aged 55 +	−0.453	−0.479	−0.345	−0.351
Aged 15–19, female	0.011	n.s.	n.s.	n.s.
Aged 20–24, female	0.065	0.050	0.092	0.101
Aged 25–29, female	0.057	0.044	0.110	0.118
Aged 35–39, female	−0.024	n.s.	n.s.	n.s.
Aged 40–44, female	−0.030	n.s.	n.s.	n.s.
Aged 45–49, female	−0.036	−0.011	0.084	0.099
Aged 50–54, female	−0.025	n.s.	n.s.	n.s.
Aged 55 +, female	n.s.	n.s.	n.s.	n.s.
Victoria		−0.016	0.039	0.043
Queensland		0.079	0.044	0.053
South Australia		−0.010	n.s.	n.s.
Western Australia		0.057	0.054	0.073
Tasmania		−0.011*	−0.051	−0.062
Northern Territory		0.035	−0.096	−0.102
Australian Capital Territory		0.022	n.s.	n.s.
Major city		−0.043	n.s.	n.s.
Probability of the base caseb	0.696	0.767	0.690	0.637
Pseudo R-Squared	0.0903	0.1176	0.1063	0.1164
Number of observations	721 797	590 940	8 989	8 626

Part B: Socioeconomic and other variables

	Total population		Indigenous population	
Explanatory variables[a]	Model 1	Model 2	Model 3	Model 4
Secondary school student		−0.049	n.s.	n.s.
Tertiary student		0.039*	0.044	n.s.
Part-time student		−0.024	n.s.	n.s.
Completed Year 9 or less		−0.022	−0.042	−0.037
Completed Year 10 or 11		−0.006	−0.029	n.s.
Does not have any qualifications		−0.078	−0.102	−0.113
Has a Diploma or Certificate only		−0.046	n.s.	n.s.
Speaks another language and English well		−0.012	−0.207	−0.201
Speaks another language and English not well or not at all		0.040	−0.333	−0.341
Never married		−0.012	0.051	0.069
Divorced, separated or widowed		0.093	0.134	0.163
Has had at least one child (for females)		−0.029	n.s.	n.s.
Has a 'core activity' need for assistance		0.020	n.s.	n.s.
Provides unpaid child care (all)		0.009	0.031	0.028*
Provides unpaid child care for children other than own		0.008	n.s.	n.s.
Provides unpaid assistance for someone with a disability		−0.027	−0.036	−0.035
Not employed		0.022	0.026	0.044
Owner or manager of enterprise or contributing family worker		−0.019	n.s.	n.s.
Employed in the government sector		−0.024	−0.063	−0.053
Employed part-time		−0.019	−0.075	−0.071
Undertook volunteer work		−0.033	n.s.	n.s.
Low individual income (less than $250pw)		−0.015	−0.084	−0.090
High individual income ($1,000pw or more)		0.027	0.039	0.037*
Lives in a mixed Indigenous and non-Indigenous household				0.080
Probability of the base case[b]	0.696	0.767	0.690	0.637
Pseudo R-Squared	0.0903	0.1176	0.1063	0.1164
Number of observations	721 797	590 940	8 989	8 626

[a.] n.s. = Those variables that were not significant at the 10% level of significance.

* = Those variables that were significant at the 10% level of significance but not the 5% level.

[b.] The base case for the total population is non-Indigenous. For all estimates, the base case is aged 30–34 years and in addition, for Models 2–4 (for the total population and for the Indigenous estimates), the base case lives in New South Wales, outside a major city, is not a student, has completed Year 12, has a university degree, speaks English only, is currently married, has not had any children, did not change usual residence in the last five years, does not provide unpaid child care or assistance to someone with a disability, is employed as an employee in the private sector, works full-time, did not undertake volunteer work, and has an income between $250 and $1 000 per week. For Model 4, an additional characteristic of the base case is that they are living in an Indigenous-only household.

Source: Customised calculations using the 2006 5% CSF, ABS Census of Population and Housing

The results for Model 1 confirm that the relatively high rates of residential mobility recorded for the Indigenous population nationally are a result of Indigenous Australians being disproportionately found in the age groups who are more likely to change usual residence. Once differences across the lifecourse have been controlled for, Indigenous Australians are actually significantly less likely to change usual residence over a five-year period than the non-Indigenous population. After controlling for the other characteristics included in Model 2, the difference between Indigenous and non-Indigenous Australians in the predicted probability of moving is even greater still.

There are a number of interesting marginal effects from the Model 3 estimates, especially when compared to the results for the total population. For the total population, living in a major city is associated with a lower probability of having changed usual residence compared to the base case. For the Indigenous population, however, there was no significant difference. Aggregate results presented in Biddle (2009a) showed a large difference between the remote and non-remote population in terms of the propensity to move. It would appear that this difference may be driven by other observed characteristics.

Indigenous tertiary students are more likely to have changed their place of usual residence than non-students. This was also the case for the total population and is not surprising given the uneven geographic spread of tertiary institutions in Australia. However, there was no significant difference between secondary school students and non-students for the Indigenous population. For the total population, attendance at secondary school appears to impose a large cost on residential mobility. This does not appear to be the case for the Indigenous population.

Other apparent constraints on residential mobility for the total population, namely having had children (for females) and undertaking voluntary work, were also not found to be significant for the Indigenous population.

The set of variables with the largest marginal effects for the Indigenous population are the for language spoken at home, with those who speak a language other than English much less likely to have changed usual residence. The greatest difference is for those who are also reported to either not speak English well or not speak it at all. It may be the case that these individuals genuinely have much lower movement propensities. However, the size of the marginal effect may also have been driven by the way in which the concept of usual residence is framed on the census form.

The final Model 4 presented in Table 4.1 includes an additional variable on whether a particular Indigenous Australian lives in a household that contains non-Indigenous usual residents. Indigenous Australians who do live in such households have a significantly higher probability of having changed usual residence than those who live in households with Indigenous residents only. Not only do the results in Table 4.1 show that non-Indigenous Australians have a higher rate of residential mobility than Indigenous Australians once other characteristics are controlled for, they also show that Indigenous Australians who live with non-Indigenous Australians also have a higher probability of changing usual residence than those who live in Indigenous-only households.

The key determinants of residential mobility are likely to be very different for children as opposed to adults. In particular, mobility decisions are likely to be made on their behalf by parents or guardians. While these decisions may take into account the particular characteristics of the child (including their educational attendance), they are also likely to be influenced by the employment, family and social circumstances of responsible adults.

The results presented in Table 4.2 are based on analysis of the same dependent variable as Table 4.1 (the probability of changing usual residence between 2001 and 2006). However, the analysis is restricted to people aged 5–14 years at the time of the 2006 Census. Clearly, a number of the explanatory variables that were applicable for adults are not applicable for children – marriage, employment, high school completion – and these are left out of the models.

A number of additional characteristics – like whether or not the child lives in a single-parent family – have been included. There are three things to keep in mind when interpreting these household or family-level variables that bear repeating. Firstly, they are only defined for people who were enumerated in a private dwelling that is their own place of usual residence. People in non-private dwellings and those away from their place of usual residence are therefore excluded from the analysis in Models 2, 3 and 4. Secondly, the household characteristics are defined at the end of the period, rather than at the start. This is of course true for a number of other explanatory variables, however, it is a particular issue for the analysis of migration as the very act of migration can have significant impacts on family structure.

The final thing to keep in mind when interpreting the household or family-level variables is that households or families are delineated by the ABS using definitions that do not necessarily reflect the diversity of Indigenous experiences. This is a point that will be returned to in subsequent chapters, especially in Chapter 9 which focuses on outcomes across the Indigenous childhood. These limitations aside, there are a number of insights that one can gain by analysing residential mobility for Indigenous and non-Indigenous children.

Table 4.2 Factors associated with the probability of changing place of usual residence, population aged 5–14 years, 2001–06

Explanatory variables[a]	Total population		Indigenous population	
	Model 1	Model 2	Model 3	Model 4
Indigenous	0.027	−0.062		
Female	0.009	0.010	n.s.	n.s.
Aged 5–9	0.085	0.074	n.s.	n.s.
Aged 5–9, female	n.s.	n.s.	0.072	0.070
Victoria		−0.041	n.s.	n.s.
Queensland		0.116	n.s.	n.s.
South Australia		−0.034	0.072*	0.068*
Western Australia		0.106	0.083	0.094
Tasmania		n.s.	n.s.	n.s.
Northern Territory		n.s.	−0.127	−0.101
Australian Capital Territory		n.s.	n.s.	n.s.
Major city		−0.041	0.050	n.s.
Speaks another language and English well		0.031	−0.254	−0.193
Speaks another language and English not well or not at all		0.128	−0.418	−0.330
Preschool student		0.065	n.s.	n.s.
Primary or infants student		0.038	n.s.	n.s.
Not a student		n.s.	n.s.	n.s.
Non-government student		−0.041	−0.085	−0.080
Lives in a single-parent family		0.127	0.037	0.054
Lives in a household without anyone employed		0.065	0.035*	0.051
Lives in a household where no-one has completed Year 12		−0.020	n.s.	n.s.
Lives in a household with Indigenous and non-Indigenous adults				0.112
Lives in a household with non-Indigenous adults only				0.204
Probability of the base case[b]	0.430	0.390	0.447	0.352
Pseudo R-Squared	0.0052	0.0310	0.0543	0.0674
Number of observations	101 903	99 137	3 819	3 815

[a.] n.s. = Those variables that were not significant at the 10% level of significance.
* = Those variables that were significant at the 10% level of significance but not the 5% level.

[b.] The base case for the total population is non-Indigenous. For all estimates, the base case is aged 10–14 years and in addition, for Models 2–4 (for the total population and for the Indigenous estimates), the base case lives in New South Wales, outside a major city, speaks English only, is a high school student, attends a government school, lives in a couple family with children, has someone in the household employed, and has someone in the household who has completed Year 12. For Model 4, an additional characteristic of the base case is that they are living in an Indigenous-only household.

Source: Customised calculations using the 2006 5% CSF, ABS Census of Population and Housing

Perhaps the most interesting result from Table 4.2 is the difference in the Indigenous coefficient between Models 1 and 2. When only age and sex are controlled for, Indigenous children were more likely to have changed their place of usual residence over the previous five years. However, after controlling for geography and a limited set of individual, family and household variables, Indigenous children were estimated to have a lower predicted probability than an otherwise identical non-Indigenous child. In other words, the higher observed residential mobility for Indigenous children and Indigenous males in particular that was shown in Fig. 4.1, is driven mainly by other observed characteristics.

Indigenous children are less likely to be attending a non-government school, as shown later in this monograph and in Biddle (2007). This variable was found to have a negative association with migration. On the other hand, Indigenous children are more likely to live in a single-parent family or a household without anyone employed. Both of these characteristics were associated with a higher probability of changing usual residence.

There were two major differences between the results from the estimates for Indigenous children only (Model 3) and children from the total population aged 5–14. For the total population, living in a major city was associated with a lower probability of changing usual residence. However, the situation was reversed for the Indigenous population, who had a significantly higher probability. The interaction between remoteness and residential mobility is clearly different for the Indigenous compared to the non-Indigenous population. In addition, speaking a language other than English was associated with a substantially lower probability of having changed usual residence for Indigenous children, whereas for the total population the association was positive.

The final Model presented in Table 4.2 contains two variables that control for the Indigenous status of adult members of the household. Compared to an Indigenous child who lives in a household where all adults are Indigenous, a child who lives in a household with both Indigenous and non-Indigenous adults, or (especially) a child who lives in a household with non-Indigenous adults only, is significantly and substantially more likely to have changed usual residence over the previous five years. As was found with adults, not only does being Indigenous reduce the level of residential mobility (once other characteristics are controlled for) – so too does living in a household with Indigenous adults.

Temporary mobility

Not all population movement involves a permanent change in a person's place of usual residence. Rather, people are often away from their place of usual residence for a night or more on a temporary basis. This could be for work, to visit family or as part of a holiday. For the Indigenous population, ceremonial practices and duties, seasonal factors and the lack of mainstream services in their area of usual residence also create a need and desire to be temporarily away from home (Prout 2008).

Like long-term residential mobility, temporary mobility also has implications for the provision of services. Furthermore, there are distinctive patterns to temporary mobility across the lifecourse that impact on, or are driven by the types of services demanded by people away from their place of usual residence.

Patterns in temporary mobility across the lifecourse are summarised in Fig. 4.2. The measure used – the proportion of the population away from their place of usual residence – is a crude proxy for a few reasons. Firstly, the definition of usual residence is problematic for the Indigenous population in general and the remote Indigenous population in particular (Morphy 2006). Secondly, the census is deliberately set at a time when the number of people away from home is likely to be minimised (that is, outside of school holidays and major sporting events). Thirdly, because the census is a snapshot at a particular point in time, it is likely to miss any seasonal variation. These caveats aside, the census snapshot does show some interesting lifecourse variation (conditional on the collection methodology).

Fig. 4.2 Probability of being away from place of usual residence, 2006

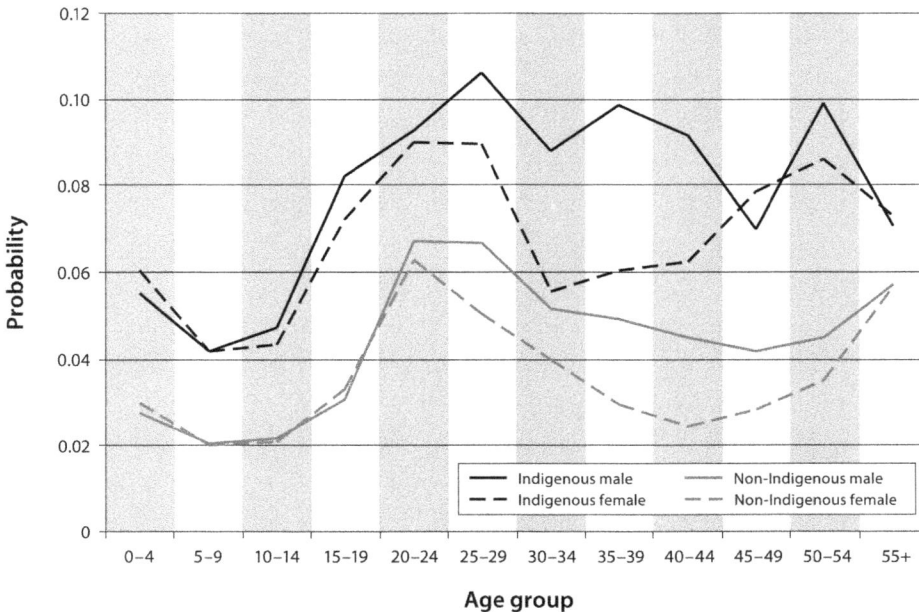

Source: Customised calculations using the 2006 5% CSF

The patterns of temporary mobility are similar to patterns for residential mobility, at least up until a person's late-twenties. Rates start off reasonably high, decline during school age and then reach a peak in a person's mid- to late-twenties. Rates of temporary mobility then decline only slightly for Indigenous and non-Indigenous males, but then decline sharply for females. Beyond the peak child-bearing and child-rearing age (around 45 years) the rates of temporary mobility then increase for females, reaching rough parity with males aged 55 years and over.

Apart from the divergence between males and females between the ages of 30 and 44, the other major difference between the results presented in Fig. 4.2 and results presented earlier in Fig. 4.1 is the consistent gap between the respective Indigenous and non-Indigenous populations. While the Indigenous population has higher rates of residential mobility for only a few age cohorts, they have higher rates of temporary mobility across the lifecourse.

Modelling temporary mobility across the lifecourse

The dependent variable for the analysis of temporary mobility is the probability of a person aged 15 years and over[3] being away from their place of usual residence on the night of the census. As it is not possible to create household-level variables for people away from their place of usual residence, it is not possible to include a fourth model with household-level explanatory variables.

---

3   Because it was not possible to use household-level variables for the temporary mobility estimations, there were very few explanatory variables available for 0–14 year olds, and hence a separate estimate is not presented. A simple analysis that controls for age, geography and education attendance showed a significant positive difference between Indigenous and non-Indigenous children. The base case and Indigenous marginal effects for these estimations is given in Table 10.1.

Table 4.3 Factors associated with the probability of being away from place of usual residence on census night, 2006

Part A: Demographic and geographic variables

Explanatory variablesa	Total population		Indigenous population
	Model 1	Model 2	Model 3
Indigenous	0.039	0.024	
Female	−0.013	−0.004*	−0.036
Aged 15–19	−0.021	n.s.	n.s.
Aged 20–24	0.016	0.017	n.s.
Aged 25–29	0.015	0.011	n.s.
Aged 35–39	n.s.	n.s.	n.s.
Aged 40–44	−0.006	n.s.	n.s.
Aged 45–49	−0.010	−0.008	−0.024*
Aged 50–54	−0.007	−0.006	n.s.
Aged 55 +	0.005	0.004	−0.023*
Aged 15–19, female	0.020	0.013	n.s.
Aged 20–24, female	0.011	n.s.	0.046*
Aged 25–29, female	n.s.	n.s.	n.s.
Aged 35–39, female	−0.011	−0.009	n.s.
Aged 40–44, female	−0.014	−0.012	n.s.
Aged 45–49, female	−0.005	n.s.	0.125
Aged 50–54, female	n.s.	n.s.	0.051*
Aged 55 +, female	0.015	0.013	0.090
Victoria		n.s.	n.s.
Queensland		n.s.	n.s.
South Australia		0.004	0.025
Western Australia		0.010	0.039
Tasmania		−0.006	n.s.
Northern Territory		0.009	0.022
Australian Capital Territory		0.009	n.s.
Major city		−0.020	−0.021
Probability of the base caseb	0.051	0.053	0.065
Pseudo R-Squared	0.0104	0.0348	0.0456
Number of observations	733 982	580 455	8 946

Part B: Socioeconomic and other variables

	Total population		Indigenous population
Explanatory variables[a]	Model 1	Model 2	Model 3
Secondary school student		−0.028	−0.025
Tertiary student		0.005	0.024*
Part-time student		−0.008	−0.025*
Completed Year 9 or less		n.s.	n.s.
Completed Year 10 or 11		n.s.	n.s.
Does not have any qualifications		−0.006	n.s.
Has a Diploma or Certificate only		n.s.	n.s.
Speaks another language and English well		−0.018	n.s.
Speaks another language and English not well or not at all		−0.027	n.s.
Never married		0.014	0.016
Divorced, separated or widowed		0.011	n.s.
Has had at least one child (for females)		−0.005	n.s.
Changed usual residence in the last 5 years		n.s.	n.s.
Changed usual residence in the last year		0.013	0.046
Has a 'core activity' need for assistance		−0.003	n.s.
Provides unpaid child care (all)		−0.017	n.s.
Provides unpaid child care for children other than own		0.024	n.s.
Provides unpaid assistance for someone with a disability		n.s.	n.s.
Not employed		0.025	0.022
Owner or manager of enterprise or contributing family worker		0.002	n.s.
Employed in the government sector		−0.002	n.s.
Employed part-time		−0.007	−0.020
Undertook volunteer work		0.005	0.019
Low individual income (less than $250pw)		−0.007	−0.013
High individual income ($1,000pw or more)		0.028	0.030
Probability of the base case[b]	0.051	0.053	0.065
Pseudo R-Squared	0.0104	0.0348	0.0456
Number of observations	733 982	580 455	8 946

[a] n.s. = Those variables that were not significant at the 10% level of significance.

* = Those variables that were significant at the 10% level of significance but not the 5% level.

[b] The base case for the total population is non-Indigenous. For all estimates, the base case is male and aged 30–34 years and in addition, for Models 2–3 and for the Indigenous estimates, the base case lives in New South Wales, outside a major city, is not a student, has completed Year 12, has a university degree, speaks English only, is currently married, has not had any children, did not change usual residence in the last five years, does not provide unpaid child care or assistance to someone with a disability, is employed as an employee in the private sector, works full-time, did not undertake volunteer work, and has an income between $250 and $1 000 per week.

Source: Customised calculations using the 2006 5% CSF, ABS Census of Population and Housing

Unlike the analysis of residential mobility presented in Table 4.1, the results presented in Table 4.3 show that Indigenous Australians have a significantly higher probability of being temporarily mobile (that is, away from their place of usual residence on the night of the census) compared to the non-Indigenous population. While the size of the marginal effect declines slightly when other characteristics are controlled for (in Model 2), the difference between Indigenous and non-Indigenous Australians is still significant and quite large relative to the probability of the base case.

There are a number of other characteristics that have a significant and reasonably large association with the probability of being away from one's place of usual residence. Secondary students have a significantly lower probability than those not participating in education, whereas Australians not in a registered marriage have a significantly higher probability than people who are. Interestingly, Australians not employed have a higher probability of being away from their place of usual residence than those who are employed. It would appear that the fact that many people travel for work does not outweigh the stronger ties to an area that results from being not employed.

A female who has had a child is estimated to have a lower probability of being away from her place of usual residence than a female who has not. The size of the marginal effect, however, is quite small. On the other hand, the (negative) marginal effect for providing unpaid child care is substantially larger. Given females are substantially more likely to provide such care, it would appear that it is current responsibilities as opposed to historical fertility decisions that is driving the difference between males and females in the rates of temporary mobility between the ages of 25 and 54, shown in Fig. 4.2.

Unlike the previous tables in this and other chapters, there were no individual-level variables that have an association in the opposite direction for the Indigenous population compared to the total population. There are, however, a few variables for which the magnitude of the marginal effect is much larger for the Indigenous estimates.

Across the total population, having changed usual residence in the preceding year is associated with a higher probability of being away from that new place of usual residence on census night. However, the marginal effect for the Indigenous population is more than three times as large, showing that residential mobility has a much greater association with temporary mobility for the Indigenous population. Similarly, those who undertook voluntary work in the 12 months preceding the census are much more likely to be away from their usual residence. Given age and employment status is controlled for, this may be because some of this volunteer work is undertaken away from a person's area of usual residence. If so, then this is much more likely to be the case for Indigenous Australians.

Despite the above insights, a quick look at the Pseudo R-Squared values for the estimates in Table 4.3 show that much of the variation in rates of temporary mobility remains unexplained. A more accurate measure that would arguably reduce the amount of unobservable variation is the number of nights a person spent away from their place of usual residence over a 12-month period. On the other hand though, such a measure would be prone to substantial recall bias. Ultimately, as discussed in Bell (2004) and taken in this paper from Biddle and Prout (2009: 322) 'the census will never be able to measure the duration of stay, frequency of movement, periodicity and seasonality – components of such population dynamics that have critical importance for policy makers'. These caveats notwithstanding, the results presented in this section show important lifecourse variation and significant differences between Indigenous and non-Indigenous Australians.

Migration and mobility across the Indigenous lifecourse

One of the major complicating factors for service delivery and program evaluation is residential and temporary mobility. In planning the type and location of capital expenditure, it is important to know not only how many people are in a particular area at a particular point in time (current demand), but also how many people are likely to be there over the life of the infrastructure (future demand). Furthermore, it is not only residents of an area that demand services, but also people who are there on a temporary basis – hence the importance of the concept of a service population.

There is a stereotype that Indigenous Australians are highly mobile. This is certainly true in aggregate terms, with Indigenous Australians more likely to have changed their place of usual residence over a five-year period, and more likely to be away from their place of usual residence on the night of the census. However, these aggregate figures hide significant variation by geography (Biddle 2009; Biddle and Prout 2009) and, as shown in this chapter, by demography and socioeconomic outcomes. Once age is controlled for, Indigenous adults are in fact less likely to have changed their place of usual residence than non-Indigenous Australians. This is also true for Indigenous children once other socioeconomic characteristics have been controlled for. Indigenous Australians still have higher rates of temporary mobility once other characteristics have been controlled for, although the difference is dramatically reduced.

Ultimately, what the results in this chapter show is that there is more difference across the lifecourse and by socioeconomic status within the Indigenous population than there are differences between Indigenous and non-Indigenous

Australians. If other characteristics beyond those controlled for in the census were ex;plored, it is likely that this observation would be strengthened. The census is somewhat of a blunt instrument for capturing Indigenous mobility processes. Nonetheless, it is clear that if service providers want a good prediction in terms of mobility of the demand for services now and into the future factors like education participation, employment and child rearing responsibilities are a much better guide than Indigenous status.

5. Education participation

Australians who complete additional years of education experience a range of positive outcomes throughout their lives. Their incomes may be higher, employment easier to obtain and their health better (Borland 2002; Card 2001; Wolfe and Haveman 2001). There are likely to be spillover effects to the household and community as a result of the individual's investment in education. People with higher education levels may act as positive role models for others around them, thereby increasing overall levels of education. A more highly educated population may also lead to more active engagement in democracy, community governance and resource management. Wei (2004) estimated that the contribution of investment in education to the stock of human capital in Australia has increased quite considerably since the early 1980s, further confirming the emphasis that is placed on the importance of education.

While it is difficult to construct completely accurate estimates of the returns to education in the absence of experimental or at the very least longitudinal data, analysis of available cross-sectional data suggests that they are at least as high for the Indigenous compared to the non-Indigenous population. Daly (1995), Junankar and Liu (2003), Hunter (2004), and Biddle (2006a, 2006b) show that the employment, income and health benefits of completing Year 12 are quite high for the Indigenous population and often higher than for the non-Indigenous population. Biddle (2007) also showed consistently high predicted income and employment benefits of education by geography and education sector, as well as large health benefits. It is not surprising, therefore, that reducing the gap in education attendance and attainment between Indigenous and non-Indigenous Australians is one of the focuses of COAG's Closing the Gap agenda.

According to the 2006 Census, only 23.9 per cent of the Indigenous population aged 15 years and over has completed high school – slightly less than half the rate for the non-Indigenous population (49.7%).[1] More than three-quarters (76.3%) of the Indigenous population aged 15 years and over have not completed either a degree or trade qualification, which is 1.41 times the rate for the non-Indigenous population (54.1%). In many ways, these national summary figures from the 2006 Census represent only a small part of the educational marginalisation faced by Indigenous Australians, with other indicators showing equally high levels of disengagement. For example, daily attendance rates for government primary

---

1   These figures are slightly different to those published by the ABS, as those who are currently at school are excluded from the analysis, as are those who did not state their usual residence on census night. However, these exclusions have no substantive impact on conclusions from the data.

schools in 2006 were estimated to be around 86 per cent for Indigenous students nationally, compared to 93 per cent for non-Indigenous students (Department of Education, Employment and Workplace Relations (DEEWR) 2008). The gap is even larger for secondary schools, with a national median of 79 per cent attendance for Indigenous government secondary school students compared to close to 90 per cent for their non-Indigenous counterparts.

Low rates of attendance are both a cause and an effect of poor academic achievement. In Australia all Year 3, 5 and 7 students are assessed across the areas of literacy and numeracy. According to DEEWR, 'the nationally agreed literacy and numeracy benchmarks for Years 3, 5 and 7 represent minimum standards of performance below which students will have difficulty progressing satisfactorily at school' (DEEWR 2008: 52). In 2006, across all three year levels and across reading, writing and numeracy, Indigenous students trail the national average. The gap (in terms of the difference in the percentage of the population who achieved the minimum benchmark) ranges from 13 percentage points for Year 3 reading to 32 percentage points for Year 7 numeracy (DEEWR 2008). In general, the gap tends to widen as Indigenous students progress to higher grades.

While the benefits of education for the Indigenous population and the gaps that currently exist are well recognised, there are a number of constraints in meeting the government's targets and a number of these constraints are summarised below. More detail is given in Biddle (2010), in a study which takes a human capital approach to Indigenous education marginalisation and focuses on the larger social and economic costs of education for the Indigenous population. A summary of the discussion is outlined below.

Relative concentration in remote Australia

While the majority of Indigenous Australians live in regional or urban Australia, there is still a greater concentration of Indigenous Australians in remote Australia compared to the non-Indigenous population. Access to schools in remote Australia is far less consistent than in other parts of the country, and can be significantly affected by seasonal variation and the student's access to economic resources.

Low English language ability

According to the 2006 Census, a greater percentage of non-Indigenous Australians aged 5–15 years speak a language other than English at home (14.1%), compared to Indigenous Australians (12.8%). However, of those that do speak a language other than English, Indigenous Australians aged 5–15 years are much more likely to be reported as speaking English not well or not at all

(20.2%), compared to their non-Indigenous population counterparts (6.1%). Unless schools are supportive of such language constraints, formal education for people from a non-English speaking background is likely to be more difficult and their latent cognitive abilities undervalued.

High geographic mobility

As shown in the previous chapter, Indigenous Australians of school age are more likely to change usual residence than non-Indigenous Australians in the same age group (at least before other characteristics are controlled). Even more so, Indigenous youth are more likely to be away from their place of usual residence on a temporary basis. Once again, unless supported by the school, both types of mobility can be disruptive for a student's academic progress.

Role models and peer effects

An Indigenous 15–17 year old who lives in an area with few Indigenous adults who have completed Year 12, or few Indigenous youth of their own age attending high school, are less likely to be attending high school themselves. Furthermore, Indigenous youth living in a household with low levels of education are also less likely to be attending education, with all these associations holding after controlling for an extensive range of individual, household and area-level variables. A lack of role models and peers with experience in, or positive feelings towards, formal education can make it much less likely that a youth will see education as being worthwhile.

Exposure to the criminal justice system

Indigenous youth are much more likely to have been arrested and incarcerated than the non-Indigenous population. Hunter and Schwab (1998) looked at household and socioeconomic factors in trying to explain education participation. They find that having been arrested was a strong predictor for not attending high school. Furthermore, early school leaving is also likely to be a predictor of youth involvement in criminal activity leading to further disengagement from formal education.

Poor health

There is a large body of international literature that has identified the relationship between health and education outcomes (Wolfe and Haveman 2001). However, Zubrick et al. (2006) is the only large-scale empirical study to look at the relationship between physical and emotional health of Indigenous children on the one hand and education participation on the other. The authors found that higher rates of absence from school due to health problems and emotional or behavioural difficulties both had a significant association with poor academic performance.

The gap in early childhood education

Quality preschool education can have substantial positive effects for the children that attend, easing the transition to school and providing a boost to a child's self esteem as well as their future scholastic ability (Barnett 1995, 1998). Heckman and Masterov (2005) also outline a number of effects on non-cognitive ability and social, economic and emotional wellbeing. While there are no empirical studies that test the effect of preschool education for Indigenous Australians, the general finding that quality preschool education benefits children who are least likely to otherwise do well at school means that reducing the gap between Indigenous and non-Indigenous Australians in terms of preschool attendance is one way in which future education disparities could be reduced.

Economic costs of undertaking education

Undertaking formal education requires significant investment from the individual and their family. The highest cost is in terms of income foregone, however there are also likely to be direct costs including fees and course materials. Indigenous university students report higher levels of economic disadvantage than other students, with one in four reporting that they regularly go without food and other necessities because they cannot afford them (Universities Australia 2007). These economic costs may be compounded by a lack of amenities at home, including adequate space to undertake home-based study and lack of access to information and communications technology (Biddle 2007).

While education completion rates reflect a historic lack of engagement with formal education, the results presented in this chapter show that current rates of participation are also substantially lower for the Indigenous compared to the non-Indigenous population. Circumstances and conditions before a child reaches 15 years of age are likely to determine to a large extent the decision regarding whether to continue on at school or not. Unfortunately though, there is very little education-related information on the census for individuals aged 6–14 years. All members of that age group are assumed to be participating in education, even if other empirical evidence shows that this is not necessarily the case (Taylor 2010). Furthermore, there is no information on the probability of actually attending school on a given day, despite the recognition that rates of attendance can have significant effects on a student's progress.

Despite the above limitations, there are a number of measures on the census that, when viewed from a lifecourse perspective, can give significant insights into Indigenous education participation. Accordingly, the results presented in this chapter are divided into three sections. The results in the first section look at the probability of participating in any type of post-compulsory education (that is, formal education for ages 15 years and over). Recognising that not all education has the same level of economic benefit, the second section of results focuses on non-school students and considers the factors associated with attending a university as opposed to another type of tertiary institution. The results in the final section return to high school students and consider the probability of attending a non-government as opposed to a government school.

Post-compulsory education participation

The first set of results presented in this paper shows the probability of participating in education across adulthood (15 years and over). All forms of education are grouped together in the graph, including high-school, vocational education and training (VET) – often referred to as technical and further education (or TAFE), and university (undergraduate and postgraduate).

Fig. 5.1 Probability of participating in education, age 15 years and over, 2006

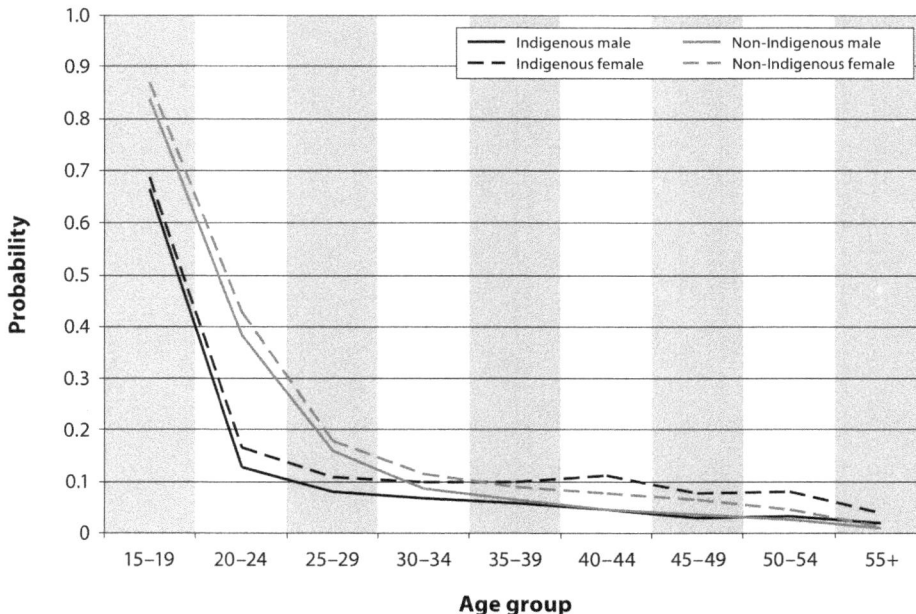

Source: Customised calculations using the 2006 5% CSF

Clearly (and not surprisingly), education participation is highest amongst 15–19 year olds. Around 85 per cent of non-Indigenous 15–19 year olds were participating in some form of education, according to the 2006 Census. This is substantially higher than the participation rate for the Indigenous population, which is around 67 per cent. Both percentages decline substantially into the next five-year age group (20–24 year olds), however the decline is much larger for the Indigenous compared to the non-Indigenous population. Around 15 per cent of Indigenous Australians of that age group were participating in education, compared to 40 per cent of the non-Indigenous population.

There are some differences by gender for these two age groups, with Indigenous and non-Indigenous females having higher rates of participation than males. However, while significant, these differences are minor compared to the differences between the respective Indigenous and non-Indigenous populations. The differences in education between Indigenous and non-Indigenous Australians reduce substantially from the 25–29 year age group and beyond. This part of the graph is a little difficult to interpret due to the scale used, so it is replicated in Fig. 5.2 with more appropriate values on the y-axis.

Fig. 5.2 Probability of participating in education, age 25–55 years plus, 2006

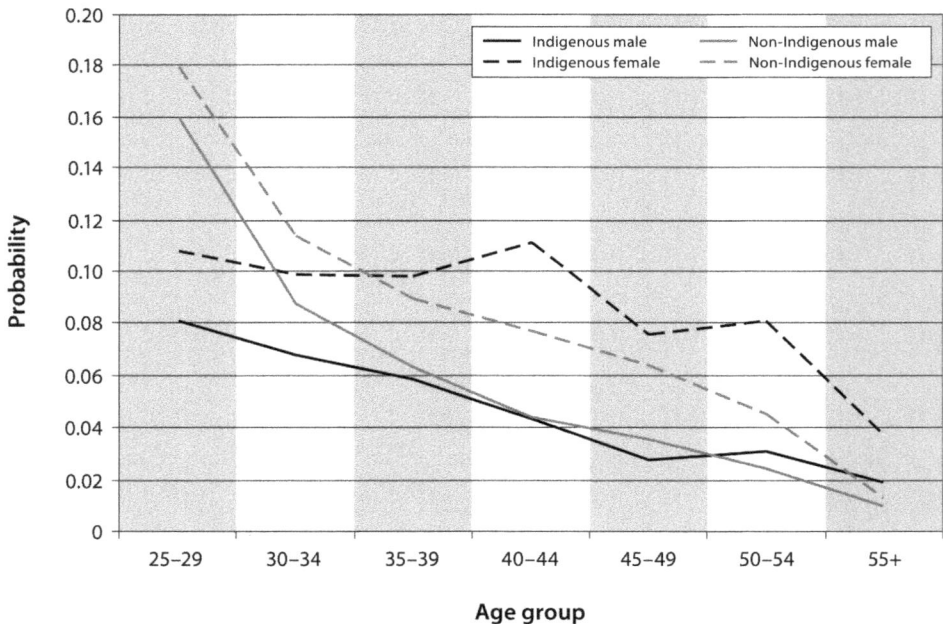

Source: Customised calculations using the 2006 5% CSF, ABS Census of Population and Housing

For both genders, participation rates converge around the 35–39 year age group. For females, the level of participation for this age group is around 10 per cent; for males it is around 6 per cent. Beyond this age group, participation rates for Indigenous and non-Indigenous males stay reasonably similar, whereas participation rates for Indigenous females are higher than for non-Indigenous females. For females, therefore, there is some catch-up in terms of education attainment from mature age students.

Modelling post-compulsory education across the lifecourse

There are three main findings from Figures 5.1 and 5.2. Education participation is highest amongst the young; females have higher rates of participation than males; and Indigenous Australians have substantially lower rates of participation when young, but similar or higher rates of participation from the mid-thirties onwards. In this section, we consider whether these stylised facts hold after controlling for other characteristics. Reflecting the substantially different rates of participation for the young compared to the mature aged, and the different factors influencing the education decision, education participation is modelled separately for 15–24 year olds (Table 5.1) compared to ages 25 years and over (Table 5.2).

Table 5.1 Factors associated with the probability of participating in education, population aged 15–24 years who were not attending high school, 2006

Explanatory variables[a]	Total population		Indigenous population[c]	
	Model 1	Model 2	Model 3	Model 4
Indigenous	−0.219	−0.152		
Female	0.044	0.091	0.076	0.074
Aged 15–19	0.454	0.418	0.402	0.384
Aged 15–19, female	n.s.	−0.023	−0.033	−0.029*
Victoria		0.033	0.078	0.073
Queensland		−0.066	−0.018*	−0.018*
South Australia		−0.022	n.s.	n.s.
Western Australia		−0.056	−0.026*	−0.023*
Tasmania		0.045	n.s.	n.s.
Northern Territory		−0.115	−0.036	−0.043
Australian Capital Territory		0.053	n.s.	n.s.
Major city		0.077	0.043	0.039

Changed usual residence in the last 5 years		n.s.	n.s.	n.s.
Changed usual residence in the last year		−0.062	n.s.	n.s.
Completed Year 9 or less		−0.043	−0.055	−0.050
Completed Year 10 or 11		−0.117	−0.042	−0.038
Has a degree or higher		−0.184	n.s.	n.s.
Has a Diploma or Certificate only		n.s.	−0.054*	−0.051*
Speaks another language and English well		0.165	−0.028*	−0.027*
Speaks another language and English not well or not at all		0.205	n.s.	n.s.
Never married		0.148	0.113	0.084*
Divorced, separated or widowedc		n.s.	***	***
Has had at least one child (for females)		−0.187	−0.074	−0.067
Has a 'core activity' need for assistance		−0.079	n.s.	n.s.
Provides unpaid child care (all)		−0.090	n.s.	n.s.
Provides unpaid child care for children other than own		0.102	n.s.	n.s.
Provides unpaid assistance for someone with a disability		n.s.	n.s.	n.s.
Lives in a mixed Indigenous and non-Indigenous household				0.036
Probability of the base caseb	0.382	0.293	0.086	0.079
Pseudo R-Squared	0.1753	0.2116	0.2240	0.2297
Number of observations	121 551	90 386	2 640	2 524

[a.] n.s. = Those variables that were not significant at the 10% level of significance.

* = Those variables that were significant at the 10% level of significance but not the 5% level.

[b.] The base case for the total population is non-Indigenous. For all estimates, the base case is aged 20–24 years and in addition, for Models 2–4 (for the total population and for the Indigenous estimates), the base case lives in New South Wales, outside a major city, did not change usual residence in the last five years, has completed Year 12, does not have any qualifications, speaks English only, is currently married, has not had any children, and does not provide unpaid child care or assistance to someone with a disability. For Model 4, an additional characteristic of the base case is that they are living in an Indigenous-only household.

[c.] All Indigenous Australians in the sample who were divorced, separated or widowed were not participating in education. They were excluded from the estimates in Models 3–4.

Source: Customised calculations using the 2006 5% CSF, ABS Census of Population and Housing

The results from Model 1 confirm that young Indigenous adults are less likely to be participating in education than their non-Indigenous contemporaries. While the results from Model 2 show that after controlling for a range of other characteristics (including a person's prior education attainment) the difference between Indigenous and non-Indigenous Australians in the sample decreases. However, the coefficient is still significant and the marginal effect is still quite large. There are a number of interesting results from Models 3 and 4 regarding the factors associated with education participation for Indigenous 15–24 year olds. However, the result with perhaps the greatest policy significance is the finding that Indigenous females who have had at least one child are significantly and substantially less likely to be attending education than other females. As mentioned earlier, it is difficult to establish causality with this relationship. It is easy to understand why a young female with a child or children would find participating in education more difficult and more costly. However, it may also be the case that females who would not otherwise consider participating in education (for unobservable reasons) would see the opportunity cost of having children as being reasonably low. Chances are that both explanations are valid and therefore reducing the high fertility rates of young Indigenous females (shown in Chapter 3), or making education less of a burden for females with children, is likely to reduce at least in part the gap between Indigenous and non-Indigenous females in terms of education participation.

As interesting perhaps as the variables that were significant in Models 3 and 4, is variables that were not significant. Some of these variables may become significant with a larger sample size. However, 2 640 observations should be sufficient to pick up most effects. It is interesting, therefore, that young Indigenous adults who changed usual residence in the previous year or in the previous five years do not have a higher probability of participation compared to young Indigenous adults who did not move over the period. It is likely that there are reverse-causality effects that are impacting in opposite directions.

The results presented in Table 5.2 replicate the analysis for Australians aged 25 years and over, focusing on non-school education. There are a few observations in the sample where a person aged 25 years and over is attending high school. These observations are excluded from the analysis as the motivations for non-school compared to high school attendance at that age are likely to be quite different. Looking at the results presented in Model 1, after controlling for age and sex, there is no significant difference between Indigenous and non-Indigenous Australians aged 25 years and over in terms of education participation. This is compared to a probability that was 0.219 lower for those aged 15–24 years (shown in Table 5.1). Furthermore, Model 2 shows that after controlling for the set of socioeconomic controls available on the 5% CSF, Indigenous Australians aged 25 years and over have a significantly higher probability of attending education than a non-Indigenous Australian with otherwise identical (observable) characteristics.

Table 5.2 Factors associated with the probability of participating in education, population aged 25 years and over, 2006

Part A: Demographic and geographic variables

Explanatory variables[a]	Total population		Indigenous population	
	Model 1	Model 2	Model 3	Model 4
Indigenous	n.s.	0.016		
Female	0.027	0.021	n.s.	n.s.
Aged 25–29	0.071	0.036	n.s.	n.s.
Aged 35–39	−0.024	−0.011	n.s.	n.s.
Aged 40–44	−0.043	−0.019	n.s.	n.s.
Aged 45–49	−0.052	−0.025	−0.040	−0.043
Aged 50–54	−0.063	−0.031	−0.043	−0.049
Aged 55 +	−0.077	−0.040	−0.063	−0.064
Aged 25–29, female	−0.011	−0.007	n.s.	n.s.
Aged 35–39, female	0.006*	0.009	n.s.	n.s.
Aged 40–44, female	0.023	0.020	0.061*	0.063*
Aged 45–49, female	0.023	0.023	n.s.	n.s.
Aged 50–54, female	0.022	0.023	n.s.	n.s.
Aged 55 +, female	−0.007	0.006	n.s.	n.s.
Victoria		−0.003	n.s.	n.s.
Queensland		−0.002*	−0.022	−0.023
South Australia		0.007	n.s.	n.s.
Western Australia		−0.003	−0.025	−0.023*
Tasmania		0.013	n.s.	n.s.
Northern Territory		0.006*	−0.034	−0.034
Australian Capital Territory		0.019	n.s.	n.s.
Major city		n.s.	n.s.	n.s.
Probability of the base case[b]	0.087	0.047	0.082	0.085
Pseudo R-Squared	0.0984	0.1241	0.1000	0.0980
Number of observations	612 431	518 121	6 993	6 731

Part B: Socioeconomic and other variables

Explanatory variables[a]	Total population		Indigenous population	
	Model 1	Model 2	Model 3	Model 4
Changed usual residence in the last 5 years		0.012	n.s.	n.s.
Changed usual residence in the last year		n.s.	n.s.	n.s.
Completed Year 9 or less		−0.026	−0.053	−0.052
Completed Year 10 or 11		−0.019	−0.034	−0.037
Has a degree or higher		0.037	0.117	0.129
Has a Diploma or Certificate only		−0.009	n.s.	−0.025
Speaks another language and English well		0.015	0.027*	n.s.
Speaks another language and English not well or not at all		0.063	0.080	n.s.
Never married		0.021	n.s.	n.s.
Divorced, separated or widowed		0.024	0.022	0.023*
Has had at least one child (for females)		−0.010	n.s.	n.s.
Has a 'core activity' need for assistance		n.s.	n.s.	n.s.
Provides unpaid child care (all)		n.s.	−0.014	n.s.
Provides unpaid child care for children other than own		0.004	n.s.	n.s.
Provides unpaid assistance for someone with a disability		0.010	n.s.	n.s.
Lives in a mixed Indigenous and non-Indigenous household				n.s.
Probability of the base case[b]	0.087	0.047	0.082	0.085
Pseudo R-Squared	0.0984	0.1241	0.1000	0.0980
Number of observations	612 431	518 121	6 993	6 731

[a.] n.s. = Those variables that were not significant at the 10% level of significance.

* = Those variables that were significant at the 10% level of significance but not the 5% level.

[b.] The base case for the total population is non-Indigenous. For all estimates, the base case is aged 30–34 years and in addition, for Models 2–4 (for the total population and for the Indigenous estimates), the base case lives in New South Wales, outside a major city, did not change usual residence in the last five years, has completed Year 12, does not have any qualifications, speaks English only, is currently married, has not had any children, and does not provide unpaid child care or assistance to someone with a disability. For Model 4, an additional characteristic of the base case is that they are living in an Indigenous-only household.

Source: Customised calculations using the 2006 5% CSF, ABS Census of Population and Housing

The predicted difference in Model 2 between Indigenous and non-Indigenous Australians of 0.016 may not seem large, especially when compared to the corresponding marginal effect of −0.152 in Table 5.1. However, when it is compared to the probability of the relevant base case (0.047), the relative size of the difference becomes apparent. Biddle (2007) showed that in 2001, Indigenous Australians on average participated in education at a later age than non-Indigenous Australians. By combining a modelling approach with a lifecourse perspective, it has been possible in this chapter to show the even more important finding that mature-age Indigenous Australians with similar characteristics are participating in education at a higher rate than non-Indigenous Australians. While it is important to note that Indigenous Australians aged 25 years and over are more likely to undertake education than their non-Indigenous counterparts, it is also important to keep in mind that even when viewed over the lifecourse, Indigenous education attainment is still substantially lower. That is, the proportion of the population with some form of qualifications does not come close to converging (Biddle 2010). This not only highlights the importance of bridging the even larger gap amongst 15–24 year olds, but also understanding the factors that are associated with Indigenous education participation so as to identify constraints on raising the rate of participation even further. The results presented in Models 3 and 4 are therefore quite instructive. Indigenous Australians who have not completed Year 12 are significantly less likely to be attending education than those who have. Given that the decision to continue on at high school is made at a much younger age than the ages in the sample, there is unlikely to be any reverse causality present in this relationship (that is, individuals opting for high school as opposed to non-school education). It would seem, therefore, that high school education encourages, rather than substitutes for education later in life. Similarly, individuals with a university degree are more likely to be participating in education than individuals without any qualifications.

A final interesting point from Table 5.2 is that females who have had at least one child do not have a significantly different probability of attending education than females without children. This is in stark contrast to the findings presented in Table 5.1 (for 15–24 year olds), which showed that high rates of fertility were associated with lower levels of education participation amongst young adults. While this does not seem to be the case amongst females aged 25 years and over, there is also not a positive coefficient, meaning that there is no catch-up later in life for females who have children when they are young.

University participation

Not all types of education have the same economic or social benefits. Not surprisingly, individuals with a university education have higher income and employment prospects than those who have completed a certificate or diploma only. However, the direct and indirect costs of attending university (including income foregone) are also higher. Even after taking this into account, Biddle (2007) found higher predicted income and employment benefits from university education as opposed to VET.[2] The educational disadvantage summarised in the previous section may be even greater still when one focuses on university as opposed to other tertiary education.

So, while Indigenous adults may participate in formal education at comparable rates to their non-Indigenous counterparts (at least beyond the age of 25), it is important to consider whether there are significant differences in the type of education that is being undertaken and whether this varies across the lifecourse. The percentage of students aged 15 years and over who were studying at a university as opposed to another tertiary institution is shown in Fig. 5.3. Individuals attending high school are excluded from the analysis, as are those not attending any form of education.

Fig. 5.3 Probability of a tertiary student participating in university education, 2006

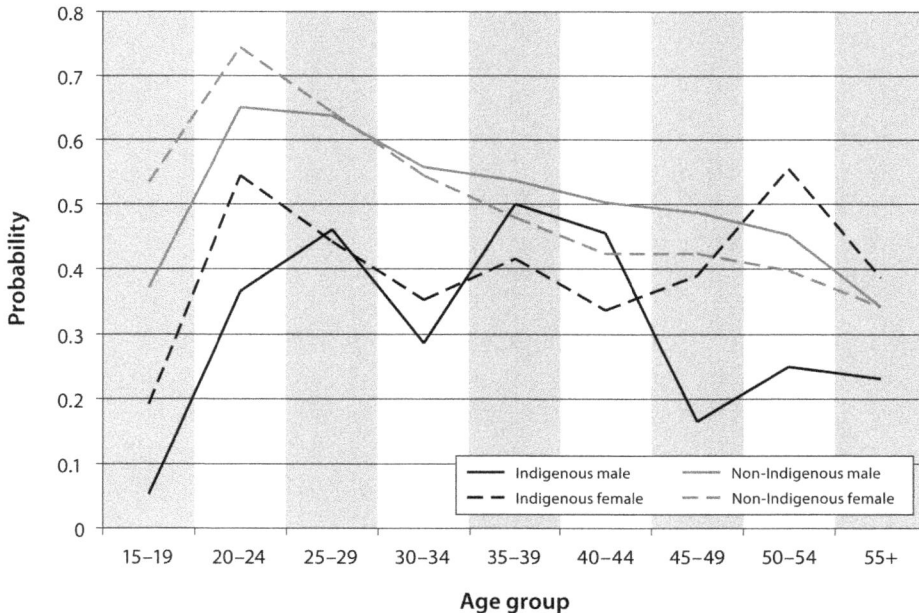

Source: Customised calculations using the 2006 5% CSF, ABS Census of Population and Housing

---

2   There are also likely to be substantial differences depending on the type of degree undertaken. However, the sample of Indigenous university students is not sufficiently large to undertake such a delineated analysis.

For non-Indigenous male and female tertiary students, the peak age of university attendance is the early twenties. More than 70 per cent of non-Indigenous female tertiary students of that age were attending university, alongside around 65 per cent of non-Indigenous males. For the Indigenous population, on the other hand, there is not only more volatility across the lifecourse, but attendance at university stays reasonably high (that is, as a proportion of tertiary students). Indeed, for the 50–54 and 55–plus age groups, Indigenous female tertiary students had a higher rate of university participation compared to non-Indigenous male and female tertiary students.

Modelling university participation across the lifecourse

The results for the factors associated with university participation are presented in Fig. 5.3. Once again, the sample is restricted to individuals attending some form of tertiary education. The results from Model 1 show that Indigenous tertiary students are significantly less likely to be attending a university as opposed to another form of tertiary institution after controlling for age and sex. With a marginal effect of −0.189 compared to the base case of 0.557, the gap in university education is quite substantial. However, when other characteristics are controlled for (in Model 2), the difference is no longer significant. Indigenous tertiary education students are no less likely to be attending university than non-Indigenous Australians with similar observed characteristics. While the insignificant result in Model 2 may appear to be somewhat heartening at first glance, the conclusion is a little less positive when one considers the explanatory variables that draw out most of the variance in university attendance. Specifically, people with lower previous levels of education (both in terms of high school and post-school education) are substantially less likely to be attending university. So, while the lower levels of participation found in Model 1 are not anything to do with indigeneity per se, they do appear to be related to education marginalisation from a young age.

Table 5.3 Factors associated with the probability of attending a university, tertiary education students, 2006

Part A: Demographic and geographic variables

Explanatory variables[a]	Total population		Indigenous population	
	Model 1	Model 2	Model 3	Model 4
Indigenous	−0.189	n.s.		
Female	n.s.	0.028	0.245	0.260
Aged 15–19	−0.190	−0.079	n.s.	n.s.
Aged 20–24	0.091	0.099	n.s.	n.s.
Aged 25–29	0.079	0.059	0.327	0.274
Aged 35–39	n.s.	0.037	0.439	0.461
Aged 40–44	−0.051	0.053	0.435	0.452
Aged 45–49	−0.071	0.057	n.s.	n.s.
Aged 50–54	−0.105	n.s.	n.s.	n.s.
Aged 55 +	−0.213	−0.091	n.s.	n.s.
Aged 15–19, female	0.164	0.094	n.s.	n.s.
Aged 20–24, female	0.117	0.083	n.s.	n.s.
Aged 25–29, female	n.s.	n.s.	n.s.	n.s.
Aged 35–39, female	−0.046	n.s.	−0.250	−0.188
Aged 40–44, female	−0.068	−0.051	−0.287	−0.200
Aged 45–49, female	−0.047	n.s.	n.s.	n.s.
Aged 50–54, female	n.s.	n.s.	n.s.	n.s.
Aged 55 +, female	n.s.	n.s.	n.s.	n.s.
Victoria		0.033	n.s.	n.s.
Queensland		0.090	n.s.	n.s.
South Australia		0.033	n.s.	n.s.
Western Australia		0.075	n.s.	n.s.
Tasmania		0.072	n.s.	n.s.
Northern Territory		0.211	0.301	0.496
Australian Capital Territory		0.066	n.s.	n.s.
Major city		0.073	0.158	0.161
Probability of the base case[b]	0.557	0.467	0.317	0.212
Pseudo R-Squared	0.0479	0.1848	0.2652	0.2864
Number of observations	64 164	54 828	837	787

Part B: Socioeconomic and other variables

Explanatory variables[a]	Total population		Indigenous population	
	Model 1	Model 2	Model 3	Model 4
Changed usual residence in the last 5 years		0.029	0.083	n.s.
Changed usual residence in the last year		n.s.	n.s.	n.s.
Completed Year 9 or less		−0.388	−0.291	−0.199
Completed Year 10 or 11		−0.321	−0.224	−0.160
Has a degree or higher		0.219	0.326	0.312
Has a Diploma or Certificate only		−0.296	−0.273	−0.192
Speaks another language and English well		n.s.	n.s.	−0.134
Speaks another language and English not well or not at all		−0.298	−0.285	−0.196
Never married		0.032	−0.089	n.s.
Divorced, separated or widowed		n.s.	0.151	0.188
Has had at least one child (for females)		−0.037	n.s.	n.s.
Has a 'core activity' need for assistance		−0.229	n.s.	n.s.
Provides unpaid child care (all)		n.s.	−0.098	n.s.
Provides unpaid child care for children other than own		n.s.	n.s.	n.s.
Provides unpaid assistance for someone with a disability		−0.016	n.s.	n.s.
Lives in a mixed Indigenous and non-Indigenous household				n.s.
Probability of the base case[b]	0.557	0.467	0.317	0.212
Pseudo R-Squared	0.0479	0.1848	0.2652	0.2864
Number of observations	64 164	54 828	837	787

[a.] n.s. = Those variables that were not significant at the 10% level of significance.

 * = Those variables that were significant at the 10% level of significance but not the 5% level

[b.] The base case for the total population is non-Indigenous. For all estimates, the base case is aged 20–24 years and in addition, for Models 2–4 (for the total population and for the Indigenous estimates), the base case lives in New South Wales, outside a major city, did not change usual residence in the last five years, has completed Year 12, does not have any qualifications, speaks English only, is currently married, has not had any children, and does not provide unpaid child care or assistance to someone with a disability. For Model 4, an additional characteristic of the base case is that they are living in an Indigenous-only household.

Source: Customised calculations using the 2006 5% CSF, ABS Census of Population and Housing

Non-government school attendance

Results presented in the previous sections showed that Indigenous Australians aged 25 years and over are more likely to be participating in education than a non-Indigenous Australian with similar observable characteristics. However, Biddle (2010) showed that this does not result in sufficient catch-up across the lifecourse to bring parity in participation in education completion. In addition, the results presented in Table 5.2 also showed that individuals who complete high school are more likely to undertake education later in life than those who do not, with the results presented in Table 5.3 showing that they are more likely to be attending university as opposed to other tertiary institutions. Finally, the benefits of education accrue over the lifecourse, so a person who undertakes education when they are 35 years old is likely to receive fewer lifetime benefits than people who complete the same level of education when they are young. For all three reasons, the factors that shape the high school decision clearly matter.

One factor that had not been included in any empirical analysis of Indigenous high school completion or participation is a person's cognitive and non-cognitive ability. According to Carneiro and Heckman (2003), Tobias (2003), and discussed in detail with regards to Indigenous Australians in Biddle (2010), students with relatively high ability are more likely to complete high school because they either have higher benefits from, or lower costs associated with, education. While it is unlikely that the distribution of natural ability across the Indigenous population is any different to the distribution for the non-Indigenous population, by the time a person reaches late secondary school there are a number of institutional or external factors that are likely to have had an impact.

The skills that are rewarded through the education system and the contemporary labour market are only one set from a larger range of abilities. As the Indigenous population makes up only a small percentage of the total population, the abilities that they value are less likely to be amongst the abilities that are rewarded. One policy response to this is to better accept and integrate into the school system the abilities of Indigenous students. A further impediment to the development of ability is likely to be intergenerational. That is, because the adult Indigenous population has been constrained in their educational attainment, they may be less able to prepare their children for Western school and assist in other ways throughout their school career.

One institutional factor that may impede skills development is the relatively low rates of preschool attendance for the Indigenous population. This low rate of attendance is likely to influence how ready a child is to start school. Biddle (2007) showed that Indigenous three, four and five year olds are less likely to attend preschool than the non-Indigenous population. A large part of this difference was explained by household and family level socioeconomic characteristics. However, having an Indigenous preschool worker in the area, also has a positive association. While school preparedness and attendance at a good quality preschool is important for the development of a person's cognitive and non-cognitive ability, so too are the amount of resources devoted to a person's education throughout their school life. Students who attend schools that are well resourced are likely to have greater access to their teacher, an improved range of educational resources, and possibly greater attention to their individual curriculum needs. For students from a low socioeconomic background, the resources channelled through their schools are crucial in at least partly addressing the relative lack of resources they receive towards their own education and development outside school. In addition to preschool attendance, therefore, Indigenous Australians may have lower levels of skills development when they reach late secondary school because of the level of resources available to them throughout their earlier school career. This in turn may be influenced by the type of school that a child attends, including whether they attend a government or non-government school.

The school system in Australia can be categorised into three broad sectors. The first, the government sector, is provided by State governments, does not charge school fees and has an obligation to provide a place for every eligible student regardless of background or financial position. In 2006, 70.9 per cent of primary students and 61.8 per cent of secondary students were attending government schools. Non-government schools, on the other hand, do charge school fees, although these school fees make up varying proportions of their total revenue. While these schools have a range of affiliations, the largest is the Catholic school system — which accounts for 19.1 per cent of primary and 21.5 per cent of secondary school students. Other non-government (or independent) schools made up the remaining 10.0 per cent of primary and 16.7 per cent of secondary school students (ABS 2006a).

The proportion of students attending non-government schools has increased quite substantially in the last 30–40 years. This has been caused in part by Commonwealth Government funding to non-government schools that began in the early 1950s and has increased reasonably steadily (even on a per-capita basis) since. Ryan and Watson (2004) show that the increase in funding has not led to a fall in school fees charged by non-government schools, but rather an increase in the amount of resources devoted to each student. This in turn has led to the maintenance of numbers of students with relatively high socioeconomic status attending non-government schools (and independent schools in particular). In Australia the resources devoted to students in non-government schools is on average higher than in government schools (Le and Miller 2003). Le and Miller also showed that even after controlling for the type of student who attends, non-government school students had a higher rate of school completion than the students in government schools. Hence, because Indigenous Australians attend non-government schools at a relatively low rate, their skills development may lag behind that of the non-Indigenous population, explaining some of the gap in school completion.

There are a number of factors that are likely to influence whether a child attends a non-government as opposed to a government school. These can be broadly categorised into three types: access, equity and preferences. Identifying factors that have a significant and substantial association with the probability of an Indigenous student attending a non-government school, as well as how these associations differ from the non-Indigenous population, will help in developing policy responses to low school completion rates. Furthermore, it is important to test whether the probability of attendance is still different for the Indigenous population after controlling for the observable characteristics of the individual.

Modelling non-government school attendance

The dependent variable in the following analysis is the probability that an infants, primary or secondary student (aged 5–19 years) is attending a non-government school as opposed to a government school. While there are likely to be differences between the outcomes of students attending a Catholic school as opposed to an 'other' non-government school, the sample size does not allow for a separate analysis of the two. Three sets of explanatory variables are used for the following estimations that have not been used up until now in this paper. The first is a control for whether the student is in infants or primary school as opposed to secondary school. Recognising that there are considerable resource requirements related to attendance at a non-government school, variables are also included (at the household level) in an attempt to control for current and permanent income or wealth. The first of these is the equivalised income of the household in which the child lives, with the base case having an equivalised income in the middle two quartiles, and a variable each for whether the household is in the first or fourth quartile. The other explanatory variable is for whether or not a person lives in a house that is owned or being purchased by a household member, with the base case being a household occupied under private or community rental. This is used as a proxy (albeit an imperfect one) for household wealth.

Table 5.4 Factors associated with the probability of attending a non-government school, for infants, primary and secondary school students, 2001–06

Explanatory variables[a]	Total population		Indigenous population	
	Model 1	Model 2	Model 3	Model 4
Indigenous	−0.173	−0.087		
Female	0.017	0.017	0.068	0.062
Aged 5–9	−0.016	n.s.	0.039*	0.036*
Aged 15–19	0.066	−0.020	n.s.	n.s.
Aged 5–9, female	−0.014	−0.017	−0.064	−0.059
Aged 15–19, female	n.s.	n.s.	n.s.	n.s.
Victoria		0.016	−0.048	−0.043*
Queensland		0.007*	n.s.	n.s.
South Australia		0.032	n.s.	n.s.
Western Australia		0.012	0.066	0.068
Tasmania		n.s.	n.s.	n.s.
Northern Territory		0.045	n.s.	0.044*
Australian Capital Territory		n.s.	0.125	0.107*
Major city		0.045	0.030	0.026
Changed usual residence in the last 5 years		−0.011	n.s.	n.s.
Changed usual residence in the last year		n.s.	n.s.	n.s.
Speaks another language and English well		n.s.	n.s.	0.048*
Speaks another language and English not well or not at all		n.s.	−0.105	−0.094
Primary or infants student		−0.081	−0.032*	−0.028*
Lives in a single-parent family		−0.034	−0.026	n.s.
Lives in a household without anyone employed		−0.024	−0.053	−0.048
Lives in a household where no-one has completed Year 12		−0.102	−0.028	−0.024
Household equivalised income in bottom quartile		−0.059	n.s.	n.s.
Household equivalised income in top quartile		0.162	0.101	0.094
Home owned or being purchased		0.121	0.098	0.086
Lives in a household with Indigenous and non-Indigenous adults				0.027
Lives in a household with non-Indigenous adults only				n.s.
Probability of the base case[b]	0.333	0.324	0.165	0.149
Pseudo R-Squared	0.0095	0.0580	0.0615	0.0625
Number of observations	144 645	123 252	4 092	4 089

[a.] n.s. = Those variables that were not significant at the 10% level of significance.

* = Those variables that were significant at the 10% level of significance but not the 5% level

b. The base case for the total population is non-Indigenous. For all estimates, the base case is aged 10–14 years and in addition, for Models 2–4 (for the total population and for the Indigenous estimates), the base case lives in New South Wales, outside a major city, speaks English only, is a high school student, lives in a couple family with children, has someone in the household employed, has someone in the household who has completed Year 12, lives in a household with equivalised income in the middle two quartiles, and lives in a dwelling that is not owned or being purchased. For Model 4, an additional characteristic of the base case is that they are living in an Indigenous-only household.

Source: Customised calculations using the 2006 5% CSF, ABS Census of Population and Housing

The results from Model 1 show that after controlling for age and gender only, Indigenous school students are significantly and substantially less likely to be attending a non-government as opposed to government school. To put the magnitude of the difference into perspective, a non-Indigenous male aged 10–14 years has a predicted probability of attending a non-government school equal to 0.333. An Indigenous male of the same age has a predicted probability of 0.160, less than half that of their non-Indigenous counterpart. This difference reduces substantially once other socioeconomic characteristics are controlled for (from −0.173 to −0.087), however it is still significant and, relative to other variables in the model, quite large. For example, the difference between Indigenous and non-Indigenous Australians in terms of non-government school participation is greater than the difference between an infants or primary school student and one attending secondary school, as well as the difference between someone who lives in a household with equivalised income in the bottom rather than the middle two quartiles.

Clearly, much of the difference between Indigenous and non-Indigenous Australians in non-government school participation results from the lower socioeconomic status of Indigenous students and their household. Models 3 and 4 also demonstrate that socioeconomic outcomes are associated with variation within the Indigenous population. Indigenous students who live in a household where no-one is employed or no-one has completed Year 12 are less likely to be attending a non-government school than the base case, whereas Indigenous students who live in a household where the equivalised income is in the top quintile, or who own or are purchasing their home are more likely to be attending.

Education participation across the Indigenous lifecourse

Although there is debate around the margins in terms of the size of any direct effect, individuals with higher levels of education tend to have better health, better employment prospects and a higher standard of living. Quite rightly, therefore, education is one of the centrepieces of COAG's Closing the Gap agenda and one of three components of the United Nations Development Programme's Human Development Index. Low levels of education participation and attainment comprises a large part of the explanation for the ongoing socioeconomic disadvantage faced by Indigenous Australians.

Focusing on education participation in adulthood, there are three main stylised facts from previous research that are confirmed from the analysis presented in this paper. Not surprisingly, education participation is highest amongst the young, females have higher rates of participation than males, and Indigenous Australians have substantially lower rates of participation when young. One of the more important findings from the analysis, however, is that Indigenous Australians have higher rates of participation from the mid-thirties onwards, especially after controlling for other characteristics. This suggests a different education lifecourse for Indigenous Australians. To a certain extent, the education that Indigenous adults undertake is likely to bring lower economic benefits than for the average non-Indigenous Australian. Not only does the education occur much later in life, leading to less time for the benefits to accrue, but it is more likely to take the form of VET rather than university study. While this latter difference disappears once other characteristics are controlled for, this is mainly because of lower levels of high school education for the Indigenous population. What happens in adolescence and young adulthood in terms of education attainment clearly has large and long-lasting effects throughout the lifecourse. If one also accepts that attendance at a non-government school brings advantages to the student (and evidence presented in Le and Miller (2003) suggests that it does), then the results presented in this chapter have also shown that throughout their school career Indigenous Australians are likely to be at a disadvantage compared to the average non-Indigenous Australian. This may explain the substantially lower levels of education participation during the part of the lifecourse generally associated with skills development.

There are two obvious policy responses to this situation. The first would be to reduce the education disadvantage faced by students attending a government as opposed to non-government school. To the extent that school resources (including the salary offered to teachers) explains this disadvantage, a redirection of funds from non-government to government schools would potentially contribute towards COAG's Closing the Gap targets. However, such a policy change is likely to be politically difficult, given the number of voters who have attended or who currently have children attending a non-government school. The second policy response would be to increase the number of Indigenous students attending a non-government school. This would potentially occur through a reduction in socioeconomic disadvantage. However, this could only realistically be seen as a long-term goal and, furthermore, there is still a large gap between Indigenous and non-Indigenous students after controlling for socioeconomic status. An alternative option would be to mandate a certain number of Indigenous-specific scholarships be made available for any non-government school to receive government funds. The two drawbacks of a policy such as this are that it ignores the large number of disadvantaged non-Indigenous Australians unable to afford the fees required to attend a non-government school, and that taking high-achieving Indigenous students out of government schools has the potential to disadvantage the Indigenous students that remain behind through the loss of positive peer group effects (Biddle 2007). Whatever the policy response, the results presented in this section have highlighted the potential for differential access to high-resource non-government schools, which may pose some difficulties for COAG in achieving the Closing the Gap targets.

6. Employment

Alongside key education and health outcomes, the other main target that underpins COAG's Closing the Gap agenda is to 'halve the gap' in Indigenous employment outcomes within a decade (by 2018). Stable, well-paid employment remains one of the key protective factors against poverty and exclusion, so the focus on Indigenous employment in the government's Closing the Gap targets is therefore both necessary and prudent. Without substantial improvements in Indigenous labour force outcomes, none of the other targets are likely to be met.

Taking results from the 2006 Census as a proxy for the baseline, a halving of the gap between Indigenous and non-Indigenous Australians in employment would entail an increase in the percentage of the population aged 15 years and over and employed from 43.2 to 51.9 per cent (assuming the non-Indigenous rate stays constant). There are a number of factors that are likely to make meeting this target difficult, as outlined below. The biggest constraint on meeting COAG's employment Closing the Gap targets is the projected growth of the working-age population over the period. As shown in Fig. 1.1 earlier in this monograph, a much greater proportion of Indigenous Australians were aged under 25 at the time of the 2006 Census compared to the non-Indigenous population. Over the subsequent decade, many of these Indigenous youth will be entering the age at which they start to look for their first job, or a stable career. Biddle and Taylor (2009) project that the Indigenous population aged 15 years and over will grow from 322 780 in 2006 to 428 169 in 2016. According to Biddle, Taylor and Yap (2009), an additional 45 528 jobs will need to be found over the period simply to maintain the level of employment at its current low level.

Adding to the difficulty in finding jobs for new entrants into the labour market (not to mention reducing the employment gap) are proposed changes to the Community Development Employment Projects (CDEP) Program. Beginning in 1977, the CDEP Program allows Indigenous Australians to forego social security benefits and instead receive a form of wages for employment. According to the (former) ATSIC (2002), 'The scheme is designed to provide meaningful employment opportunities for Aboriginal and Torres Strait Islander peoples as well as enabling Aboriginal and Torres Strait Islander communities to manage their own affairs and to gain economic and social equity'.

At least up until the time of the 2006 Census, the CDEP Program made up a substantial component of the labour market of Indigenous people. According to estimates in Biddle, Taylor and Yap (2008), employment in the program made up nearly one-quarter (23.4%) of the total employed Indigenous labour force.

However, participation in the scheme was primarily in remote Australia, and there were 14 regions out of a total of 37 across Australia where individuals in CDEP jobs made up 50 per cent or more of the employed. In late 2008, the Australian Government announced a number of changes to the CDEP Program that has the potential to have substantial impacts on the labour market prospects of Indigenous Australians. While the removal of CDEP positions from non-remote locations mostly reflects previous trends, the changes in remote Australia are potentially more drastic. In particular, there will be no new participants in remote Australia; current participants will be removed from the scheme permanently if they take a break from the scheme for more than two weeks; and the scheme will be stopped entirely from 30 June 2011. Once the removal of the CDEP Program has been factored into their projections, Biddle, Taylor and Yap (2009) estimate that a total of around 80 000 additional jobs will be required to keep Indigenous employment at its current level and 117 000 additional jobs will be required in total to meet the target of halving the employment gap.

The two issues combined (population growth and changes to the CDEP Program) influence the number of additional jobs that will be required to meet COAG's Closing the Gap targets. However, to be able to obtain and maintain these jobs, Indigenous Australians will need to be able to compete with the non-Indigenous population. This has always been the case to a large extent in cities and large regional towns, where Indigenous-specific jobs are scarce relative to the size of the population. However, with the withdrawal of the CDEP Program – the largest existing Indigenous labour market program – this is going to be increasingly the case across Australia. As shown in the previous chapter, however, Indigenous Australians continue to have lower levels of education participation than non-Indigenous Australians, with incomplete catch-up across the lifecourse.

There is also evidence that, even with the same level of qualifications and skills, Indigenous Australians are less likely to be employed than an otherwise identical non-Indigenous Australian. Hunter (2004) showed the potential for this discrimination through a decomposition analysis of the 2001 Census. Going further, Booth, Leigh and Varganova (2009) showed that an otherwise identical resume submitted with an Indigenous name is significantly less likely to receive a positive response than a resume with an Anglo-Saxon name. Finally, unpublished analysis of the HILDA survey showed that Indigenous Australians were more likely to report that they were discriminated against both applying for a job and in their current job.

The final constraint on halving the gap in Indigenous and non-Indigenous employment outcomes are the labour supply preferences of Indigenous Australians themselves. It is clear from the respective unemployment figures at the time of the 2006 Census (15.6% for the Indigenous population compared to 5.1% for the non-Indigenous population) that there is a large percentage of the Indigenous population who would like to work but are unable to find a job. However, there may also be a number of Indigenous Australians who have a preference for working outside the mainstream labour market (Altman 2009) or who are unable to work because of poor health or disability. This is captured by the 45.5 per cent of Indigenous adults that are not in the labour force according to the 2006 Census (that is, not working or not actively looking for work), compared to 35.0 per cent of non-Indigenous adults. These differences are greater still when the small proportion of Indigenous Australians of retirement age is taken into account.

Results presented in Chapter 3 of this monograph showed that Indigenous females are likely to have more children across the lifecourse, with the difference greatest amongst teenagers and females in their twenties. Childbirth and child-rearing are likely to substantially reduce the net benefits of working. This may be through direct economic costs of working (through having to pay childcare fees) or indirectly through the perceived effect on child development. There are, however, Indigenous-specific constraints on labour supply that will make it harder to bring the employment rate of Indigenous Australians closer into line with that of the non-Indigenous population. Whether it is because of 'passive welfare' (Pearson 2009: 159), the relatively high opportunity costs of working as opposed to remaining unemployed (Daly and Hunter 1999), or alternative activities in the 'hybrid economy' (Altman 2009: 9), a number of authors argue that, on average across the two populations, the incentive or inclination to undertake work in the wage economy is lower for Indigenous Australians than non-Indigenous Australians.

So, while employment remains a key avenue for poverty reduction, it is also important to keep in mind variation in Indigenous aspirations to participate in the mainstream labour market. Recognising these competing aims, the analysis presented in this chapter considers the distribution of various aspects of Indigenous employment across the lifecourse and the factors associated with them. The analysis begins with the simplest measure, the probability of an adult 15 years and over being employed. However, not all employment is equal and hence the second and third sections of the chapter consider the probability of being in part-time employment and employed as a Manager or Professional respectively. Both sets of analysis focus on the employed.

The final set of analysis in the chapter attempts to extend the discussion of employment across the lifecourse beyond the mainstream labour market. Unfortunately, there is very little information on non-mainstream employment in the census, especially as it relates to participation in the hybrid economy. However, a new question included in the 2006 Census is whether or not a person undertook volunteer work for an organisation or group during the 12 months that preceded the census. The analysis presented in the final section of results in this section is the first to explicitly consider variation in the probability of undertaking volunteer work across the lifecourse and whether this varies by Indigenous status. In another first, we also consider the factors associated with undertaking unpaid domestic work.

Employment

More than most other variables, employment across the lifecourse follows a distinctly cyclical pattern. Employment generally starts in earnest for people aged 15 years and over, with individuals either leaving school or undertaking part-time work in conjunction with their studies. The probability of employment then increases substantially as individuals leave compulsory and then post-compulsory education, with the 25–54 year age group generally taken to be prime working age. The major exception to this is time taken out of the labour force to raise children (especially for females). Beyond the age of 55, individuals begin to retire, with the exact age of retirement depending on health, wealth, superannuation benefits and the type of job the person has access to. This employment profile is clearly reflected in Fig. 6.1. However, the question posed in the remainder of this section is the extent to which this lifecourse pattern varies for the Indigenous population.

Fig. 6.1 Probability of being employed, Indigenous and non-Indigenous males and females aged 15 years and over, 2006

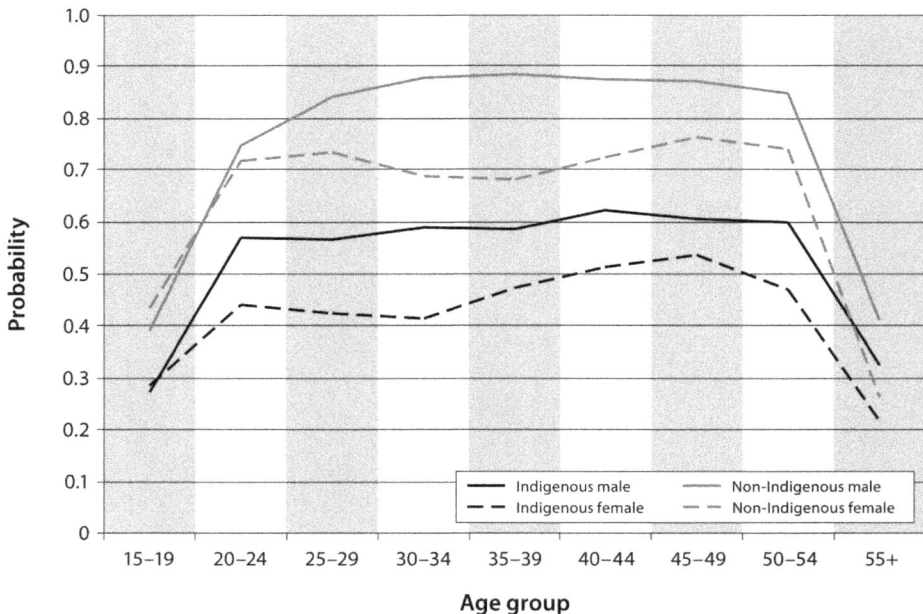

Source: Customised calculations using the 2006 5% CSF, ABS Census of Population and Housing

The results presented in Fig. 6.1 show that the shape of the distribution of employment across the lifecourse is quite similar for Indigenous compared to non-Indigenous males and females. The one major difference is the much earlier divergence between Indigenous males and females in terms of employment probabilities, with Indigenous males aged 20–24 years being substantially more likely to work than Indigenous females of the same age. The relative difference for the non-Indigenous population of this age group is, in comparison, quite minor. The higher rates of fertility amongst relatively young Indigenous females (identified in Chapter 3) are clearly reflected in the above employment figures. Ultimately, the biggest difference between the Indigenous and non-Indigenous population is the actual probability of being employed. It is not the patterns across the lifecourse that are different, but the overall level of employment.

Modelling Indigenous employment across the lifecourse

Results using the probability of a person being employed as the dependent variable of interest are given in Table 6.1. The marginal effects for the Indigenous population from Model 1 are quite large. After controlling for age and sex only, the results show that an Indigenous male aged 30–34 years has a probability of being employed that is 0.172 points lower than the probability of a non-Indigenous male of the same age. However, when one compares the results presented in Model 2 with results from Model 1, it is clear that much of the predicted difference between Indigenous and non-Indigenous Australians in terms of the probability of being employed is because of other observed characteristics. The magnitude of the marginal effect falls to −0.032 after controlling for these characteristics.

Table 6.1 Factors associated with the probability of being employed, population aged 15 years and over, 2006

Part A: Demographic and geographic variables

Explanatory variables[a]	Total population		Indigenous population	
	Model 1	Model 2	Model 3	Model 4
Indigenous	−0.172	−0.032		
Female	−0.191	−0.032	n.s.	n.s.
Aged 15–19	−0.483	−0.038	−0.031	−0.048
Aged 20–24	−0.129	−0.010	n.s.	n.s.
Aged 25–29	−0.037	−0.003	n.s.	n.s.
Aged 35–39	0.005	n.s.	n.s.	n.s.
Aged 40–44	n.s.	−0.003	n.s.	n.s.
Aged 45–49	−0.008	−0.006	n.s.	n.s.
Aged 50–54	−0.030	−0.017	n.s.	n.s.
Aged 55 +	−0.464	−0.275	−0.119	−0.151
Aged 15–19, female	0.097	0.018	0.017	0.023*
Aged 20–24, female	0.081	0.014	n.s.	n.s.
Aged 25–29, female	0.051	0.006	n.s.	n.s.
Aged 35–39, female	−0.008	0.006	0.020	0.028
Aged 40–44, female	0.023	0.013	0.023	0.031
Aged 45–49, female	0.047	0.017	0.028	0.043
Aged 50–54, female	0.049	0.018	0.028	0.043
Aged 55 +, female	0.045	0.020	0.028	0.041
Victoria		0.002	n.s.	n.s.
Queensland		0.004	0.009	0.017
South Australia		0.001	n.s.	n.s.
Western Australia		0.005	n.s.	n.s.
Tasmania		−0.003	n.s.	n.s.
Northern Territory		0.012	n.s.	n.s.
Australian Capital Territory		0.009	n.s.	n.s.
Major city		n.s.	n.s.	n.s.
Probability of the base case[b]	0.878	0.977	0.960	0.934
Pseudo R-Squared	0.1668	0.2665	0.1893	0.1913
Number of observations	734 824	606 289	9 559	9 183

Part B: Socioeconomic and other variables

Explanatory variables[a]	Total population		Indigenous population	
	Model 1	Model 2	Model 3	Model 4
Changed usual residence in the last 5 years		−0.002	n.s.	−0.009*
Changed usual residence in the last year		−0.004	−0.015	−0.027
Secondary school student		−0.140	−0.139	−0.182
Tertiary student		−0.099	−0.085	−0.121
Part-time student		0.021	0.035	0.058
Completed Year 9 or less		−0.046	−0.107	−0.132
Completed Year 10 or 11		−0.009	−0.029	−0.038
Does not have any qualifications		−0.038	−0.109	−0.151
Has a Diploma or Certificate only		−0.010	−0.018	−0.029
Speaks another language and English well		−0.020	−0.012	n.s.
Speaks another language and English not well or not at all		−0.091	−0.055	−0.062
Never married		−0.025	−0.047	−0.046
Divorced, separated or widowed		−0.012	−0.021	−0.015
Has had at least one child (for females)		−0.070	−0.110	−0.145
Has a 'core activity' need for assistance		−0.304	−0.274	−0.341
Provides unpaid child care (all)		−0.009	n.s.	n.s.
Provides unpaid child care for children other than own		0.006	n.s.	n.s.
Provides unpaid assistance for someone with a disability		−0.012	−0.027	−0.043
Lives in a mixed Indigenous and non-Indigenous household				0.033
Probability of the base case[b]	0.878	0.977	0.960	0.934
Pseudo R-Squared	0.1668	0.2665	0.1893	0.1913
Number of observations	734 824	606 289	9 559	9 183

[a.] n.s. = Those variables that were not significant at the 10% level of significance.

* = Those variables that were significant at the 10% level of significance but not the 5% level

[b.] The base case for the total population is non-Indigenous. For all estimates, the base case is aged 30–34 years and in addition, for Models 2–4 (for the total population and for the Indigenous estimates), the base case lives in New South Wales, outside a major city, did not change usual residence in the last five years, has completed Year 12, does not have any qualifications, is not studying, speaks English only, is currently married, has not had any children, and does not provide unpaid child care or assistance to someone with a disability. For Model 4, an additional characteristic of the base case is that they are living in an Indigenous-only household.

Source: Customised calculations using the 2006 5% CSF, ABS Census of Population and Housing

A number of the characteristics in the model have a strong association with the probability of being employed for the Indigenous population. Interestingly though, Indigenous Australians who live in a major city do not have a significantly different probability than Indigenous Australians who live in the rest of Australia. This supports to a certain extent the finding in Biddle (2009c) that, at least at the time of the 2006 Census when the CDEP Program was a large employer, there were plenty of jobs in the areas in which Indigenous Australians lived (relative to the usual resident population). It is simply that Indigenous Australians aren't being hired to fill them.

One of the reasons that Indigenous Australians have a lower probability of being employed would appear to be their lower levels of school completion and qualifications. The base case Indigenous male in Model 3 (who has completed Year 12 and has a degree) has a predicted probability of being employed of 0.960. This is not very different to the predicted probability of a non-Indigenous male with identical observed characteristics in Model 2 (0.977). However, if all other characteristics are held constant with the exception of the Indigenous male having completed Year 9 or less and not having any qualifications, the predicted probability falls to 0.744. This predicted probability is substantially different to that of an otherwise identical non-Indigenous male (0.893). It is not only that Indigenous Australians have lower levels of education than non-Indigenous Australians – it would appear that being unskilled has a bigger association with poor employment prospects for Indigenous Australians. Another variable for which the association in Model 3 is much larger than the association in Model 2, is having had at least one child (for females). Once again, it would appear that not only do Indigenous females have higher fertility rates, the association with having had children is also larger.

Part-time employment

While there are some benefits of employment that are present regardless of the type of job, others are more conditional. From a purely mechanical point of view, people who work part-time are likely to receive lower weekly wages or salaries, purely because they work fewer hours. In addition though, many part-time jobs at the time of the census were likely to be part of the CDEP Program, where wages per hour are also lower. On the other hand, the flexibility inherent in part-time employment can be quite desirable for people in a variety of situations. In particular, people who are studying, people who have caring responsibility for young children or other family members, people who are close to, or beyond retirement age, and people (especially Indigenous Australians) with commitments to, or a desire to participate in the non-market sector.

The percentage of the employed population whose main job was part-time as opposed to full-time is shown in Fig. 6.2. Not surprisingly, the age group with the highest probability of being employed part-time (conditional on being employed at all) is the 15–19 years group. Even in this age group, females have a substantially higher probability than males. It is, however, the only age group where the non-Indigenous population has a substantially higher probability than the Indigenous population. This more than likely reflects the greater level of education participation amongst this age group for the former (non-Indigenous population) relative to the latter (Indigenous population).

Beyond the 15–19 year age group, there are significantly different patterns for Indigenous compared to non-Indigenous Australians. For the former, the probability declines substantially over the next five years but is then relatively stable across the next six age groups. There is only a small gradual decline in the probability for Indigenous males over this age range, with a small increase for 30–34 years age group for Indigenous females and a gradual decline beyond that age group. The decrease in probability is much greater for non-Indigenous males, reaching a low of around 10 per cent of the employed population for the 30–54 age group. For non-Indigenous females, the probability declines substantially into the 25–29 year age group, then increases over the next two age groups (when child care responsibilities are highest). For non-Indigenous males and females as well as Indigenous females, there is a significant increase in the probability of working part-time in the 55–plus age group compared to the 50–54 year age group. For Indigenous males on the other hand, the increase is more modest. This may reflect a relative lack of part-time jobs for Indigenous males or, perhaps in addition, a necessity to continue working full-time given a lack of retirement savings.

Fig. 6.2 Probability of being employed part-time, employed population aged 15 years and over, 2006

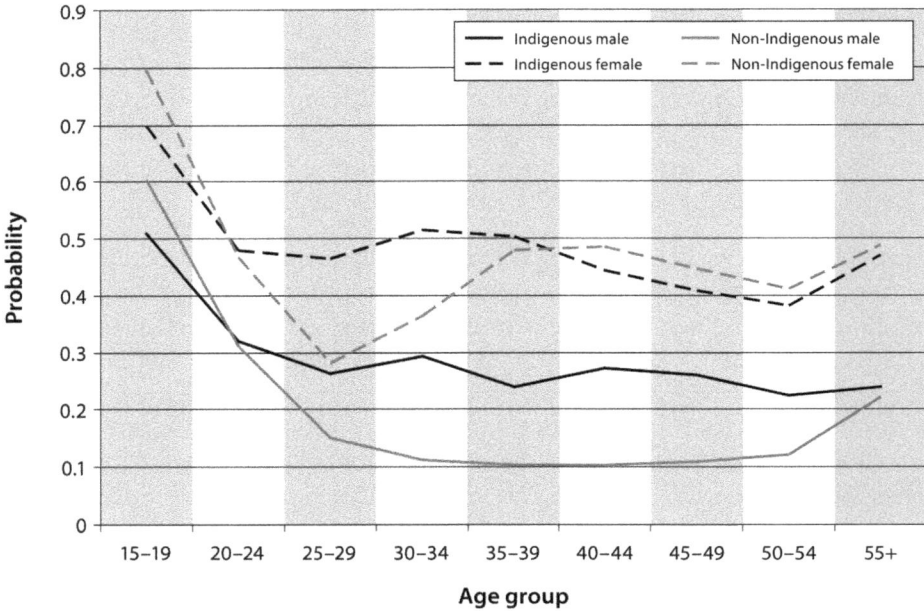

Source: Customised calculations using the 2006 5% CSF, ABS Census of Population and Housing

Modelling part-time work across the lifecourse

A very complicated set of lifecourse patterns for part-time work, with distinct peaks and troughs for all four groups is indicated in Fig. 6.2. The modelling presented in Table 6.2 considers the extent to which these patterns and differences can be explained by other observable characteristics. In addition to the explanatory variables used in the previous section, we also controlled for whether or not the person is employed in the government as opposed to private sector.

Table 6.2 Factors associated with the probability of being employed part-time, employed population aged 15 years and over, 2006

Part A: Demographic and geographic variables

Explanatory variables[a]	Total population		Indigenous population	
	Model 1	Model 2	Model 3	Model 4
Indigenous	0.043	0.036		
Female	0.253	0.103	0.105	0.113
Aged 15–19	0.485	0.127	n.s.	n.s.
Aged 20–24	0.197	0.068	n.s.	n.s.
Aged 25–29	0.037	0.015	n.s.	n.s.
Aged 35–39	−0.008	−0.006	−0.048	−0.068
Aged 40–44	−0.008	−0.004*	n.s.	n.s.
Aged 45–49	n.s.	0.005	−0.039*	−0.054*
Aged 50–54	0.007	0.021	−0.063	−0.081
Aged 55 +	0.109	0.114	−0.066	−0.089
Aged 15–19, female	−0.048	−0.018	n.s.	n.s.
Aged 20–24, female	−0.065	−0.024	n.s.	n.s.
Aged 25–29, female	−0.061	−0.022	n.s.	n.s.
Aged 35–39, female	0.076	0.022	n.s.	n.s.
Aged 40–44, female	0.080	0.012	n.s.	n.s.
Aged 45–49, female	0.049	−0.008	n.s.	n.s.
Aged 50–54, female	0.015	−0.028	n.s.	n.s.
Aged 55 +, female	−0.024	−0.046	n.s.	n.s.
Victoria		0.004	n.s.	n.s.
Queensland		−0.003	n.s.	n.s.
South Australia		0.010	n.s.	n.s.
Western Australia		0.002*	0.044	0.047
Tasmania		0.012	n.s.	n.s.
Northern Territory		−0.020	0.061	0.059
Australian Capital Territory		−0.011	−0.069	−0.093
Major city		n.s.	n.s.	n.s.
Probability of the base case[b]	0.114	0.073	0.136	0.185
Pseudo R-Squared	0.1209	0.2067	0.1405	0.1448
Number of observations	438 950	383 906	4 633	4 475

Part B: Socioeconomic and other variables

	Total population		Indigenous population	
Explanatory variables[a]	Model 1	Model 2	Model 3	Model 4
Changed usual residence in the last 5 years		−0.006	−0.046	−0.053
Changed usual residence in the last year		−0.006	−0.020*	−0.029
Secondary school student		0.607	0.586	0.609
Tertiary student		0.542	0.209	0.236
Part-time student		−0.072	−0.100	−0.130
Completed Year 9 or less		0.015	0.120	0.131
Completed Year 10 or 11		n.s.	0.029	0.032
Does not have any qualifications		0.022	0.139	0.155
Has a Diploma or Certificate only		0.008	0.039*	0.045*
Speaks another language and English well		−0.004	0.099	0.101
Speaks another language and English not well or not at all		0.017	0.157	0.140*
Never married		0.015	0.021*	n.s.
Divorced, separated or widowed		−0.010	n.s.	n.s.
Has had at least one child (for females)		0.174	0.064	0.073
Has a 'core activity' need for assistance		0.185	0.096	0.118
Provides unpaid child care (all)		0.035	0.031	0.039
Provides unpaid child care for children other than own		n.s.	n.s.	n.s.
Provides unpaid assistance for someone with a disability		0.022	n.s.	n.s.
Employed in the government sector		−0.024	n.s.	n.s.
Lives in a mixed Indigenous and non-Indigenous household				−0.053
Probability of the base case[b]	0.114	0.073	0.136	0.185
Pseudo R-Squared	0.1209	0.2067	0.1405	0.1448
Number of observations	438 950	383 906	4 633	4 475

[a.] n.s. = Those variables that were not significant at the 10% level of significance.

* = Those variables that were significant at the 10% level of significance but not the 5% level

[b.] The base case for the total population is non-Indigenous. For all estimates, the base case is aged 30–34 years and in addition, for Models 2–4 (for the total population and for the Indigenous estimates), the base case lives in New South Wales, outside a major city, did not change usual residence in the last five years, has completed Year 12, does not have any qualifications, is not studying, speaks English only, is currently married, has not had any children, and does not provide unpaid child care or assistance to someone with a disability. In addition, the base case person is employed in the private as opposed to government sector. For Model 4, an additional characteristic of the base case is that they are living in an Indigenous-only household.

Source: Customised calculations using the 2006 5% CSF, ABS Census of Population and Housing

Model 1 shows that, on average, employed Indigenous Australians are more likely to be working part-time than non-Indigenous Australians of the same age and sex. The marginal effects for whether or not a person is female and whether or not they are aged 15–19 years (compared to 30–34 years) clearly dominate the model. However, relative to the probability of the base case (0.114), a marginal effect of 0.043 is still reasonably large. Unlike the marginal effect for females and the young, the marginal effect for Indigenous Australians does not decline substantially once other characteristics are controlled for (in Model 2).

Not surprisingly, students – and in particular secondary school students – were significantly more likely to be working part-time than individuals who were not studying at all. The other variable in the model that indicates potentially large time constraints, females who have had at least one child, was also positive and significant. However, it is interesting to note that the size of the marginal effect was much larger for the total population (Model 2) than it was for the Indigenous population only (Models 3 and 4). This may be an indication that Indigenous females with children who were working had greater resource requirements than otherwise identical non-Indigenous females, because of single parenthood or because their partners had relatively low incomes.

The above two variables, as well as the variables for having a 'core activity' need for assistance and for providing unpaid child care were all likely to be related to labour supply. Greater time constraints imply a relative preference for part-time as opposed to full-time work. However, there are a number of other variables with large, positive marginal effects that probably indicate difficulties in finding full-time as opposed to part-time work. In particular, Indigenous Australians who have not completed Year 12 are much more likely to be working part-time as opposed to full-time, as are those without qualifications. Importantly, the marginal effects for these variables are much larger for Indigenous compared to non-Indigenous Australians, showing that low-skilled Indigenous Australians are much more likely to be working part-time than low-skilled non-Indigenous Australians.

Managerial and professional employment

The previous section focused on part-time employment and showed that both before and after controlling for other characteristics, working Indigenous Australians were more likely to be in a part-time job (as opposed to a full-time job) compared to working non-Indigenous Australians. The number of hours that a person works clearly influences their level of remuneration. However, so too does a person's occupational status. According to the Australian and New Zealand Standard Classification of Occupations (ANZSCO) in the 2006 Census, median income for Managers who were employed full-time was $1 087 per week, whereas for employed Professionals it was $1 207 per week. The former category includes: Chief Executives; General Managers; Farmers and Farm Managers; Specialist Managers; as well as Hospitality, Retail and Service Managers. Professional occupations are found across a diverse range of industries in the government and private sector, but are generally occupations that require a bachelor degree or higher (ABS 2006b). Examples include teachers, doctors, lawyers as well as information and communication technology professionals.

Not only do Managers and Professionals have higher income on average than other occupation groupings (the next highest group in the ANZSCO, Technicians and Trades Workers, had a median income of $801), they also hold a level of prestige within the community that other occupations do not. Furthermore, the working conditions in these occupations are likely to be more pleasant on average than the conditions in other occupations, including the level of autonomy held by workers. These more favourable working conditions can result in an ability and desire to remain productive for a much longer period of time, extending the potential number of years that a person can work across the lifecourse.

Managers and Professionals have been one of the fastest growing groups of occupations over recent years (Birrell and Rapson 2006). In order for Indigenous Australians to take advantage of continued growth in demand for highly skilled labour, it is important to understand the factors that are associated with their current rate of employment. The percentage of Indigenous and non-Indigenous Australians identified as being employed as a Manager or Professional according to the 2006 Census is presented in Fig 6.3. Once again, the focus is on individuals who were employed only.

Of the four demographic groupings in the 15–19 year age group, Indigenous males have the highest probability of being a Manager or Professional. At 30.8 per cent, this is slightly higher than the probability for non-Indigenous males (24.9%), but substantially higher than the probability for Indigenous and non-Indigenous females (8.1% and 4.3% respectively). This higher probability is likely to reflect the lower age at which males in general and Indigenous males in particular leave school. Unlike the three other age groups, there is no substantial increase in the probability of being employed as a Manager or Professional across the lifecourse for Indigenous males (conditional on being employed at all). The probability for an Indigenous male worker aged 35–39 years when the probability peaks (36.1%) is only slightly higher than the probability at the start of working life. This flat age profile means that non-Indigenous males and females overtake Indigenous males by the 20–24 year age group, with Indigenous females having a higher probability by the 25–29 year age group.

Fig. 6.3 Probability of being employed as a Manager or Professional, employed population, 2006

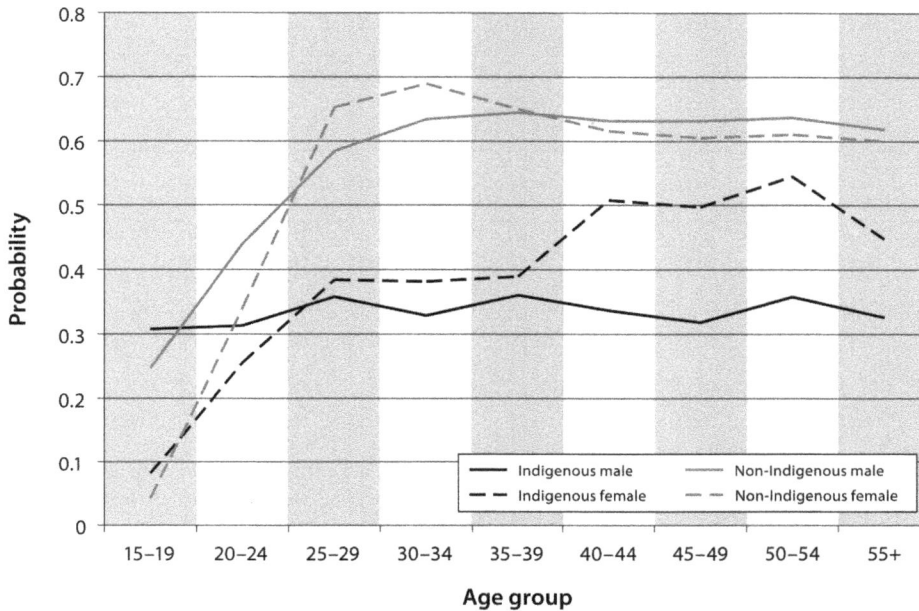

Source: Customised calculations using the 2006 5% CSF, ABS Census of Population and Housing

Modelling managerial and professional employment across the lifecourse

The previous figure showed distinct lifecourse patterns for all four demographic groupings. Table 6.3 uses the probability of being employed as a Manager or Professional (conditional on being employed) as the dependent variable to test the extent to which these patterns and differences are explained by other characteristics. The results presented in Model 1 in Table 6.3 confirm that, after controlling for age and sex only, employed Indigenous Australians are less likely to be employed as a Manager or Professional compared to their employed non-Indigenous counterparts. While the Indigenous status variable is negative and significant in Model 2 as well, the size of the estimated marginal effect declines substantially (from −0.208 to −0.045). It would appear that the main reason why Indigenous workers have a lower probability than non-Indigenous workers is to be found in other characteristics.

Table 6.3 Factors associated with the probability of being employed as a Manager or Professional, employed population, 2006

Part A: Demographic and geographic variables

Explanatory variables[a]	Total population		Indigenous population	
	Model 1	Model 2	Model 3	Model 4
Indigenous	−0.208	−0.045		
Female	0.056	n.s.	n.s.	n.s.
Aged 15–19	−0.378	0.009	0.066	0.068
Aged 20–24	−0.191	−0.009	0.045	0.040*
Aged 25–29	−0.050	−0.006	n.s.	n.s.
Aged 35–39	0.012	0.008	n.s.	n.s.
Aged 40–44	n.s.	0.010	0.044*	n.s.
Aged 45–49	n.s.	0.010	n.s.	n.s.
Aged 50–54	n.s.	0.012	0.061	0.065
Aged 55 +	−0.015	0.016	0.058	0.061
Aged 15–19, female	−0.435	−0.216	−0.262	−0.302
Aged 20–24, female	−0.163	−0.076	n.s.	n.s.
Aged 25–29, female	n.s.	−0.015	n.s.	n.s.
Aged 35–39, female	−0.053	n.s.	n.s.	n.s.
Aged 40–44, female	−0.072	n.s.	n.s.	n.s.
Aged 45–49, female	−0.084	0.006*	n.s.	n.s.
Aged 50–54, female	−0.084	0.011	n.s.	n.s.
Aged 55 +, female	−0.076	0.018	n.s.	n.s.
Victoria		n.s.	n.s.	n.s.
Queensland		−0.010	−0.060	−0.059
South Australia		−0.003	−0.086	−0.078
Western Australia		n.s.	−0.036*	n.s.
Tasmania		−0.005*	n.s.	n.s.
Northern Territory		n.s.	n.s.	n.s.
Australian Capital Territory		0.027	n.s.	n.s.
Major city		−0.002	0.021*	n.s.
Probability of the base case[b]	0.633	0.930	0.880	0.872
Pseudo R-Squared	0.0496	0.2415	0.2259	0.2274
Number of observations	322 637	281 932	3 196	3 084

Part B: Socioeconomic and other variables

Explanatory variables[a]	Total population		Indigenous population	
	Model 1	Model 2	Model 3	Model 4
Changed usual residence in the last 5 years		n.s.	n.s.	n.s.
Changed usual residence in the last year		n.s.	n.s.	n.s.
Secondary school student		−0.248	n.s.	n.s.
Tertiary student		−0.093	n.s.	n.s.
Part-time student		0.062	0.054*	n.s.
Completed Year 9 or less		−0.093	−0.186	−0.186
Completed Year 10 or 11		−0.044	−0.055	−0.054
Does not have any qualifications		−0.433	−0.628	−0.637
Has a Diploma or Certificate only		−0.176	−0.315	−0.326
Speaks another language and English well		−0.050	−0.061	−0.076
Speaks another language and English not well or not at all		−0.125	n.s.	n.s.
Never married		−0.032	n.s.	n.s.
Divorced, separated or widowed		−0.029	n.s.	n.s.
Has had at least one child (for females)		−0.035	0.037	n.s.
Has a 'core activity' need for assistance		−0.065	n.s.	n.s.
Provides unpaid child care (all)		0.005	n.s.	n.s.
Provides unpaid child care for children other than own		−0.006	n.s.	n.s.
Provides unpaid assistance for someone with a disability		n.s.	n.s.	n.s.
Employed in the government sector		0.027	0.029	0.033
Lives in a mixed Indigenous and non-Indigenous household				n.s.
Probability of the base case[b]	0.633	0.930	0.880	0.872
Pseudo R-Squared	0.0496	0.2415	0.2259	0.2274
Number of observations	322 637	281 932	3 196	3 084

[a.] n.s. = Those variables that were not significant at the 10% level of significance.

 * = Those variables that were significant at the 10% level of significance but not the 5% level

[b.] The base case for the total population is non-Indigenous. For all estimates, the base case is aged 30–34 years and in addition, for Models 2–4 (for the total population and for the Indigenous estimates), the base case lives in New South Wales, outside a major city, did not change usual residence in the last five years, has completed Year 12, does not have any qualifications, is not studying, speaks English only, is currently married, has not had any children, and does not provide unpaid child care or assistance to someone with a disability. In addition, the base case person is employed in the private as opposed to government sector. For Model 4, an additional characteristic of the base case is that they are living in an Indigenous-only household.

Source: Customised calculations using the 2006 5% CSF, ABS Census of Population and Housing

As seen in Table 6.1, education explained most of the difference between the Indigenous and non-Indigenous population (in Model 2 in employment as a Manager or Professional), as well as differences within the Indigenous population (in Models 3 and 4). To put the magnitude of the differences by education in perspective, an Indigenous male who has completed Year 12 and has a degree (and has all the other characteristics of the base case) has a predicted probability of being a Manager or Professional equal to 0.880. A non-Indigenous male with similar characteristics has a predicted probability of 0.930 – not too much higher. On the other hand, an Indigenous male who has completed Year 9 or less only and does not have any qualifications (but otherwise identical characteristics) has a probability of 0.066, compared to a non-Indigenous male with the same characteristics with a probability of 0.404. Once again, not only do Indigenous Australians have lower levels of education, it would seem that a lack of skills has a bigger effect as well.

Voluntary and unpaid domestic work

Not all productive work that takes place in an economy is in the form of paid employment. Volunteer work and unpaid domestic work both contribute to output of goods and services, even if they are not reflected in labour market statistics or a country's gross domestic product. Individuals who undertake volunteer work provide a number of services that may otherwise need to be provided by government. These services benefit disproportionately the most vulnerable members of society. Unpaid domestic work provides benefits to the household (for example cleaning, cooking, or general maintenance) that would otherwise need to be paid for from the income of those in paid employment. Using the National Aboriginal and Torres Strait Islander Survey (NATSIS 1994), Smith and Roach (1996) analysed the extent of Indigenous involvement in voluntary work. The authors found that Indigenous volunteers were generally younger with differing peak involvement for males and females, were likely to be in the participating in the mainstream labour force and lived outside capital cities.. The most common type of Indigenous voluntary work after discounting subsistence work was working within community organisations. However, the NATSIS does not have a non-Indigenous comparison.

For the first time, the 2006 Census included separate questions on whether or not a person undertook voluntary work for an organisation or group in the preceding 12 months, as well as whether they undertook unpaid domestic work. For the latter, individuals were also asked to estimate the number of hours in the previous week with the options being: less than 5 hours; 5–14 hours; 15–29 hours; and 30 hours or more. The next part of this section considers the probability and factors associated with voluntary work across the lifecourse, while the final part of the section repeats this analysis for unpaid domestic work. This is the first time such analysis comparing voluntary and unpaid domestic work by the Indigenous and non-Indigenous Australian population has been undertaken.

Summarising voluntary work across the lifecourse

The probability of undertaking voluntary work starts off highest for non-Indigenous females at around 20.7 per cent of the population, with Indigenous males and females both having substantially lower probabilities (11.5% and 12.2% respectively). The probability for non-Indigenous males (15.9%) falls somewhere in between. These probabilities then decline for non-Indigenous males and females such that Indigenous and non-Indigenous males, as well as Indigenous and non-Indigenous females, have roughly the same probabilities in the 30–34 year age group. The probabilities for non-Indigenous females diverge once more such that at the peak age for this group (40–44 years), the probability for this demographic group is 8 to 9 percentage points above that of the other three groups.

Fig. 6.4 Probability of undertaking volunteer work, 2006

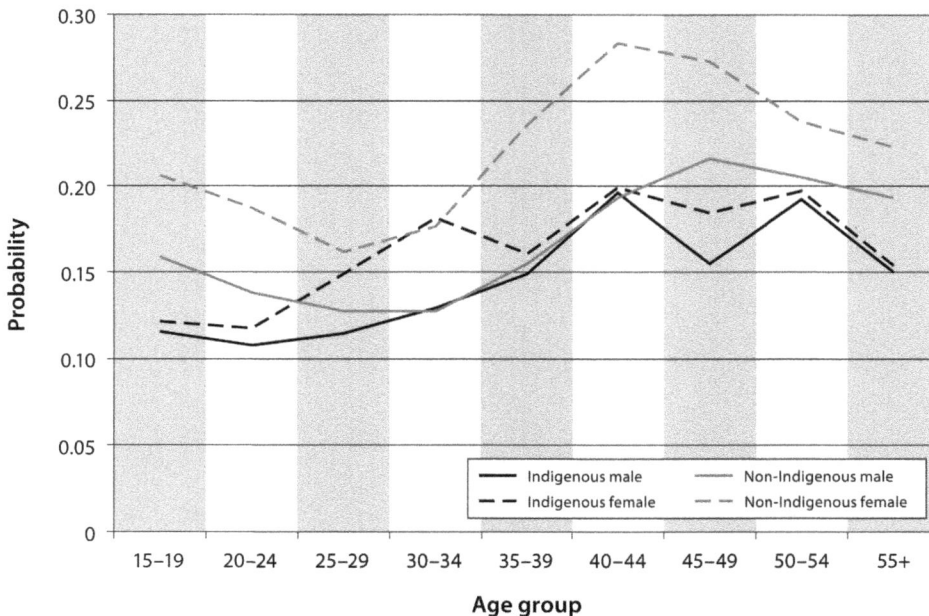

Source: Customised calculations using the 2006 5% CSF, ABS Census of Population and Housing

Modelling voluntary work across the lifecourse

While the levels are different, Fig. 6.4 shows that the patterns of voluntary work across the lifecourse are similar for non-Indigenous males and females, with Indigenous males and females also having a similar shape, apart from during the late-twenties and early-thirties. The results presented in Table 6.4 consider whether other characteristics of the individual are associated with voluntary work and, if so, the extent to which the differences presented in Fig. 6.4 remain, after controlling for these characteristics.

Reflecting the fact that there is a trade-off in many ways between undertaking voluntary work and undertaking paid work, Models 2–4 include a variable for the person not being employed, whether or not they are employed part-time, whether or not they are employed in the public sector, and whether or not they are an owner or manager of a business or a contributing family worker. The base case for the analysis is therefore a person who is employed full-time in the private sector as an employee who does not own the business.

Table 6.4 Factors associated with the probability of having undertaken voluntary work for an organisation or group in the previous 12 months, population aged 15 years and over, 2006

Part A: Demographic and geographic variables

| Explanatory variables[a] | Total population | | Indigenous population | |
	Model 1	Model 2	Model 3	Model 4
Indigenous	−0.031	−0.030		
Female	0.050	0.037	n.s.	n.s.
Aged 15–19	0.031	0.028	n.s.	n.s.
Aged 20–24	0.010	0.036	n.s.	n.s.
Aged 25–29	n.s.	0.023	n.s.	n.s.
Aged 35–39	0.027	0.025	n.s.	n.s.
Aged 40–44	0.067	0.086	0.109	0.113
Aged 45–49	0.088	0.114	0.075	0.084
Aged 50–54	0.078	0.107	0.133	0.136
Aged 55 +	0.066	0.107	0.100	0.104
Aged 15–19, female	−0.007*	n.s.	n.s.	n.s.
Aged 20–24, female	n.s.	n.s.	−0.074*	n.s.
Aged 25–29, female	−0.012	−0.022	n.s.	n.s.
Aged 35–39, female	0.018	0.045	−0.069*	n.s.
Aged 40–44, female	0.016	0.055	−0.075*	−0.075
Aged 45–49, female	−0.007	0.033	n.s.	n.s.
Aged 50–54, female	−0.020	0.016	n.s.	n.s.
Aged 55 +, female	−0.022	0.041	n.s.	n.s.
Victoria		n.s.	n.s.	n.s.
Queensland		0.008	n.s.	n.s.
South Australia		0.034	n.s.	n.s.
Western Australia		−0.008	n.s.	n.s.
Tasmania		−0.037	n.s.	n.s.
Northern Territory		−0.016	−0.091	−0.088
Australian Capital Territory		0.041	n.s.	n.s.
Major city		−0.080	−0.020*	−0.019*
Probability of the base case[b]	0.128	0.253	0.240	0.222
Pseudo R-Squared	0.0107	0.0783	0.0867	0.0868
Number of observations	712 317	590 457	9 189	8 820

Part B: Socioeconomic and other variables

Explanatory variables[a]	Total population		Indigenous population	
	Model 1	Model 2	Model 3	Model 4
Changed usual residence in the last 5 years		−0.024	n.s.	n.s.
Changed usual residence in the last year		−0.009	n.s.	n.s.
Secondary school student		0.177	0.129	0.109
Tertiary student		0.147	0.143	0.146
Part-time student		−0.035	n.s.	n.s.
Completed Year 9 or less		−0.098	−0.108	−0.102
Completed Year 10 or 11		−0.050	−0.088	−0.081
Does not have any qualifications		−0.120	−0.115	−0.109
Has a Diploma or Certificate only		−0.070	−0.041*	−0.040*
Speaks another language and English well		−0.101	n.s.	n.s.
Speaks another language and English not well or not at all		−0.168	−0.133	−0.113
Never married		−0.039	−0.049	−0.041
Divorced, separated or widowed		−0.041	−0.036	−0.032*
Has had at least one child (for females)		−0.033	n.s.	n.s.
Has a 'core activity' need for assistance		−0.099	n.s.	n.s.
Provides unpaid child care (all)		0.067	0.081	0.078
Provides unpaid child care for children other than own		0.055	0.056	0.055
Provides unpaid assistance for someone with a disability		0.100	0.132	0.125
Not employed		0.077	n.s.	n.s.
Owner or manager of a business or contributing family worker		0.052	0.058	0.056*
Employed in the government sector		0.031	0.037	0.039
Employed part-time		0.056	n.s.	0.028*
Lives in a mixed Indigenous and non-Indigenous household				n.s.
Probability of the base case[b]	0.128	0.253	0.240	0.222
Pseudo R-Squared	0.0107	0.0783	0.0867	0.0868
Number of observations	712 317	590 457	9 189	8 820

[a.] n.s. = Those variables that were not significant at the 10% level of significance.

* = Those variables that were significant at the 10% level of significance but not the 5% level

[b.] The base case for the total population is non-Indigenous. For all estimates, the base case is aged 30–34 years and in addition, for Models 2–4 (for the total population and for the Indigenous estimates), the base case lives in New South Wales, outside a major city, did not change usual residence in the last five years, has completed Year 12, does not have any qualifications, is not studying, speaks English only, is currently married, has not had any children, and does not provide unpaid child care or assistance to someone with a disability. In addition, the base case person is employed full-time in the private sector as an employee who does not own the business. For Model 4, an additional characteristic of the base case is that they are living in an Indigenous-only household.

Source: Customised calculations using the 2006 5% CSF, ABS Census of Population and Housing

The results presented in Table 6.4 confirm that Indigenous Australians are less likely to report that they undertook voluntary work in the 12 months preceding the census than non-Indigenous Australians. This was true after controlling for age and sex only (in Model 1), as well as a range of other observable characteristics (in Model 2). It may be the case that the type of voluntary work undertaken by Indigenous Australians is underreported in the census. In particular, the voluntary work that Indigenous Australians undertake may not be for an organisation or group, but as an individual or through informal networks. However, taking the question on the census at face value, the results presented in Table 6.4 are an indication that voluntary work may be less common for Indigenous Australians compared to non-Indigenous Australians across the lifecourse. This lower probability is potentially problematic for two reasons. Firstly, given the spatial concentration of Indigenous Australians by suburb and neighbourhood (Biddle 2009c) and the likelihood that a large proportion of voluntary work that is undertaken takes place in one's local area, these results may be an indication that less voluntary work is being undertaken in the areas in which Indigenous Australians live. The second reason to be concerned about the results for Models 1 and 2 in Table 6.4 regards the benefits that voluntary work can bring to the individual undertaking it. This includes the development of one's skills as well as the social and community interaction that voluntary work can bring (Thoits and Hewitt 2001).

While the results from Models 1 and 2 provide strong evidence for Indigenous Australians being less likely to undertake voluntary work than non-Indigenous Australians, the results from Models 3 and 4 show that there is also significant variation within the Indigenous population. There appears to be a strong association with education. In terms of education participation, secondary and tertiary students are more likely to undertake voluntary work than those who are not studying. In terms of education completion, people with lower levels of education are generally less likely to undertake voluntary work than people who have completed Year 12 or who have a degree. It is interesting to note that for the total population (Model 2), individuals who were not in paid employment are more likely to undertake voluntary work than individuals who are employed. This is the expected situation given the additional hours available to individuals who are not working. However, for the Indigenous population there is no significant difference between those who are employed and those not employed, nor a significant difference between people working part-time and full-time (at least at the 5% level of significance). For the non-Indigenous population, voluntary work and paid employment appear to be substitutes. For the Indigenous population, on the other hand, they appear to be unrelated.

Unpaid domestic work across the lifecourse

The final type of work considered in this chapter is unpaid domestic work. Fig. 6.5 gives the percentage of the Indigenous and non-Indigenous male and female population aged 15 years and over who undertook one hour or more of unpaid domestic work in the week preceding the census. It shows that females were more likely to report that they undertook at least one hour or more of unpaid domestic work per week than males and, for both sexes and for all ages, non-Indigenous Australians had a higher probability than Indigenous Australians. For all four age groups the probability increases up until a person's early thirties, levels off for the next 15–20 years, and then declines for the 55–plus population.

Undertaking one hour or more per week of domestic work is a reasonably low threshold. Indeed, apart from Indigenous males aged 15–19 years, all other age and demographic group combinations had a probability greater than 0.5. For non-Indigenous females aged 30–49, more than 90 per cent of the population reported working at least one hour. Undertaking relatively low numbers of hours is unlikely to impact significantly on other leisure or work activities, and hence Fig. 6.6 replicates the above analysis using the more stringent cut-off of undertaking five hours or more per week of domestic work.

Fig. 6.5 Probability of undertaking unpaid domestic work, 2006

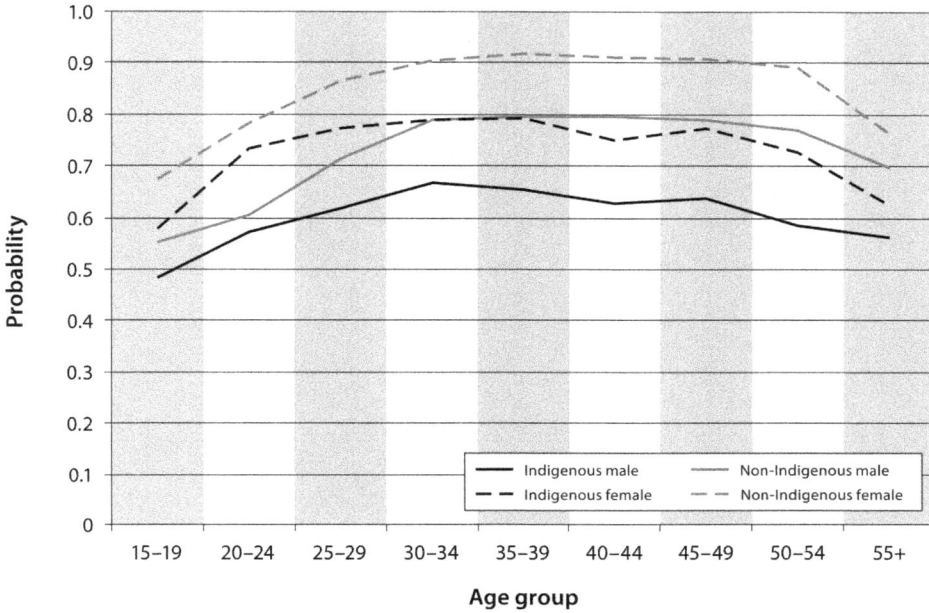

Source: Customised calculations using the 2006 5% CSF, ABS Census of Population and Housing

Fig. 6.6 Probability of undertaking five hours or more of unpaid domestic work, 2006

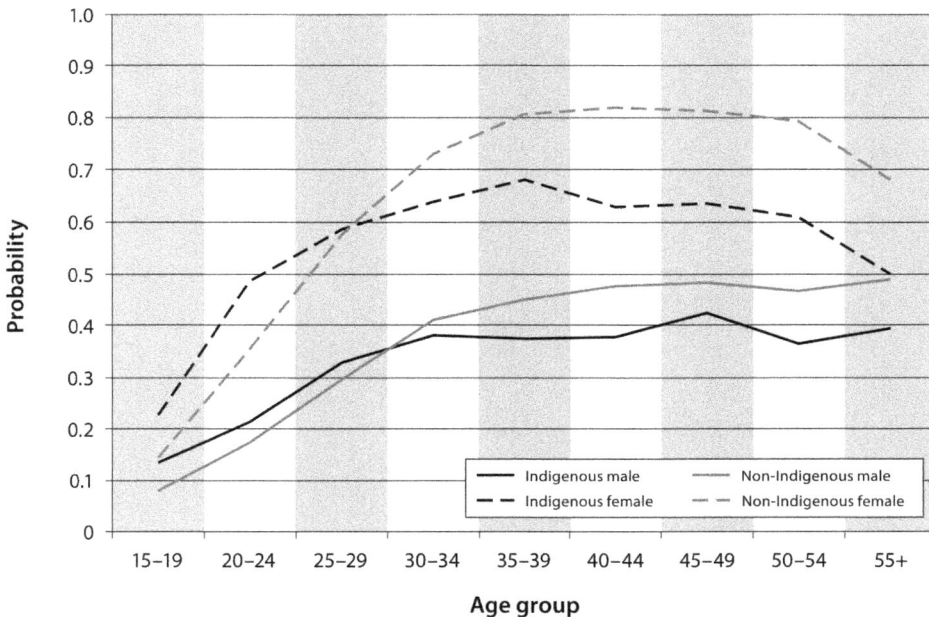

Source: Customised calculations using the 2006 5% CSF, ABS Census of Population and Housing

By restricting the threshold to five hours or more per week, Fig. 6.6 shows a much greater degree of variation across the lifecourse than was found in Fig. 6.5. The main stylised fact remains that females are more likely to report doing unpaid work than males, and non-Indigenous Australians are more likely to report doing unpaid work than Indigenous Australians. However, the differences between males and females are much greater when the higher threshold is used, whereas the differences between Indigenous and non-Indigenous Australians reduce. Indeed, up to and including the 25–29 year age group, the probability for Indigenous males and females is higher than non-Indigenous males and females respectively. This last finding may be related to the greater level of child care responsibility for Indigenous Australians of this age, as shown earlier in this volume.

Modelling unpaid domestic work across the lifecourse

The final model in this section looks at the factors associated with undertaking unpaid domestic work. Given the greater variation across the lifecourse found when using the stricter threshold and the relatively small impact on leisure or paid work from undertaking unpaid domestic work for 1–4 hours only, the dependent variable for the following analysis is undertaking unpaid work for five hours or more per week (compared to zero hours or 1–4 hours).

Table 6.5 Factors associated with the probability of undertaking unpaid domestic work, 2006

Part A: Demographic and geographic variables

Explanatory variables[a]	Total population		Indigenous population	
	Model 1	Model 2	Model 3	Model 4
Indigenous	−0.056	−0.083		
Female	0.318	0.199	0.124	0.131
Aged 15–19	−0.330	−0.234	−0.146	−0.144
Aged 20–24	−0.237	−0.161	−0.110	−0.112
Aged 25–29	−0.113	−0.057	n.s.	n.s.
Aged 35–39	0.040	n.s.	n.s.	n.s.
Aged 40–44	0.065	0.018	n.s.	n.s.
Aged 45–49	0.070	0.040	0.076	0.075
Aged 50–54	0.054	0.053	n.s.	n.s.
Aged 55 +	0.079	0.086	0.084	0.089
Aged 15–19, female	−0.174	−0.072	n.s.	n.s.
Aged 20–24, female	−0.094	−0.024	0.086*	0.077*
Aged 25–29, female	−0.042	n.s.	n.s.	n.s.
Aged 35–39, female	0.055	0.033	0.087*	n.s.
Aged 40–44, female	0.049	0.037	n.s.	n.s.
Aged 45–49, female	0.035	0.041	n.s.	n.s.
Aged 50–54, female	0.024	0.021	n.s.	n.s.
Aged 55 +, female	−0.127	−0.099	−0.073*	−0.074*
Victoria		0.007	n.s.	n.s.
Queensland		0.017	−0.031	−0.026*
South Australia		0.039	n.s.	n.s.
Western Australia		0.016	−0.073	−0.063
Tasmania		0.011	n.s.	n.s.
Northern Territory		n.s.	−0.098	−0.087
Australian Capital Territory		0.050	n.s.	n.s.
Major city		−0.034	n.s.	n.s.
Probability of the base case[b]	0.412	0.407	0.404	0.389
Pseudo R-Squared	0.1304	0.2167	0.1822	0.1779
Number of observations	707 583	584 939	9 076	8 710

Part B: Socioeconomic and other variables

Explanatory variables[a]	Total population		Indigenous population	
	Model 1	Model 2	Model 3	Model 4
Changed usual residence in the last 5 years		0.023	0.033	0.037
Changed usual residence in the last year		0.005	n.s.	n.s.
Secondary school student		−0.175	−0.151	−0.140
Tertiary student		−0.080	n.s.	n.s.
Part-time student		0.086	n.s.	n.s.
Completed Year 9 or less		−0.046	−0.059	−0.052
Completed Year 10 or 11		n.s.	n.s.	n.s.
Does not have any qualifications		−0.065	−0.099	−0.099
Has a Diploma or Certificate only		−0.008	n.s.	n.s.
Speaks another language and English well		−0.087	n.s.	n.s.
Speaks another language and English not well or not at all		−0.141	−0.217	−0.202
Never married		−0.097	−0.102	−0.094
Divorced, separated or widowed		−0.097	−0.076	−0.069
Has had at least one child (for females)		0.157	0.095	0.096
Has a 'core activity' need for assistance		−0.256	−0.122	−0.105
Provides unpaid child care (all)		0.180	0.228	0.228
Provides unpaid child care for children other than own		0.006*	n.s.	n.s.
Provides unpaid assistance for someone with a disability		0.170	0.175	0.168
Not employed		0.130	0.064	0.061
Owner or manager of a business or contributing family worker		−0.036	0.066	0.060*
Employed in the government sector		0.069	0.066	0.063
Employed part-time		0.089	0.069	0.068
Undertook voluntary work in the preceding 12 months		0.101	0.111	0.113
Lives in a mixed Indigenous and non-Indigenous household				0.025
Probability of the base case[b]	0.412	0.407	0.404	0.389
Pseudo R-Squared	0.1304	0.2167	0.1822	0.1779
Number of observations	707 583	584 939	9 076	8 710

[a.] n.s. = Those variables that were not significant at the 10% level of significance.

* = Those variables that were significant at the 10% level of significance but not the 5% level

[b.] The base case for the total population is non-Indigenous. For all estimates, the base case is aged 30–34 years and in addition, for Models 2–4 (for the total population and for the Indigenous estimates), the base case lives in New South Wales, outside a major city, did not change usual residence in the last five years, has completed Year 12, does not have any qualifications, is not studying, speaks English only, is currently married, has not had any children, and does not provide unpaid child care or assistance to someone with a disability. In addition, the base case person is employed full-time in the private sector as an employee who does not own the business and did not undertake voluntary work in the preceding 12 months. For Model 4, an additional characteristic of the base case is that they are living in an Indigenous-only household.

Source: Customised calculations using the 2006 5% CSF, ABS Census of Population and Housing

While Model 1 shows that Indigenous Australians were less likely to report undertaking five or more hours of unpaid work than non-Indigenous Australians after controlling for age and sex, it is interesting to note that the difference actually increases after controlling for other characteristics. For example, Indigenous females were more likely to have had children than non-Indigenous Australians and more likely to not be employed. If employed, they were more likely to be in the government sector or employed part-time. All these characteristics were shown in Model 2 to be positively associated with undertaking unpaid work and hence, once they are controlled for, the predicted difference between Indigenous and non-Indigenous Australians increases.

Employment across the Indigenous lifecourse

The analysis presented in this chapter was motivated to a certain extent by the target set by COAG to halve the gap in employment percentages between Indigenous and non-Indigenous Australians by 2018. As mentioned above, this focus on employment is sensible given the link between employment and other socioeconomic outcomes. While the results presented in this chapter confirmed that Indigenous males and females were significantly less likely to be employed at all points across the lifecourse than their non-Indigenous counterparts, it was also shown that once observable characteristics had been controlled for, the differences declined substantially.

The policy implications of this finding are clear. To reduce the employment disparity between Indigenous and non-Indigenous Australians, the main focus should be on the characteristics they bring to the labour market. This includes the obvious need to improve education and skills. However, less obvious factors like child-rearing, and the poor health of the individual and those they are taking care of, cannot be ignored. Importantly, there was no significant difference between Indigenous Australians who lived in major cities compared to Indigenous Australians who live in the rest of the country. That is, there is no evidence from this analysis that encouraging Indigenous Australians to change location will lead to significant change in employment outcomes. Rather, the focus should be on making sure Indigenous Australians have the skills and training to compete for the jobs that are available in the areas in which they currently live.

In many ways, reducing the gap between Indigenous and non-Indigenous Australians in terms of the percentage of the population employed is just the first step in reducing labour market disadvantage. Even after focusing on the employed only, Indigenous Australians were shown to be less likely to be employed full-time and less likely to be employed as a Manager or Professional. Both of these employment types are associated with better conditions and higher pay. For both types of employment, the gap between Indigenous and non-Indigenous Australians decreased substantially after controlling for other factors. Once again, it would seem that observable factors explain much of the difference between Indigenous and non-Indigenous Australians in terms of hours worked and occupation.

It is not clear whether the decision by COAG to focus on halving as opposed to fully closing the gap between Indigenous and non-Indigenous Australians in terms of employment was due to a realistic assessment of the chances of achieving the latter, or because of a recognition that not all Indigenous Australians desire to maintain a full-time job in the mainstream labour market. Results presented in previous chapters have clearly shown the large gaps between some of the determinants of employment, including education and fertility, highlighting the need for a realistic assessment of what can be achieved. However, it is unfortunate that many of the alternative activities in arts, craft, hunting, gathering and fishing (what Altman (2009) refers to as the hybrid economy) that Indigenous Australians are disproportionately engaged in are not well captured by large-scale, nationally representative surveys.

Two non-market activities that are captured in the census are working as a volunteer and unpaid domestic work. The results presented in this chapter are the first detailed comparative analysis of the variation in these two activities between Indigenous and non-Indigenous Australians and across the lifecourse. For both of these activities (but particularly for unpaid domestic work), females are more likely to participate than males. Furthermore, after controlling for age and sex, Indigenous Australians are less likely to participate than the non-Indigenous population.

It is difficult to identify clear policy implications from the analysis of volunteering and unpaid domestic work presented in this chapter. In terms of unpaid domestic work, the differences between Indigenous and non-Indigenous Australians may reflect the larger household size of the former and the greater sharing of domestic work. Perhaps the most relevant finding from the analysis was that for the Indigenous population, volunteering and paid work appear to act as complements, whereas for the non-Indigenous population they appear to be substitutes. This may be an indication of a lack of access to formal volunteering opportunities for Indigenous Australians who are not employed, and an indication of volunteer organisations and services not being available in the areas in which Indigenous Australians live. On the other hand though, it may simply be the case that the type of volunteer and community work that Indigenous Australians are engaged in is not well captured by the census, as demonstrated by the slightly higher percentage of people who reported that they participated in voluntary work according to the 2002 NATSISS (ABS 2004).

7. Housing

Adequate housing is a fundamental human need for survival and protection from the environment (HREOC 1996). However, there are significant groups of people who continue to live in public places, in shelters, or any makeshift bed they can find. According to the 2001 Census, the rate of homelessness[1] for Indigenous Australians was 3.5 times the rate for non-Indigenous Australians (ABS and AIHW 2005). The lack of appropriate housing means that sometimes people choose to live in public areas. This is particularly relevant for the Indigenous population for whom homelessness is sometimes viewed quite differently, both spiritually and culturally (Keys Young 1998). Memmott, Long and Chambers (2003) distinguished between 'public place dwellers' (who do not live in a boxed dwelling but argue that they are both 'placed' and 'homed'), and other homeless people who may be seeking accommodation because of relationship breakdown, escaping domestic violence, or for other reasons. The lack of resources in terms of income as well as the housing situation in Australia means there are significant barrier for securing appropriate housing (Birdsall-Jones and Shaw 2008).

In Chapter 4, the absence of health and education services locally, as well as the cultural and socially driven reasons for movement was introduced. These population movements are an added dimension to the issue of Indigenous homelessness and overcrowding. The obligation of providing familial support for kin and visitors means that overcrowding occurs more in Indigenous homes than non-Indigenous. While there are various degrees of homelessness which Indigenous people experience differently from non-Indigenous people, the census 5% Sample File does not allow for that analysis. Instead, in this chapter, the issue of housing tenure and overcrowding is analysed.

Overcrowding has significant negative impacts on a number of outcomes. The impact of inadequate housing on health outcomes has been identified historically (Gauldie 1974; Thomson, Petticrew and Morrison 2001), as well as more specifically for the Indigenous population of Australia (Bailie and Wayte 2006; Pholeros, Rainow and Torzillo 1993). The efficacy of any policy responses to high levels of overcrowding will depend heavily on the local housing market and dominant tenure type in the region. For example, AIHW (2005: 42) showed that in 2001 there was greater disparity in levels of overcrowding between

---

1   The standard definition of homelessness is classified in three levels: people without conventional accommodation; people who move frequently from one temporary shelter to another; and people in boarding houses (ABS and AIHW 2005).

Indigenous and other households in public or community rental compared to other tenure types. Furthermore, Memmott et al. (2009) identified a number of intrinsic benefits of home ownership including stability and the ability to pass a house down in the family.

The effects of overcrowding, poor quality housing and tenure type are likely to be quite different across the lifecourse. While all age groups are likely to be adversely affected by poor housing outcomes, the young in particular are more likely to be impacted, given the relationship between education participation and attendance. Furthermore, the ability and motivation to control one's housing status is also likely to vary. The housing outcomes of children are in many ways beyond their control, with agency and access to economic resources increasing into adulthood. Therefore, policies aimed at improving the housing outcomes of children will need to address the other members of the household. Housing needs are also likely to vary with the space required and the need for stability changing dramatically as one moves across the different stages of the lifecourse. That is, the type, determinants and effects of housing outcomes are all likely to differ at different points in the lifecourse.

The analysis in this chapter focuses on two aspects of Indigenous housing. In the next section, housing tenure is analysed, with differences between peope who own or are purchasing their own home, people in private rental and people in community rental considered. The section that follows considers one measure of overcrowding (the number of usual residents per bedroom), with the final section discussing the implications of the empirical results.

Housing tenure

The analysis presented in this section considers two aspects of housing tenure. The first aspect is whether or not a person is living in a dwelling that is owned or being purchased by one of the usual residents. The second aspect focuses on people who are living in a rental property, looking at whether or not the person is living in a dwelling rented from the government or community organisation, as opposed to rented in the private housing market.[2] The analysis presented in this chapter excludes people who live in non-private dwellings.

---

2   In the context of this paper, the private housing market includes dwellings rented from a parent or other relative.

Home ownership

The percentage of the population who live in a dwelling that is owned or being purchased by one of the dwelling's usual residents is shown in Fig. 7.1.

Fig. 7.1 Probability of living in a dwelling that is owned or being purchased, 2006

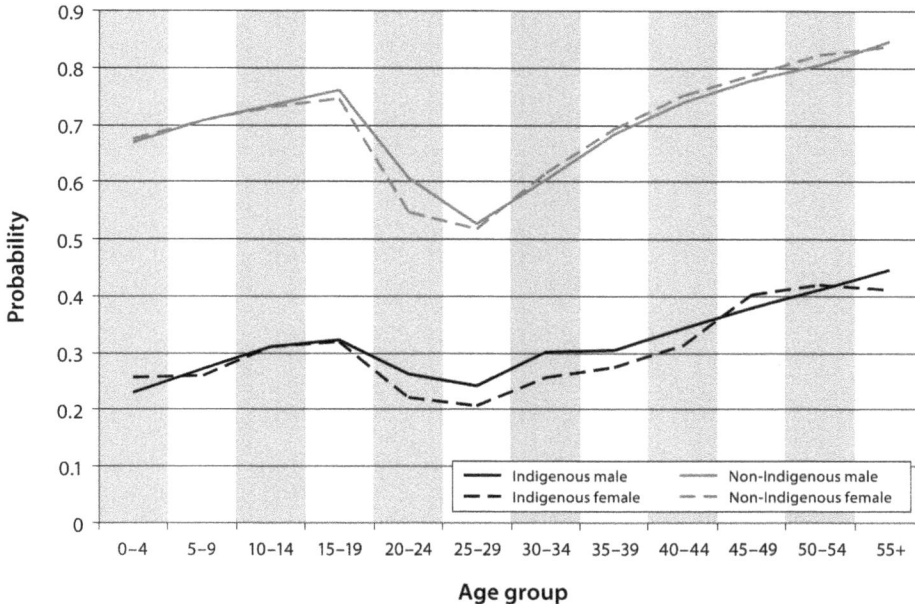

Source: Customised calculations using the 2006 5% CSF, ABS Census of Population and Housing

The patterns across the lifecourse in terms of living in an owner-occupied house are similar for Indigenous and non-Indigenous Australians. The probability starts off high (when the house is likely to be owned by a parent or guardian), declines substantially in a person's twenties as they leave home and then increases gradually as wealth is accumulated. If anything, the differences across the lifecourse are less for the Indigenous compared to the non-Indigenous population, with the former having a much flatter age profile. While the patterns are similar, the differences in home ownership between Indigenous and non-Indigenous Australians are consistently large across the lifecourse. Proportionately, Indigenous Australians are half as likely to live in an owner-occupied dwelling as non-Indigenous Australians for almost all age groups, with the difference being particularly large for children.

Modelling home ownership across the lifecourse

Table 7.1 presents the factors associated with the probability of living in a home that is owned or being purchased by a usual resident. Because the income and employment characteristics of the individual are likely to have a substantial impact on the ability to afford one's own home, the analysis is restricted to the 15 years and over age group. As expected from Fig. 7.1, the results presented in Table 7.1 confirm that Indigenous adults are significantly and substantially less likely to live in a home that is owned or being purchased by a usual resident. A comparison between Model 1 and Model 2 shows that some of this difference is removed after controlling for other characteristics of the individual. However, the difference in Model 2 of −0.252 relative to a base case of 0.872 is still very large.

Table 7.1 Factors associated with the probability of living in a dwelling that is owned or being purchased, 2006

Part A: Demographic and geographic variables

Explanatory variables[a]	Total population		Indigenous population	
	Model 1	Model 2	Model 3	Model 4
Indigenous	−0.379	−0.252		
Female	0.013	0.022	n.s.	n.s.
Aged 15–19	0.157	0.081	0.056*	n.s.
Aged 20–24	n.s.	0.047	n.s.	n.s.
Aged 25–29	−0.078	n.s.	−0.074	−0.092
Aged 35–39	0.081	0.012	−0.054	n.s.
Aged 40–44	0.135	0.022	n.s.	n.s.
Aged 45–49	0.173	0.030	n.s.	n.s.
Aged 50–54	0.200	0.040	n.s.	0.106
Aged 55 +	0.241	0.074	0.104	0.206
Aged 15–19, female	−0.031	−0.041	n.s.	n.s.
Aged 20–24, female	−0.070	−0.049	n.s.	n.s.
Aged 25–29, female	−0.020	−0.016	n.s.	n.s.
Aged 35–39, female	n.s.	0.007	n.s.	n.s.
Aged 40–44, female	n.s.	0.013	n.s.	n.s.
Aged 45–49, female	n.s.	0.015	n.s.	n.s.
Aged 50–54, female	0.012	0.022	n.s.	n.s.
Aged 55 +, female	−0.023	0.021	n.s.	n.s.
Victoria		0.030	0.061	0.073
Queensland		0.004	−0.045	−0.041
South Australia		0.020	0.037*	0.086
Western Australia		0.027	−0.040	n.s.
Tasmania		0.032	0.129	0.168
Northern Territory		−0.099	−0.069	n.s.
Australian Capital Territory		n.s.	n.s.	n.s.
Major city		n.s.	0.053	0.030
Probability of the base case[b]	0.607	0.872	0.765	0.516
Pseudo R-Squared	0.0605	0.1921	0.2014	0.2570
Number of observations	698 879	559 079	8 444	8 444

119

Part B: Socioeconomic and other variables

	Total population			Indigenous population
Explanatory variables[a]	Model 1	Model 2	Model 3	Model 4
Changed usual residence in the last 5 years		−0.213	−0.096	−0.141
Changed usual residence in the last year		−0.117	−0.092	−0.133
Secondary school student		0.063	0.143	0.197
Tertiary student		−0.006	0.063	0.080
Part-time student		n.s.	n.s.	n.s.
Completed Year 9 or less		−0.037	−0.150	−0.145
Completed Year 10 or 11		−0.012	−0.042	−0.036
Does not have any qualifications		−0.008	−0.066	−0.085
Has a Diploma or Certificate only		0.014	n.s.	n.s.
Speaks another language and English well		−0.014	−0.447	−0.342
Speaks another language and English not well or not at all		−0.039	−0.285	−0.227
Never married		−0.162	−0.230	−0.162
Divorced, separated or widowed		−0.170	−0.196	−0.120
Has had at least one child (for females)		−0.014	−0.040	n.s.
Has a 'core activity' need for assistance		−0.022	n.s.	n.s.
Provides unpaid child care (all)		0.008	n.s.	n.s.
Provides unpaid child care for children other than own		n.s.	n.s.	n.s.
Provides unpaid assistance for someone with a disability		n.s.	n.s.	n.s.
Not employed		−0.047	−0.160	−0.135
Owner or manager of enterprise or contributing family worker		0.028	0.129	0.164
Employed in the government sector		0.015	−0.030	n.s.
Employed part-time		n.s.	−0.046	−0.036*
Undertook volunteer work		0.005	0.047	0.072
Low individual income (less than $250pw)		n.s.	n.s.	n.s.
High individual income ($1,000pw or more)		0.045	0.099	0.152
Lives in a mixed Indigenous and non-Indigenous household				0.302
Probability of the base case[b]	0.607	0.872	0.765	0.516
Pseudo R-Squared	0.0605	0.1921	0.2014	0.2570
Number of observations	698 879	559 079	8 444	8 444

[a.] n.s. = Those variables that were not significant at the 10% level of significance.

* = Those variables that were significant at the 10% level of significance but not the 5% level

[b.] The base case for the total population is non-Indigenous. For all estimates, the base case is aged 30–34 years and in addition, for Models 2–4 (for the total population and for the Indigenous estimates), the base case lives in New South Wales, outside of a major city, did not change usual residence in the last five years, is not a student, has completed Year 12, has a university degree, speaks English only, is currently married, has not had any children, does not provide unpaid child care or assistance to someone with a disability, is employed as an employee in the private sector, works full-time, did not undertake volunteer work and has an income between $250 and $1 000 per week. For Model 4, an additional characteristic of the base case is that they are living in an Indigenous-only household.

Source: Customised calculations using the 2006 5% CSF, ABS Census of Population and Housing

There are a number of characteristics identified as being associated with home ownership for the Indigenous population. Interestingly, while significant, the difference between Indigenous people who live in a major city and Indigenous people who live in the rest of Australia was not large. This is supported somewhat by the results presented in Biddle (2008), who found that home ownership rates for the Indigenous population were slightly lower in major cities than they were in the rest of non-remote Australia. It is in remote as opposed to regional Australia where home ownership was found by Biddle (2008) to be lowest, and in that sense it is unfortunate that it is not possible using the 5% CSF to separately identify remote from non-remote, and in particular regional, Australia.

Individuals who changed usual residence in the previous five years were significantly less likely to live in an owner-occupied dwelling than a person who has been in the same usual residence since 2001. Given that all individuals who changed usual residence in the last year are likely to have changed usual residence in the last five years as well, the second migration variable is in addition to the first. It would seem, therefore, that recent movers have an even lower probability than people who moved in the last five years only to live in an owner-occupied dwelling. Transaction costs when buying a home are quite high and people who have changed usual residence recently are likely to delay purchasing a home until they are settled in an area. Furthermore, there is likely to be an element of reverse causality, with home ownership placing a constraint on residential mobility.

The majority of the variables in Models 3 and 4 are related in some way to access to economic resources either at the household or individual level. It is interesting, therefore, that even after controlling for these characteristics, the variable for living in a mixed Indigenous and non-Indigenous household (in Model 4) is significant and has such a large marginal effect. It is impossible to tell with the available data whether this is related to unobserved preferences or the contribution of other household members to the ability to afford a house. Nonetheless, it would appear that the composition of an Indigenous Australian's household is an important predictor of whether or not they are a home owner.

Community or government housing

While there are many costs and benefits of home ownership (financial and otherwise) there are also substantial differences depending on landlord type for people who are renting. In terms of access, community or government rental is usually rationed according to some measure of need (typically socioeconomic and demographic status), with supply also restricted. Private rental on the other hand, is usually allocated by the market. There are, however, potential access issues in the private rental market as well, including the geographic distribution of rental housing (AIHW 2005), and the ability to tap into available networks to secure rental properties from family and/or friends.

Even for a given rental property leased via an agent, access might vary depending on the characteristics of the prospective renter (Yinger 1986). Landlords or agents may be less likely to rent to a particular sex, age or ethnicity group, with family circumstances also being taken into account. Such discrimination could be statistical as opposed to taste-based in the sense that these characteristics are used as markers for other undesirable but unobserved characteristics of the applicant (for example the likelihood of not paying rent or damaging the property). Either way, there is evidence that some groups are less likely to be offered a rental place given their observed characteristics (Yinger 1986), and it is quite possible that this impacts on Indigenous Australians. Another difference between community or government housing and private rental is the cost of the rental accommodation. The former is likely to be heavily subsidised by the government or community organisation (hence the need to ration), leaving a greater share of the household budget to be spent on other goods or services. The final major difference between community or government and private rental is the security of tenure. Once access to a community or government house has been obtained, the renter often has a reasonably secure and stable housing situation (AIHW 2005). This is likely to change when the income or family composition of the household changes.

Compared to private rental, community or government rental therefore has a number of attractive aspects for many Indigenous Australians (Sanders 2005), and may even have benefits over home ownership. Focusing on people in a rented dwelling, Fig. 7.2 shows the proportion of Indigenous and non-Indigenous Australians who are renting from a government or community organisation. While there are also likely to be differences in access and outcomes for people in a community as opposed to government rental, sample sizes are not sufficiently large to analyse differences between the two. Furthermore, the distinction may not always be clear to respondents to the census.

Fig. 7.2 Probability of living in a dwelling rented from a government or community organisation, 2006

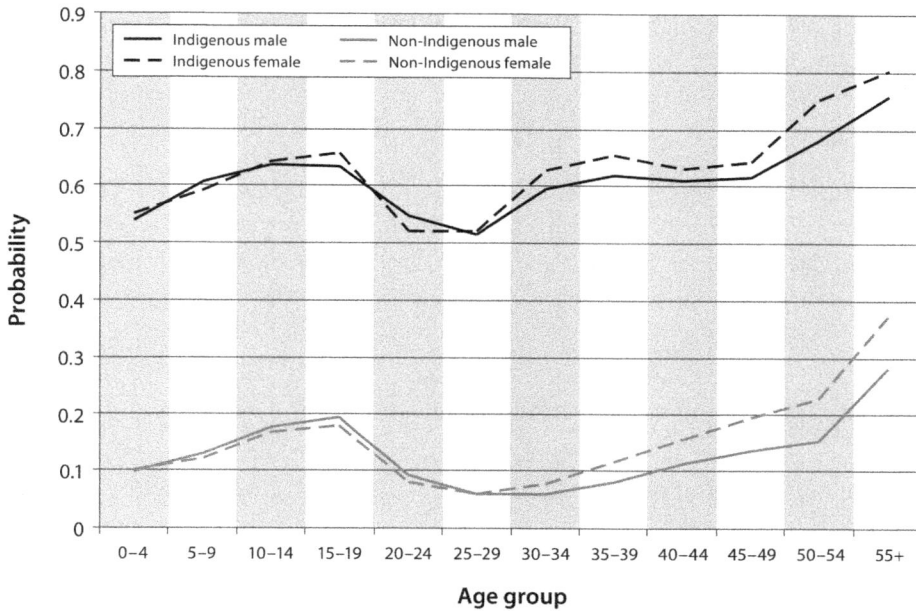

Source: Customised calculations using the 2006 5% CSF, ABS Census of Population and Housing

The probability of living in a dwelling that is rented from a government or community organisation (as opposed to private rental) starts off reasonably low for the 0–4 years age group. It then increases throughout childhood, reaching a local maximum amongst 15–19 year olds. Given the targeting of families and the elderly when it comes to the allocation of public or community housing, it is not surprising that the probability of living in such households is at its lowest during a person's twenties. The probability increases from a person's early-thirties onwards as people have families of their own, with the highest rate across the lifecourse occurring in the 55–plus age group. An interesting finding in Fig. 7.2 is the higher probability for females (from the early-thirties onwards). This likely reflects the greater proportion of single-parent females compared to single-parent males.

Similar to the findings presented in Fig. 7.1, the results in Fig. 7.2 show no discernable differences between Indigenous and non-Indigenous Australians in terms of patterns across the lifecourse. Rather, it is the difference in levels that is most striking. Proportionately speaking, Indigenous Australians in a rented dwelling are around five times more likely than non-Indigenous Australians to be in a community- or government-rented dwelling. As shown in Table 7.2, this is caused in part by the types of areas in which Indigenous Australians live and their other characteristics.

Modelling community or government housing across the lifecourse

The results presented in Table 7.2 show the factors associated with the probability of living in a dwelling that is rented from a government or community organisation, as opposed to through a private rental agreement. Once again, the analysis for the table focuses on the 15 years and over age group, and on individuals in rented dwellings only. The results presented in Table 7.2 confirm that Indigenous Australians are more likely to live in community or government rental than non-Indigenous Australians. While the magnitude of the difference declines substantially once other characteristics have been controlled for, the difference between Indigenous and non-Indigenous Australians in Model 2 is still quite large. The marginal effect for the Indigenous variable (0.175) dwarfs the predicted probability of the base case (0.030), as well as the marginal effects for all other variables. While there are significant differences by age and sex for the total population (in Model 2), this is not the case for the Indigenous population (Models 3 and 4). While the first three sets of variables (sex, age and the interaction between the two) are jointly significant, none of the individual variables are significant, even at the 10 per cent level of significance. It would seem, therefore, that the differences across the lifecourse identified in Fig. 7.2 are due to the variation in other characteristics controlled for in the model.

Table 7.2 Factors associated with the probability of living in a dwelling that is rented from a government or community organisation, population aged 15 years and over, in a rented dwelling, 2006

Part A: Demographic and geographic variables

Explanatory variables[a]	Total population		Indigenous population	
	Model 1	Model 2	Model 3	Model 4
Indigenous	0.403	0.175		
Female	0.017	−0.006	n.s.	n.s.
Aged 15–19	0.124	0.007	n.s.	n.s.
Aged 20–24	0.028	n.s.	n.s.	n.s.
Aged 25–29	n.s.	−0.004*	n.s.	n.s.
Aged 35–39	0.021	0.011	n.s.	n.s.
Aged 40–44	0.051	0.010	n.s.	n.s.
Aged 45–49	0.073	0.018	n.s.	n.s.
Aged 50–54	0.092	0.021	n.s.	n.s.
Aged 55 +	0.211	0.027	n.s.	n.s.
Aged 15–19, female	−0.018	0.007*	n.s.	n.s.
Aged 20–24, female	−0.020	n.s.	n.s.	n.s.
Aged 25–29, female	−0.012	n.s.	n.s.	n.s.
Aged 35–39, female	0.008*	−0.006	n.s.	n.s.
Aged 40–44, female	0.008*	n.s.	n.s.	n.s.
Aged 45–49, female	0.013	n.s.	n.s.	n.s.
Aged 50–54, female	0.018	n.s.	n.s.	n.s.
Aged 55 +, female	0.017	n.s.	n.s.	n.s.
Victoria		−0.007	n.s.	n.s.
Queensland		−0.006	n.s.	n.s.
South Australia		0.039	0.195	0.186
Western Australia		0.005	0.172	0.137
Tasmania		0.014	−0.112	−0.097*
Northern Territory		0.068	0.148	0.115
Australian Capital Territory		0.092	0.277	0.266
Major city		0.004	−0.089	−0.075
Probability of the base case[b]	0.061	0.030	0.279	0.437
Pseudo R-Squared	0.1234	0.3159	0.3287	0.3646
Number of observations	177 696	137 494	5 324	5 324

125

Part B: Socioeconomic and other variables

Explanatory variables[a]	Total population		Indigenous population	
	Model 1	Model 2	Model 3	Model 4
Changed usual residence in the last 5 years		−0.025	−0.198	−0.258
Changed usual residence in the last year		−0.015	−0.106	−0.123
Secondary school student		−0.020	−0.124	−0.139
Tertiary student		−0.016	−0.117	−0.150
Part-time student		0.027	0.207	0.223
Completed Year 9 or less		0.042	0.154	0.148
Completed Year 10 or 11		0.016	0.075	0.072
Does not have any qualifications		0.029	0.143	0.166
Has a Diploma or Certificate only		0.019	0.095*	0.106*
Speaks another language and English well		0.022	0.314	0.273
Speaks another language and English not well or not at all		0.025	0.391	0.352
Never married		0.039	0.090	n.s.
Divorced, separated or widowed		0.026	−0.053	−0.126
Has had at least one child (for females)		0.017	0.169	0.156
Has a 'core activity' need for assistance		0.036	n.s.	0.084
Provides unpaid child care (all)		−0.004	−0.064	−0.070
Provides unpaid child care for children other than own		n.s.	n.s.	n.s.
Provides unpaid assistance for someone with a disability		0.020	0.057	0.069
Not employed		0.066	0.214	0.187
Owner or manager of enterprise or contributing family worker		−0.019	−0.233	−0.308
Employed in the government sector		0.018	0.137	0.113
Employed part-time		0.021	0.121	0.118
Undertook volunteer work		0.002*	−0.038	n.s.
Low individual income (less than $250pw)		0.018	0.100	0.128
High individual income ($1,000pw or more)		−0.016	−0.105	−0.125
Lives in a mixed Indigenous and non-Indigenous household				−0.259
Probability of the base case[b]	0.061	0.030	0.279	0.437
Pseudo R-Squared	0.1234	0.3159	0.3287	0.3646
Number of observations	177 696	137 494	5 324	5 324

[a.] n.s. = Those variables that were not significant at the 10% level of significance.

* = Those variables that were significant at the 10% level of significance but not the 5% level

[b.] The base case for the total population is non-Indigenous. For all estimates, the base case is aged 30–34 years and in addition, for Models 2–4 (for the total population and for the Indigenous estimates), the base case lives in New South Wales, outside a major city, did not change usual residence in the last five years, is not a student, has completed Year 12, has a university degree, speaks English only, is currently married, has not had any children, does not provide unpaid child care or assistance to someone with a disability, is employed as an employee in the private sector, works full-time, did not undertake volunteer work, and has an income between $250 and $1 000 per week. For Model 4, an additional characteristic of the base case is that they are living in an Indigenous-only household.

Source: Customised calculations using the 2006 5% CSF, ABS Census of Population and Housing

Some of the variables that have been identified earlier in this paper as varying across the lifecourse and found to be significantly associated with community or government rental are residential mobility, education attendance, marital status, child rearing and employment. All of these differences are likely to reflect eligibility rules. One variable that potentially represents differential access across the Indigenous population in terms of community and government housing is living in a major city. The lower probability for those who changed usual residence in the last five years (and especially who changed usual residence in the last year) is likely to reflect the greater stability of community and government housing. This may be because individuals who move frequently are unable to access community or government housing, or it may be because that tenure type places a break on residential mobility. Either way, there is clearly a significant interaction between the two variables.

Overcrowding

There is a large (and growing) literature on the relationship between a person's housing circumstances and their health outcomes. One aspect of this literature is the adequacy of the housing stock to meet the sanitary needs of the residents (Bailie and Wayte 2006; Pholeros, Rainow and Torzillo 1993). Unfortunately, the census does not have very good information on the quality of Indigenous housing. The other aspect of housing that is covered in the literature is overcrowding. Here the link is also reasonably straightforward – the greater the concentration of people in a house, the more likely it is that communicable diseases will spread across the residents. A person's health is not the only thing that overcrowding impacts upon. Biddle (2007) showed a significant negative association between overcrowding and Indigenous education participation. Importantly, these results held after controlling for the size of the household in terms of usual residents. That is, it was not the number of people living in a house per se which had an association. Rather, the effects come from an inadequacy of the housing stock to meet the needs of Indigenous Australians, whether they live in large households or small.

This distinction highlights one of the difficulties in measuring variation in overcrowding across population subgroups (for example Indigenous compared to non-Indigenous Australians), or across different regions in Australia. That is, measures of housing utilisation that may be relevant in one context (the number of people per house) may not be relevant in other contexts. However, these cultural considerations are going to be important in almost all measures used, albeit to varying degrees. Compared to specially targeted surveys or qualitative interviewing techniques, measures of overcrowding derived from pre-existing statistical collections like the census are likely to only give partial measures of overcrowding. A measure that is used consistently across populations and regions will include people who may subjectively feel that their housing situation does not constitute overcrowding despite being measured as such. Equally, a proportion of the population are likely to subjectively feel that they are living in an overcrowded household because of their particular circumstances but not be captured in standard measures.

The most comprehensive measure available on standard census outputs is the housing utilisation measure based on the Canadian occupancy standards which takes into account the number of bedrooms in the dwelling as well as the size and demographic composition of the usual residents (Biddle 2008). Unfortunately, the housing and person information available on the 5% CSF is not sufficiently detailed to construct this occupancy measure, nor is it made available as a standard output. For this reason, the analysis in this section uses the slightly cruder proxy for overcrowding, namely the number of people per bedroom and in particular, the probability of living in a dwelling where there is more than one person per bedroom. As mentioned, Biddle (2007) showed that this variable is associated with education participation for Indigenous youth, whereas Biddle (2008) showed that the proxy for overcrowding had a very high correlation at the area level with the aforementioned housing utilisation measure (with a coefficient of 0.987).

The probability across the lifecourse of living in a dwelling with more than one person per bedroom is presented in Fig. 7.3. Clearly, the probability of living in a house with more than one person per bedroom declines with age. For the Indigenous population, this continues up until the 20–24 year age group, whereas for the non-Indigenous population, the local minimum is for the 25–29 year age group. This is not surprising, given the high incidence of siblings sharing rooms. Beyond these two ages, the probability then rises into and across the thirties and early forties as people cohabit and have children of their own.

Fig. 7.3 Probability of living in a rented dwelling with more than one person per bedroom, 2006

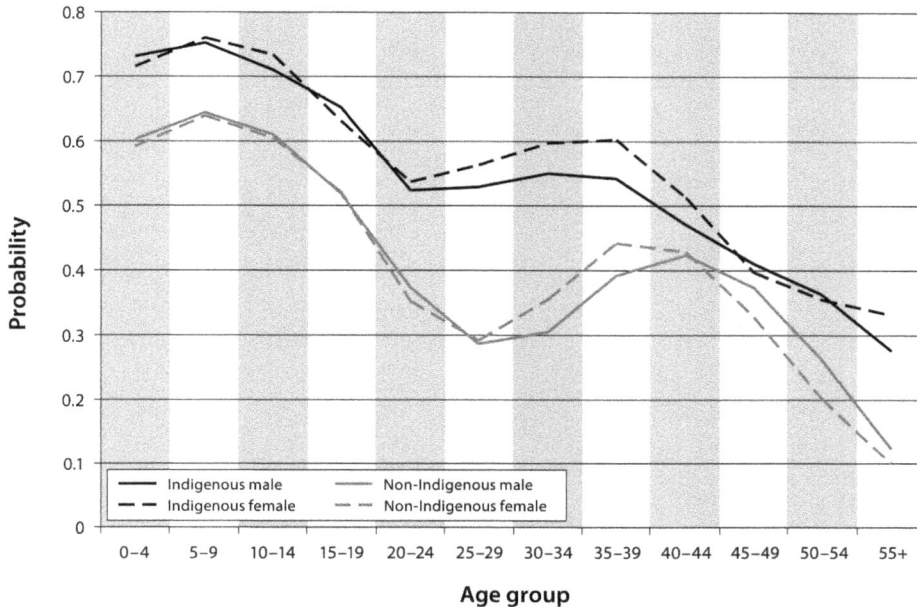

Source: Customised calculations using the 2006 5% CSF, ABS Census of Population and Housing

While there are clear lifecourse patterns to this proxy measure of overcrowding, it is also clear that there is a large and consistent gap between Indigenous and non-Indigenous Australians. Indigenous children are about 10 percentage points more likely to live in such dwellings, with the difference even greater in their late-twenties and thirties.

Modelling overcrowding across the lifecourse

Using the probability of living in a dwelling that has more than one person per bedroom as a proxy, Table 7.3 presents results that consider the factors associated with overcrowding. Given the high incidence of siblings sharing bedrooms, a situation that does not tend to be classified as overcrowding, the analysis focuses on the 15 years and over age group. In addition to the explanatory variables used in previous estimations in this chapter, the model for this dependent variable includes the tenure and structure of the dwelling as explanatory variables. The base case is a house that is owned or being purchased by one of the usual residents.

Table 7.3 Factors associated with the probability of living in a dwelling that has more than one person per bedroom, population aged 15 years and over, 2006

Part A: Demographic and geographic variables

Explanatory variables[a]	Total population		Indigenous population	
	Model 1	Model 2	Model 1	Model 2
Indigenous	0.176	0.153		
Female	0.049	−0.095	−0.065*	−0.056*
Aged 15–19	0.209	0.273	0.150	0.135
Aged 20–24	0.066	0.164	n.s.	n.s.
Aged 25–29	−0.019	0.039	n.s.	n.s.
Aged 35–39	0.085	0.046	n.s.	n.s.
Aged 40–44	0.115	0.065	−0.084	−0.067
Aged 45–49	0.067	0.041	−0.129	−0.111
Aged 50–54	−0.043	−0.039	−0.180	−0.148
Aged 55 +	−0.182	−0.174	−0.265	−0.212
Aged 15–19, female	−0.045	0.092	n.s.	n.s.
Aged 20–24, female	−0.062	0.051	n.s.	n.s.
Aged 25–29, female	−0.040	0.014	n.s.	n.s.
Aged 35–39, female	n.s.	−0.021	n.s.	n.s.
Aged 40–040, female	−0.040	−0.051	n.s.	n.s.
Aged 45–49, female	−0.083	−0.079	n.s.	n.s.
Aged 50–54, female	−0.106	−0.099	n.s.	−0.088*
Aged 55 +, female	−0.081	−0.067	n.s.	n.s.
Victoria		−0.006	−0.096	−0.088
Queensland		−0.029	0.053	0.054
South Australia		−0.032	n.s.	n.s.
Western Australia		−0.086	0.033*	0.045
Tasmania		−0.017	n.s.	n.s.
Northern Territory		0.084	0.148	0.157
Australian Capital Territory		−0.070	n.s.	n.s.
Major city		0.005	−0.085	−0.086
Probability of the base case[b]	0.306	0.277	0.421	0.318
Pseudo R-Squared	0.0823	0.1543	0.1527	0.1588
Number of observations	711 953	555 224	8 313	8 313

Part B: Socioeconomic and other variables

Explanatory variables[a]	Total population		Indigenous population	
	Model 1	Model 2	Model 1	Model 2
Changed usual residence in the last 5 years		−0.043	−0.033	−0.034
Changed usual residence in the last year		−0.011	0.032	0.025*
Secondary school student		0.017	n.s.	n.s.
Tertiary student		0.013	−0.068	−0.061
Part-time student		−0.017	n.s.	n.s.
Completed Year 9 or less		0.020	0.050	0.052
Completed Year 10 or 11		0.008	0.034	0.035
Does not have any qualifications		0.021	0.096	0.090
Has a Diploma or Certificate only		n.s.	n.s.	n.s.
Speaks another language and English well		0.117	0.118	0.127
Speaks another language and English not well or not at all		0.230	0.125	0.130
Never married		−0.101	−0.106	−0.074
Divorced, separated or widowed		−0.134	−0.108	−0.075
Has had at least one child (for females)		0.169	0.111	0.116
Has a 'core activity' need for assistance		0.027	−0.048	−0.052
Provides unpaid child care (all)		0.229	0.171	0.163
Provides unpaid child care for children other than own		−0.092	n.s.	n.s.
Provides unpaid assistance for someone with a disability		0.006	n.s.	n.s.
Not employed		−0.004*	n.s.	n.s.
Owner or manager of enterprise or contributing family worker		n.s.	−0.065	−0.063*
Employed in the government sector		−0.013	n.s.	n.s.
Employed part-time		n.s.	n.s.	n.s.
Undertook volunteer work		0.007	−0.041	−0.036
Low individual income (less than $250pw)		0.031	0.041	0.033
High individual income ($1,000pw or more)		−0.034	−0.056	−0.048
Renting from private organisation, family or friend		0.037	n.s.	0.026*
Renting from government or community organisation		0.078	0.156	0.200
Other tenure type		0.042	n.s.	n.s.
Lives in semi-detached, row or terrace house		−0.019	−0.105	−0.091
Lives in flat, unit or apartment		0.015	−0.098	−0.078
Lives in other dwelling type		0.365	0.122	0.129
Lives in a mixed Indigenous and non-Indigenous household				0.115

131

Probability of the base case[b]	0.306	0.277	0.421	0.318
Pseudo R-Squared	0.0823	0.1543	0.1527	0.1588
Number of observations	711 953	555 224	8 313	8 313

[a.] n.s. = Those variables that were not significant at the 10% level of significance.

* = Those variables that were significant at the 10% level of significance but not the 5% level

[b.] The base case for the total population is non-Indigenous. For all estimates, the base case is aged 30–34 years and in addition, for Model 2 (for the total population and for the Indigenous estimates), the base case lives in New South Wales, outside a major city, did not change usual residence in the last five years, is not a student, has completed Year 12, has a university degree, speaks English only, is currently married, has not had any children, does not provide unpaid child care or assistance to someone with a disability, is employed as an employee in the private sector, works full-time, did not undertake volunteer work, has an income between $250 and $1 000 per week and lives in a house owned or being purchased. For Model 4, an additional characteristic of the base case is that they are living in an Indigenous-only household.

Source: Customised calculations using the 2006 5% CSF, ABS Census of Population and Housing

The large marginal effect for many of the age groups shows substantial variation in this measure of overcrowding across the lifecourse. However, after controlling for this variation, there is still a significant and substantial difference between Indigenous and non-Indigenous Australians. Importantly, the difference does not change by much after controlling for other characteristics of the individual and their dwelling. That is, to the extent that the most important variables are captured in the model, it would appear that there is something consistent about Indigenous status itself that is associated with living in a dwelling with more than one person per bedroom. This may be something not captured by the census (and hence unobserved in the model) including geographic location. Alternatively, it might be related to a relative preference for such dwellings and household structure.

For the most part, characteristics that are associated with this measure of overcrowding for the total population have the same association for the Indigenous population in isolation. For variables that do have a differently signed association, the magnitudes of the marginal effects are not large. Two variables where there was found to be substantive differences are tenure type and structure of the dwelling. For the total population, dwellings that are owned or being purchased by one of the usual residents (the base case) have the lowest probability of being overcrowded. For the Indigenous population, on the other hand, dwellings that are being rented in the private rental market do not have a significantly different probability of being overcrowded as compared to owner-occupied dwelling (at least at the 5% level of significance). There is, however, a significant difference between those who are renting from a government or community organisation and those in an owner-occupied dwelling. While it is not possible to assign causality with these cross-sectional results, it is clear that there is significant interaction between tenure and household overcrowding. However, it is also clear that this interaction is different for Indigenous compared to non-Indigenous Australians.

Finally, one of the more interesting findings from the second part of Table 7.3 is that Indigenous Australians who live in a household with both Indigenous and non-Indigenous usual residents are more likely to live in a dwelling that is deemed to be overcrowded than the base case (Indigenous-only households). This is despite the fact that mixed households have on average slightly fewer usual residents than Indigenous-only households. It is interesting to note, therefore, that this is one of the few instances where the coefficient for mixed households in Model 4 is in the same direction as the Indigenous status variable in Models 1 and 2.

Housing across the Indigenous lifecourse

The results presented in this chapter have shown large differences between Indigenous and non-Indigenous Australians in terms of housing tenure and overcrowding. Importantly, these differences were consistent across the lifecourse and remained after controlling for other characteristics. One of the more relevant findings from the chapter was the interaction between the two main variables of interest. Indigenous Australians who lived in a house that was rented from a government or community organisation are significantly and substantially more likely to live in a house with more than one usual resident per bedroom compared to Indigenous Australians who own their own home or are renting in the private sector. Not everyone can afford to own their own home, and in many of the areas in which Indigenous Australians live, the private housing market is virtually non-existent. Furthermore, there are potential benefits to living in a community-rented house (Sanders 2005). Nonetheless, it needs to be made clear that there are potential trade-offs in terms of overcrowding.

Ultimately, while housing does not feature explicitly in COAG's Closing the Gap targets, there is no doubt that there are important interactions between housing and the measures that are included. Without improvements in the quality and availability of housing for the Indigenous population, it will be very difficult to make substantial inroads into health and education inequality. Conversely, without improvements in Indigenous employment, home ownership is likely to remain low, and overcrowding is likely to continue.

8. Health

The centrepiece of COAG's Closing the Gap agenda is the elimination of the life expectancy gap between Indigenous and non-Indigenous Australians. At the time the commitment was made, the available estimates posited a roughly 17-year gap between how long an Indigenous child born today would expect to live compared to the life expectancy of its non-Indigenous counterpart. Revised methodology from the ABS now estimates the life expectancy gap (as of the 2005–07 period) to be 11.5 years for males and 9.7 years for females (ABS 2008b).[1] Although it is not always thought of as such, life expectancy is a key measure that summarises differences in the lifecourse experience. Estimates of life expectancy are generally constructed as the number of years that a child born today would expect to live based on the current age distribution of deaths. In other words, the length of their lifecourse. Whatever the true estimate, it is clear that an Indigenous child born today is expected to have a shorter life, on average, than a non-Indigenous child.

Perhaps as important as the length of the lifecourse is how healthy a person is at different stages throughout their life. According to the World Health Organization (WHO 1948) 'health is a state of complete physical, mental and social wellbeing and not merely the absence of disease or infirmity'. Unfortunately, data on health and wellbeing from the census is limited at best. The census is a poor instrument for looking at health issues. However, many of the other outcomes examined in this monograph such as employment, education, housing tenure and migration are all fundamentally linked to health and wellbeing. The association between an individual's social and economic status and their health has long been established (Wilkinson and Marmot 2003), with other measures of disadvantage generally associated with worse health and higher mortality rates (Matthews, Jagger and Hancock 2006).

A new variable available on the 2006 Census that at least touches on physical wellbeing is whether or not a person reports a need for assistance in undertaking a 'core activity'. According to the ABS data dictionary (ABS 2009c: 19) 'this population is defined as people who need assistance in their day to day lives with any or all of the following core activities – self-care, body movements or communication – because of a disability, long-term health condition, or old age'.

---

1   These revisions in no way reflect an improvement in Indigenous life expectancy, but rather a complete change in methodology. Even now, the methodology used and the data underlying it is treated as experimental by the ABS and the subject of ongoing debate by experts in the field.

The first set of results presented in this section considers variation across the lifecourse in reporting a 'core activity' need for assistance, as well as the factors associated with it for the 45 years and over age group.

The final set of results in this chapter returns to life expectancy estimates and considers the percentage of a hypothetical population who are still alive after a given age. More so than the other chapters in this monograph, a consideration of health outcomes across the lifecourse using census data is severely restricted by the extensiveness of the data available. The census was not designed to capture health or wellbeing and is a very blunt instrument for this purpose. So, while the results in this section do give some new insights into the differences between Indigenous and non-Indigenous Australians in terms of their health outcomes across the lifecourse, in the final section of this chapter we discuss alternative datasets that give a more complete picture.

'Core activity' need for assistance

The probability of reporting a restriction in a 'core activity' for Indigenous and non-Indigenous males and females is graphed in Fig. 8.1. Results presented here clearly show that, at least up until the 35–39 year age group, reporting a 'core activity' need for assistance is a relatively rare event. Although the probabilities are generally higher for Indigenous compared to non-Indigenous Australians, the probability for the under 40 years age group stays under 5 per cent. To the extent that there is a difference, males tend to have a higher probability of reporting a need for assistance than females.

From the age of 40 onwards, the probability of reporting a 'core activity' need for assistance increases substantially, as does the predicted difference between Indigenous and non-Indigenous Australians. By the 60–64 year age group, 16.4 per cent of Indigenous males and 14.7 per cent of Indigenous females report a need for assistance. This is compared to 6.3 and 5.0 per cent respectively for non-Indigenous males and females. To put this disparity another way, a non-Indigenous Australian aged in their early to mid-sixties has roughly the same probability of reporting a 'core activity' need for assistance as an Indigenous Australian in their mid-forties.

Modelling 'core activity' need for assistance across the lifecourse

The dependent variable in the following analysis is the probability of an individual reporting a 'core activity' need for assistance. Given the age distribution summarised in Fig. 8.1 and the clear finding that this measure of poor health is skewed towards the end of the age distribution, the analysis is restricted to the population aged 45 years and over. The base case is the 45–49 years age group.

Fig. 8.1 Probability of reporting a 'core activity' need for assistance, 2006

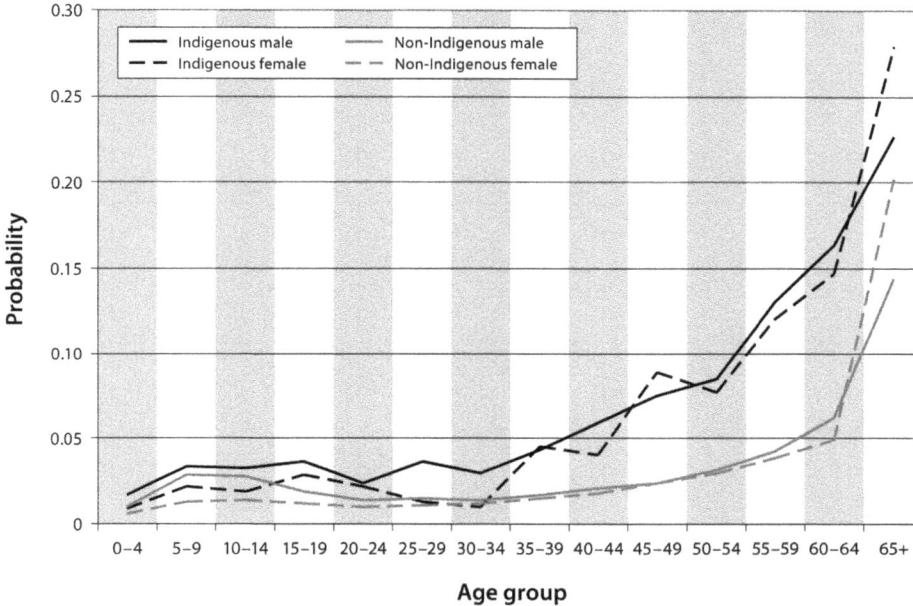

Source: Customised calculations using the 2006 5% CSF, ABS Census of Population and Housing

There is a strong potential for endogeneity and reverse causality between having a 'core activity' need for assistance and a number of the independent variables used in previous models. This is a phenomenon that is more likely to occur for this variable compared to any other dependent variable analysed in this monograph. For example, individuals who are employed or have a relatively high income are likely to be better able to afford the treatments that allow them to overcome any restrictions on their mobility or communication. On the other hand, a 'core activity' need for assistance is likely to place severe limitations on obtaining and maintaining stable, well-paid employment (indeed we used it as an explanatory variable in a number of previous estimations). Although we did not attempt to measure causality in any of the previous models, we felt it particularly important to restrict the explanatory variables in the analysis summarised in Table 8.1 to demography, geography and education.

Table 8.1 Factors associated with reporting a 'core activity' need for assistance, population 45 years and over

Explanatory variables[a]	Total population		Indigenous population	
	Model 1	Model 2	Model 3	Model 4
Indigenous	0.041	0.007		
Female	n.s.	0.002	0.023*	0.027
Aged 50–54	0.008	0.003	n.s.	n.s.
Aged 55–59	0.019	0.007	0.020	0.023
Aged 60–64	0.039	0.014	0.036	0.033
Aged 65 +	0.117	0.038	0.056	0.045
Aged 50–54, female	n.s.	n.s.	n.s.	n.s.
Aged 55–59, female	n.s.	−0.001	−0.011*	−0.012
Aged 60–64, female	−0.006	−0.003	−0.013*	−0.012
Aged 65 +, female	0.016	0.002	n.s.	n.s.
Victoria		−0.001	n.s.	n.s.
Queensland		n.s.	n.s.	n.s.
South Australia		0.000	n.s.	n.s.
Western Australia		−0.001	n.s.	n.s.
Tasmania		0.001	n.s.	n.s.
Northern Territory		−0.003	−0.009*	n.s.
Australian Capital Territory		n.s.	n.s.	n.s.
Major city		0.000	−0.006	−0.006
Completed Year 9 or less		0.012	0.023	0.023
Completed Year 10 or 11		0.001	n.s.	n.s.
Does not have any qualifications		0.007	0.029	0.022*
Has a Diploma or Certificate only		0.004	n.s.	n.s.
Speaks another language and English well		0.002	0.012	n.s.
Speaks another language and English not well or not at all		0.015	0.038	n.s.
Never married		0.012	0.008*	n.s.
Divorced, separated or widowed		0.010	0.011	0.011
Has had at least one child (for females)		−0.002	n.s.	n.s.
Lives in a mixed Indigenous and non-Indigenous household				n.s.
Probability of the base case[b]	0.023	0.006	0.019	0.017
Pseudo R-Squared	0.1002	0.1497	0.0859	0.0735
Number of observations	352 738	311 613	2 914	2 782

[a.] n.s. = Those variables that were not significant at the 10% level of significance.

* = Those variables that were significant at the 10% level of significance but not the 5% level

[b.] The base case for the total population is non-Indigenous. For all estimates, the base case is aged 45–49 years and in addition, for Models 2–4 (for the total population and for the Indigenous estimates), the base case lives in New South Wales, outside of a major city, has completed Year 12, has a university degree, speaks English only and is married. For Model 4, an additional characteristic of the base case is that they are living in an Indigenous-only household.

Source: Customised calculations using the 2006 5% CSF, ABS Census of Population and Housing

The results presented in Model 1 confirm that not only does having a 'core activity' need for assistance increase with age (especially into the 65-plus age group), but also that Indigenous Australians have a higher likelihood after controlling for age and sex. The difference associated with being Indigenous reduces substantially once other socioeconomic characteristics are controlled for both in absolute terms and relative to the base case.

Whilst lower levels of education and being single are associated with a higher probability of reporting a need for assistance (confirming the association between socioeconomic status and health), age remains the predominant predictor of disability. For the Indigenous population, living in a major city is related to having a lower probability of a 'core activity' need for assistance. This could be attributed to better access to services, in particular health services.

Survival rates

As mentioned at the start of this chapter, the census is limited in its ability to capture variation in health across the lifecourse. While providing some information, the 'core activity' need for assistance variable can only really be considered a partial measure of poor health. Before discussing alternative data sources that are more suitable for capturing physical, mental and social wellbeing in the concluding chapter, we first return to a more detailed discussion of variation in mortality rates by gender and Indigenous status.

Figures 8.2 and 8.3 provide an indication of mortality across the lifecourse by illustrating the proportion of the population still alive at the beginning of successive age cohorts. Data for these figures come from the respective life tables in ABS (2008b). The first (Fig. 8.2) graphs the percentage of population still alive for the cohorts aged 1–4 years through to 40–44 years. Given the high rate of survival over this age group, the vertical axis is restricted to 90–100 per cent of the population in order to better show the difference between the four population groups. The second (Fig. 8.3) concentrates on the cohorts aged 40–44 years through to 85 years and over.

Fig. 8.2 Hypothetical percentage of population aged 0–44 years still alive at start of five-year age cohort, 2006

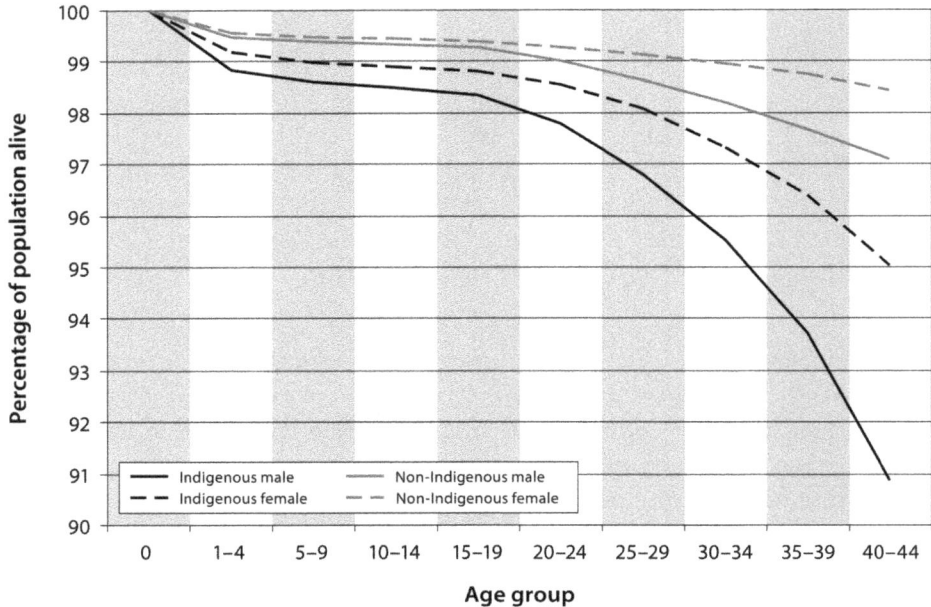

Source: ABS (2008b)

The higher likelihood of death for Indigenous males shows clearly in Fig. 8.2. While the gap starts off reasonably small in absolute terms, it widens considerable from the age of 20 onwards. Turning the analysis around somewhat and focusing on mortality as opposed to survival, Indigenous boys are 1.4 times as likely to die in the first five years of their life compared to Indigenous girls, and nearly 2.3 times as likely to die as non-Indigenous boys. While the ratio for the two groups of males stays reasonably constant, across the cohorts considered in Fig. 8.2 the gender disparity does not. Indigenous males are 1.7 times as likely to die before the age of 25 compared to Indigenous females.

The shorter life expectancy of Indigenous males is in many ways even more pronounced in Fig. 8.3. Once again, across all age cohorts, Indigenous males have the lowest proportion of the population still alive. It is over the age groups presented in Fig. 8.3 where the disparity between Indigenous and non-Indigenous females becomes apparent. An Indigenous female is 2.0 times as likely to die before reaching the age of 20 than a non-Indigenous female. By the age of 50, this ratio was predicted to have increased to 3.8 – even higher than the difference between Indigenous and non-Indigenous males (3.6 times).

Fig. 8.3 Hypothetical percentage of population aged 40–85 years still alive at start of five-year age cohort

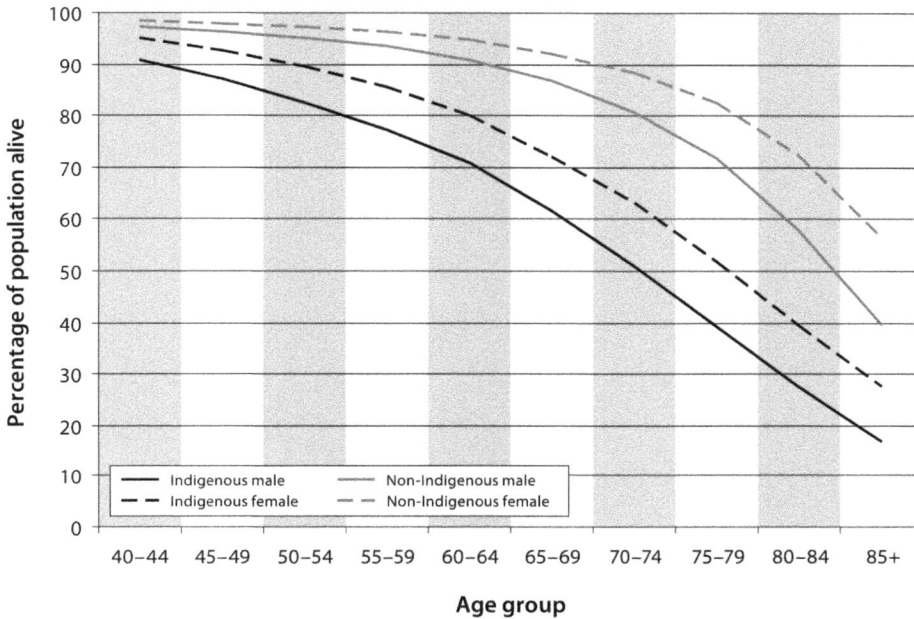

Source: ABS (2008b)

Health across the Indigenous lifecourse

While a healthy life is, and should be, one of the key focuses of government policy related to the Indigenous population, it is clear that information from the census around this issue is limited at best. The results presented show that although Indigenous Australians aged 45 years and over are significantly more likely to report a 'core activity' need for assistance, much of this difference is driven by other observed characteristics. By linking census data with deaths data, the ABS is also able to come up with an estimate of age-specific survival rates and life expectancy. An analysis of the resulting life tables shows significant differences both by Indigenous status and sex.

9. Childhood outcomes

There is a growing body of research around the concept of intergenerational disadvantage. There is strong evidence suggesting that the environment in which a child grows up influences the experience of poverty, inclusiveness and wellbeing of the child (Hérault and Kalb 2009). Statistics paint a picture of Indigenous children experiencing poorer outcomes compared to non-Indigenous children across a range of indicators such as birth weight, rates of hospitalisation, preschool participation, and reading and numeracy results (AIHW 2008). Daly and Smith (2003) looked at the wellbeing of Indigenous children using a social exclusion framework, and outlined a set of indicators as correlating strongly with outcomes of children including household income, absence of a parent, parental employment and education status, health status, and welfare reliance. These factors provide a measure of access to opportunities and investment in early childhood.

The analysis in this chapter begins with single parents themselves and how the probability of being a single parent varies across the lifecourse. The focus and the unit of analysis then turns to children and we examine whether the experience of an Indigenous child in terms of family and household characteristics differs to that of a non-Indigenous child. We look at three dependent variables: whether the child lives in a single-parent family; whether the child lives in a household without anyone employed; and whether the child lives in a household where no-one has completed Year 12. The final section of analysis looks at the interaction and intersection of these three dependent variables.

In the absence of measures of wellbeing for children in the Australian census, the range of indicators available for analysis is limited. The approach here is to consider the possible predictors of child outcomes. Understanding the types of households and the characteristics of household members in which Indigenous children live, provides an indication of the type of disadvantage that accumulates from the early stages of childhood and may carry throughout their lifecourse.

Single parenthood

Single parents are amongst the most marginalised in the community. Single parents are more likely to have lower education levels and lower labour force participations rates than the rest of the population (Daly and Smith 1998) and more likely to have lower disposable household income and be receiving government payments as their principal source of income. Single-parent households are less likely to have immediate support socially and financially (Pech and McCoull 1998) but this is not necessarily the case for Indigenous single parents who are able to draw on resources from extended kin and networks (Daly and Smith 2003). The probability of being a single parent as opposed to a parent in a registered or de facto marriage is plotted in Fig. 9.1.

Fig. 9.1 Probability of being a single parent, 2006

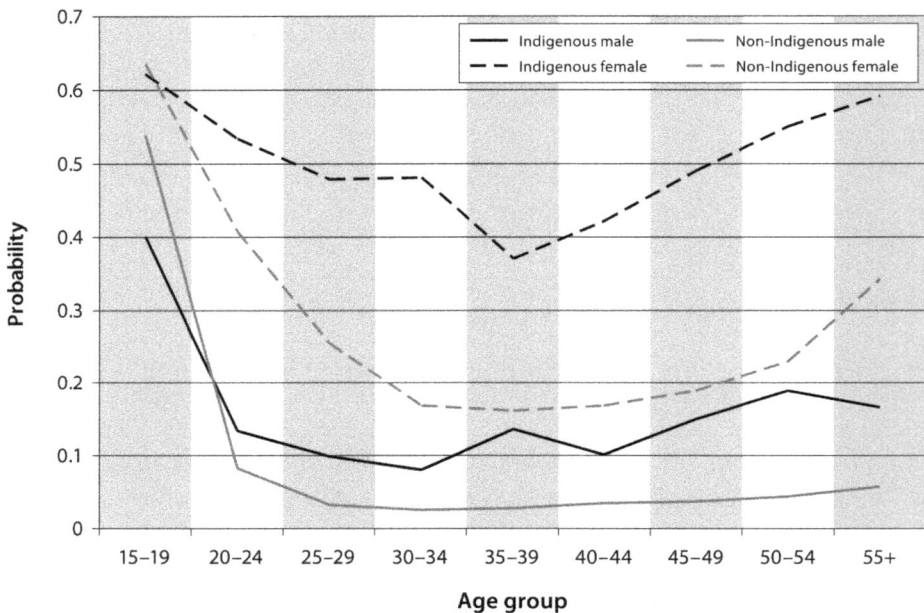

Source: Customised calculations using the 2006 5% CSF, ABS Census of Population and Housing

For both the Indigenous and non-Indigenous population, females are more likely to be single parents compared to males. While the probability of single parenthood for both Indigenous and non-Indigenous females start off quite similar, by the age of 30, an Indigenous female is approximately four times more likely to be a single parent compared to their non-Indigenous counterpart. Young non-Indigenous males have higher probability of being a single parent compared to Indigenous males, but that trend quickly changes as they transition to youth and adulthood with the Indigenous males more likely to be single parents.

An interesting pattern observed here is that the probability of being a single parent for Indigenous females remains quite high over the lifecourse. For young Indigenous females, this is likely to be because of the low rates of marriage discussed earlier and, perhaps, the large proportion of young Indigenous males who are incarcerated (ABS 2009). For older Indigenous females, this is largely due to the lower life expectancy of Indigenous males which results in widowed women being called upon to look after children of female relatives (Henry and Daly 2001).

Modelling single parenthood across the lifecourse

In Table 9.1 we look at the factors associated with being a lone parent. Model 1 once again includes demographic variables only with Model 2 and 3 including information on geography, education and English proficiency. The results in Model 1 suggest that after controlling for differences across the lifecourse Indigenous Australians are more likely to be single parents. Females also have a higher propensity to be single parents compared to males. An estimated marginal effect of 0.147 relative to the predicted probability of the base case of 0.025 suggests that the differences are quite large. After controlling for demographic, geographic and socioeconomic characteristics, Model 2 shows that Indigenous Australians are still more likely to be a single parent. However, the magnitude of that difference is less than the magnitude of the difference under Model 1. In general, the marginal effects for the Indigenous sample (Model 3) were in the same direction as the marginal effects for the total sample (Model 2). If anything though, the sizes of the marginal effects were slightly larger, in particular for the education variables.

Table 9.1 Factors associated with the probability of being a single parent, 2006

Explanatory variables[a]	Total population		Indigenous population
	Model 1	Model 2	Model 3
Indigenous	0.073	0.025	
Female	0.147	0.089	0.294
Aged 15–19	0.448	0.271	0.273
Aged 20–24	0.049	0.019	n.s.
Aged 25–29	0.006	n.s.	n.s.
Aged 35–39	n.s.	n.s.	n.s.
Aged 40–44	0.010	0.004	n.s.
Aged 45–49	0.013	0.006	0.040
Aged 50–54	0.019	0.009	0.073
Aged 55 +	0.033	0.013	n.s.
Aged 15–19, female	−0.021	−0.009	−0.031
Aged 20–24, female	0.011	0.005	n.s.
Aged 25–29, female	0.013	0.007	n.s.
Aged 35–39, female	−0.004	−0.002	−0.024
Aged 40–44, female	−0.008	−0.003	n.s.
Aged 45–49, female	−0.006	−0.002	−0.020*
Aged 50–54, female	n.s.	n.s.	−0.023*
Aged 55 +, female	0.010	0.003	n.s.
Victoria		n.s.	−0.013
Queensland		0.001	n.s.
South Australia		0.001	n.s.
Western Australia		−0.001	n.s.
Tasmania		0.002	−0.020
Northern Territory		−0.002	−0.018
Australian Capital Territory		n.s.	n.s.
Major city		0.001	0.010
Completed Year 9 or less		0.020	0.037
Completed Year 10 or 11		0.007	0.017
Does not have any qualifications		0.010	0.021*
Has a Diploma or Certificate only		0.008	0.034
Speaks another language and English well		−0.003	−0.014
Speaks another language and English not well or not at all		−0.003	n.s.
Probability of the base case[b]	0.025	0.010	0.034
Pseudo R-Squared	0.1106	0.1317	0.1385
Number of observations	180 688	164 513	3 525

a. n.s. = Those variables that were not significant at the 10% level of significance.
   * = Those variables that were significant at the 10% level of significance but not the 5% level

b. The base case for the total population is non-Indigenous. For all estimates, the base case is male and aged 30–34 years and in addition, for Model 2 and for the Indigenous estimates, the base case lives in New South Wales, outside a major city, has completed Year 12, has a university degree, and speaks English only.

Source: Customised calculations using the 2006 5% CSF, ABS Census of Population and Housing

Family and household characteristics of Indigenous children

Modelling family and household characteristics across the lifecourse

We now return to the child as the focus of our analysis. In particular, we present results from three very simple models with various family and household characteristics as the dependent variables and a limited set of explanatory variables, restricted to age, gender and geography. The first dependent variable is the probability of a child living in a single-parent family. According to the 2006 Census, 45 per cent of Indigenous children aged 15 and under live in a single-parent family, compared to 17 per cent of non-Indigenous children aged 15 and under who live in a single-parent family.

Household employment provides the resources and means for investing in child development. Employment income makes up a large proportion of a household's resources. The extent of joblessness in a household could be considered another proxy for household resources and risk of disadvantage and financial hardship. The second dependent variable in Table 9.2 is therefore the probability of a child living in a household where no-one is employed. According to the 2006 Census, 41 per cent of Indigenous children live in jobless households compared to 13 per cent of non-Indigenous children. The extent and period of joblessness is not known, because the census provides only a snapshot picture of the circumstances. Care should therefore be taken while interpreting the results in Table 9.2.

Education is a critical element of building human capital and social capital. Education provides the pathway to employment. The educational attainment of the parent, in particular that of the mother, has a significant influence on the early development and health outcomes of the child (United Nations Children's Fund 2006). The final dependent variable is therefore the probability of a child living in a household where no-one has completed Year 12. Indigenous children are more likely to be in living in households where parents have low education levels (65%), compared to non-Indigenous children (32%).

Table 9.2 Factors associated with the probability of being in a single-parent household, a jobless household and a low educational attainment household, population aged 0–14 years, 2006

Explanatory variables[a]	Single-parent household	Jobless household	Low educational attainment household
Female	n.s.	n.s.	n.s.
Indigenous	0.284	0.281	0.272
Aged 0–4	−0.078	0.013	−0.139
Aged 5–9	−0.038	0.009	−0.067
Aged 0–4, female	n.s.	n.s.	n.s.
Aged 5–9, female	n.s.	n.s.	n.s.
Victoria	n.s.	−0.013	−0.038
Queensland	0.016	−0.015	−0.025
South Australia	0.019	n.s.	n.s.
Western Australia	−0.016	−0.015	n.s.
Tasmania	0.023	0.014	0.084
Northern Territory	−0.047	−0.057	−0.061
Australian Capital Territory	−0.025	−0.073	−0.190
Major city	−0.008	−0.019	−0.126
Probability of the base case[b]	0.208	0.156	0.473
Pseudo R-Squared	0.024	0.025	0.038
Number of observations	158 234	161 466	161 466

[a] n.s. = Those variables that were not significant at the 10% level of significance.

* = Those variables that were significant at the 10% level of significance but not the 5% level

[b] The base case for the total population is non-Indigenous. For all estimates, the base case is male and aged 10–14 years, lives in New South Wales and outside a major city.

Source: Customised calculations using the 2006 5% CSF, ABS Census of Population and Housing

In Table 9.2, the results are presented at the child level and for children aged 0–14. In essence, the table looks at children living in single-parent households, jobless households and households where the adults have low educational attainment. Overall, younger children are more likely to be in jobless households, whereas the older children are more likely to be in single-parent households and low educational attainment households. Indigenous children are more likely to occupy all three states (single-parent family, jobless family and low educational attainment family) when compared to non-Indigenous children.

The interaction and intersection of family and household characteristics

While the previous sections considered the role of sole parenthood, unemployment and education separately, the combination of the various characteristics may also have lifelong impacts on the child. Figures 9.2 and 9.3 illustrate the overlapping characteristics for both Indigenous and non-Indigenous children respectively. The zone which represents overlap of all three characteristics (being in a sole-parent family, with low education attainment and jobless) is the critical point in the diagrams. From the figures, it is evident that the majority of Indigenous children experience more than one form of disadvantage. While about 5 per cent of non-Indigenous children live in single-parent families with low education attainment and unemployed, the proportion of Indigenous children in these circumstances is four times that of the non-Indigenous children. More than half of non-Indigenous children do not exhibit any of the three characteristics, but only a quarter of Indigenous children do not have any of the characteristics.

Fig. 9.2 Percentage of Indigenous child population aged 0–14 years by three characteristics of their family or household, 2006

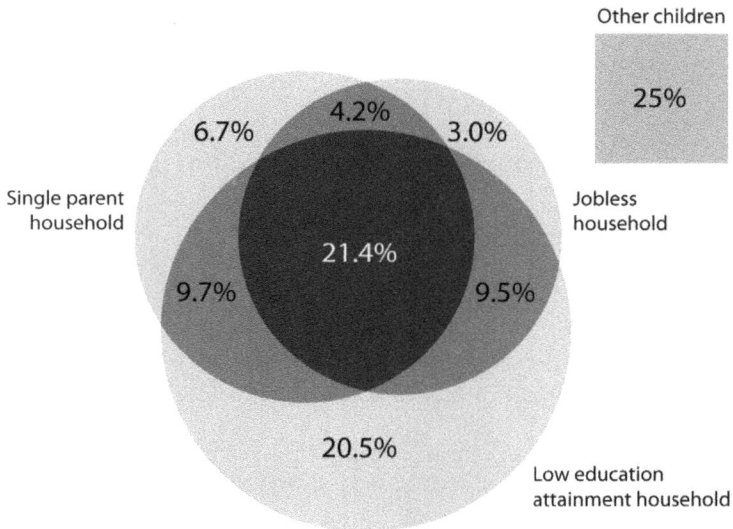

Source: Customised calculations using the 2006 5% CSF, ABS Census of Population and Housing

Fig. 9.3 Percentage of non-Indigenous child population aged 0–14 years by three characteristics of their family or household, 2006

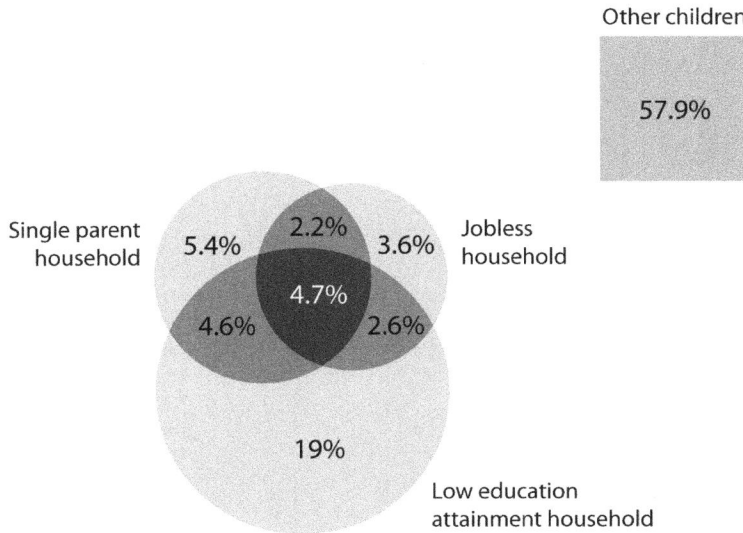

Other children

57.9%

Single parent household   5.4%   2.2%   3.6%   Jobless household

4.7%

4.6%   2.6%

19%

Low education attainment household

Source: Customised calculations using the 2006 5% CSF, ABS Census of Population and Housing

Childhood outcomes across the Indigenous lifecourse

This chapter has attempted to look at some aspects of child outcomes using the available information from the census. While the census provides very limited information at the child level, the characteristics examined here provides a little insight into the types of households in which Indigenous and non-Indigenous children live.

Indigenous women in general and young Indigenous females in particular, have the highest probability of being single parents. While they often have lower educational levels, lower labour force participation, and therefore lower household incomes, they are often living in communities where they can draw upon resources and care from kin and networks. This makes the experience of single parenthood quite different for Indigenous and non-Indigenous parents. The analysis has not looked into whether the single parent lives with their parents (that is, the child's grandparents), extended family or with other nonrelations. Policies or programs targeted at single parents may need to consider the overall social and economic situation of the single parent, and this may include the extended family and community for Indigenous families.

Indigenous children are more likely than non-Indigenous children to live in single-parent households, jobless households, and households where the adults have low educational attainment. Unfortunately, despite these measures being quite relevant for policy formulation, the factors available on the census are not well suited to explaining the variation in them. The experience of multiple disadvantage has implications for the child and the parent. Although this chapter does not attempt to address the associations between the three dimensions and how this might impact on the child's wellbeing, what is shown is the extent to which children, and in particular Indigenous children, experience all three dimensions.

The multidimensional aspect of disadvantage has implications for policy. If a single parent also has low educational attainment, and is looking to enter the workforce, policies aimed at re-skilling or job readiness might have to go hand-in-hand with the provision of child support. On the other hand, policies aimed at single parents with a job might be geared towards supportive work-life practices.

10. An Indigenous lifecourse? Implications and limitations

The overarching aim of this study is to consider whether there is something different about the Indigenous lifecourse compared to the non-Indigenous lifecourse as observed in the 5% Sample File from the 2006 Census. While it is not possible to track individual Indigenous Australians through time using this (or any other) dataset, the simple answer to this question would appear to be 'yes'. Of the 19 dependent variables for adults, there is a significant difference between Indigenous and non-Indigenous Australians for all of them, either before or after controlling for other characteristics. Furthermore, there is a significant difference between Indigenous and non-Indigenous children for all six of the estimations carried out on 0–14 year olds.

Not only are there differences between Indigenous and non-Indigenous Australians in terms of levels, there are also substantial differences in patterns across the lifecourse for a number of the dependent variables. While much of the analysis presented in this paper points to differences between the Indigenous and non-Indigenous populations, it also shows that in many cases there is as much variation within these two populations as there is between them. In a number of instances, the factors associated with the particular demographic or socioeconomic variable varies between the two populations. However, the relationship between demographic and socioeconomic variables is also shown to be vitally important.

In this final chapter, we summarise the main results from the analysis. We draw together results from all the dependent variables in order to determine what we can say about the Indigenous lifecourse and how it varies from that of the non-Indigenous population. The section that follows discusses some of the implications from the analysis in terms of policy planning. The final section of this chapter discusses the limitations of the data used in the analysis, as well as the potential scope for ongoing analysis of the Indigenous lifecourse.

An Indigenous lifecourse?

Is there a typical Indigenous lifecourse? If so, does it vary from the typical non-Indigenous lifecourse? In answer to the first question – no, probably not. There is substantial variation within the Indigenous population across the lifecourse in the incidence of the majority of the dependent variables. For example, a significant minority of Indigenous children are estimated to be living in single-parent families where no-one in their household is employed or has completed Year 12. However, almost four out of five Indigenous children did not live in such families. Indeed, there are fewer Indigenous children who have this combination of family and household characteristics (21.4%) than Indigenous children who live in couple families and a household where at least one person is employed and at least one person has completed Year 12 (25.0%).

This diversity in experience continues into adulthood. Indigenous Australians who have completed Year 12 or a post-school qualification tend to have significantly different and generally better outcomes than Indigenous Australians who have not. Furthermore, childbirth and unpaid child care is associated with a number of the education, employment and housing variables. Geographic variables make up an important part of the story for many of the dependent variables, although a lower level of disaggregation for the remoteness variable would provide more insight into the differences between Indigenous people living in regional versus remote areas.

These differences within the Indigenous population should always be kept in mind when designing policy and trying to explain outcomes. With a population of over 500 000 there is substantial diversity in the outcomes and aspirations of Indigenous Australians. While there was no typical Indigenous lifecourse that was held in common by all, or in many cases most of the population, a consideration of the average Indigenous lifecourse or (in the case of this study) the average probability of having a particular characteristic at a given age can still be informative. What's more, it is also instructive to consider whether there are differences between Indigenous and non-Indigenous Australians in the probability of having that characteristic after controlling for variation across the lifecourse.

The predicted difference between Indigenous and non-Indigenous Australians in having a particular characteristic is summarised in Table 10.1. The differences reported take into account variations across lifecourse (model 1) as well as other characteristsics (Model 2). As a reminder, a positive or negative value indicates Indigenous Australians are more or less likely to have that characteristic than non-Indigenous Australians, with the size of the marginal effect indicating the magnitude of that difference. To put these marginal effects into context, the predicted probability of the base case is also given, with the characteristics of the base case given in the tables of data throughout this volume.

Table 10.1 Summary of Indigenous marginal effects by dependent variable, 2006

Dependent variable – probability of ...	Model 1		Model 2	
	Prob. of base case	Marg. Effect	Prob. of base case	Marg. Effect
Adults aged 15 years and over				
Being in a registered or de facto marriage	0.454	−0.198	0.622	−0.107
Being in a registered as opposed to de facto marriage (those in any marriage)	0.709	−0.232	0.715	−0.200
Number of children ever born (females)	1.129	0.532	1.410	0.800
Providing unpaid child care	0.380	0.076	0.567	0.125
Changing place of usual residence between 2001 and 2006	0.696	−0.023	0.767	−0.034
Being away from place of usual residence	0.051	0.039	0.053	0.024
Participating in education (aged 15–24 years)	0.382	−0.219	0.293	−0.152
Participating in education (aged 25 years and over)	0.087	n.s.	0.047	0.016
Participating in university as opposed to another tertiary institute (tertiary students)	0.557	−0.189	0.467	n.s.
Being employed	0.878	−0.172	0.977	−0.032
Being employed part-time (those employed)	0.114	0.043	0.073	0.036
Being employed as a Manager or Professional (those employed)	0.633	−0.208	0.930	−0.045
Having undertaken voluntary work for an organisation or group in the previous 12 months	0.128	−0.031	0.253	−0.030
Having undertaken 5 hours or more of unpaid domestic work in the previous week	0.128	−0.056	0.253	−0.083
Living in a dwelling that is owned or being purchased	0.607	−0.379	0.872	−0.379
Living in a dwelling that is rented from a government or community organisation (those in a rented dwelling)	0.061	0.403	0.030	0.175
Living in a dwelling that has more than one person per bedroom	0.061	0.176	0.032	0.153
Reporting a 'core activity' need for assistance (aged 45 years and over)	0.023	0.041	0.006	0.007
Being a single parent	0.025	0.073	0.010	0.025
Children aged 0–14 years				
Changing place of usual residence between 2001 and 2006 (aged 5–14 years)	0.430	0.027	0.390	−0.062
Being away from place of usual residence	0.021	0.020	0.026	0.017
Attending a non-government school (school students)	0.333	−0.173	0.324	−0.087
Being in a single-parent family			0.208	0.284
Being in a household where no-one is employed			0.156	0.281
Being in a household where no-one has completed Year 12			0.473	0.272

155

Source: Customised calculations using the 2006 5% CSF, ABS Census of Population and Housing

To summarise Table 10.1, there is a significant difference for 18 out of the 19 dependent variables for adults, and for all of the dependent variables for children. The only variable for which there was not a significant difference between Indigenous and non-Indigenous Australians after controlling for age and sex was education participation for the 25 years and over age group. However, once other characteristics had been controlled for, Indigenous Australians in that age group were more likely to be participating in education than non-Indigenous Australians. On the other hand, despite there being a large difference in Model 1, after controlling for other characteristics, there was no significant difference between Indigenous and non-Indigenous tertiary students in terms of university attendance.

In many ways, it is not surprising that the differences between Indigenous and non-Indigenous Australians are generally significant. As mentioned in the data chapter, there were 1 002 793 respondents in the 5% CSF, of which 22 437 were identified as being Indigenous. Even after excluding observations because of non-response or age restrictions, the sample size for the majority of the estimates was large by most standards. In that sense, it is worth considering the size of the marginal effect in order to see whether the differences are qualitatively significant in addition to being statistically significant.

After controlling for observable characteristics (that is, in Model 2), there are six instances where Indigenous Australians have a predicted probability that is more than double that of the non-Indigenous population. Such a result is found for the last two of the housing variables as well as for reporting a 'core activity' need for assistance and for being a single parent. Indigenous children are also predicted to be more than twice as likely to live in a single-parent family or a household where no-one is employed. At the other extreme, non-Indigenous Australians aged 15–24 years are more than twice as likely as Indigenous Australians to be participating in education.

For the aforementioned variables especially, the difference in levels between Indigenous and non-Indigenous Australians are large, both qualitatively and statistically. However, it is not only in levels that the average Indigenous lifecourse is different to the non-Indigenous population – so too are the patterns. While it is not possible to summarise the patterns for all the variables in a single figure, the following two sets of figures highlight the differences across the lifecourse in average outcomes for two key economic variables (Fig. 10.1) and two key demographic variables (Fig. 10.2). The figures are constructed as the cumulative percentage of the adult population with each of the four possible combinations of outcomes – education and employment in Fig. 10.1, and marital status and unpaid child care in Fig. 10.2.[1]

---

1   Unlike the remainder of the analysis in this paper, the results presented in Figures 10.1 and 10.2 are based on the full census data. However, a three-year moving average is used to smooth the lines.

Fig. 10.1 Variation in education participation and work across the lifecourse, 2006

Indigenous males

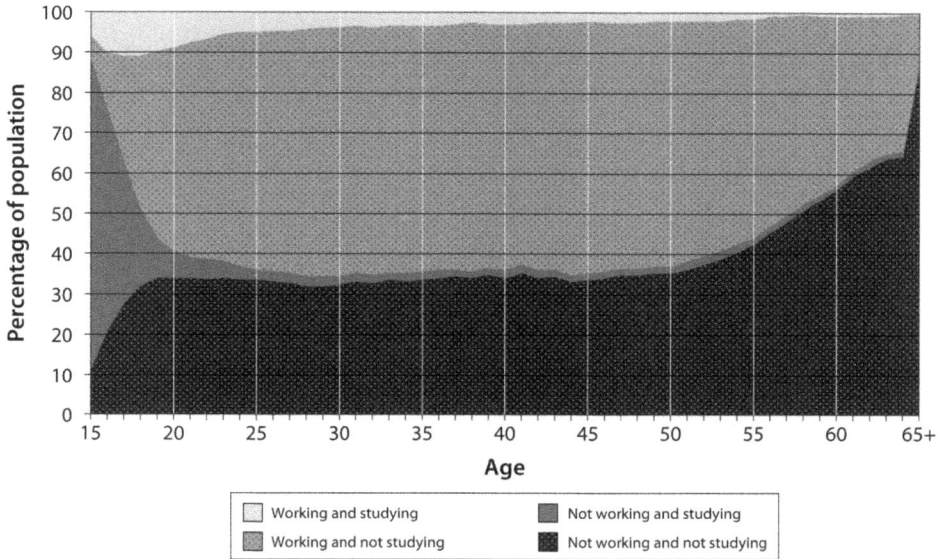

Legend:
- Working and studying
- Working and not studying
- Not working and studying
- Not working and not studying

Non-Indigenous males

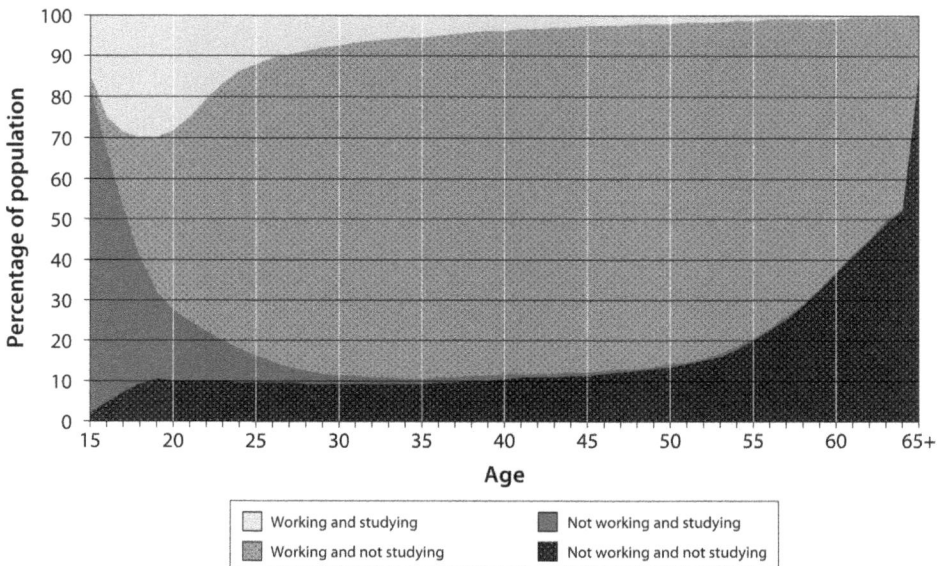

Legend:
- Working and studying
- Working and not studying
- Not working and studying
- Not working and not studying

Indigenous females

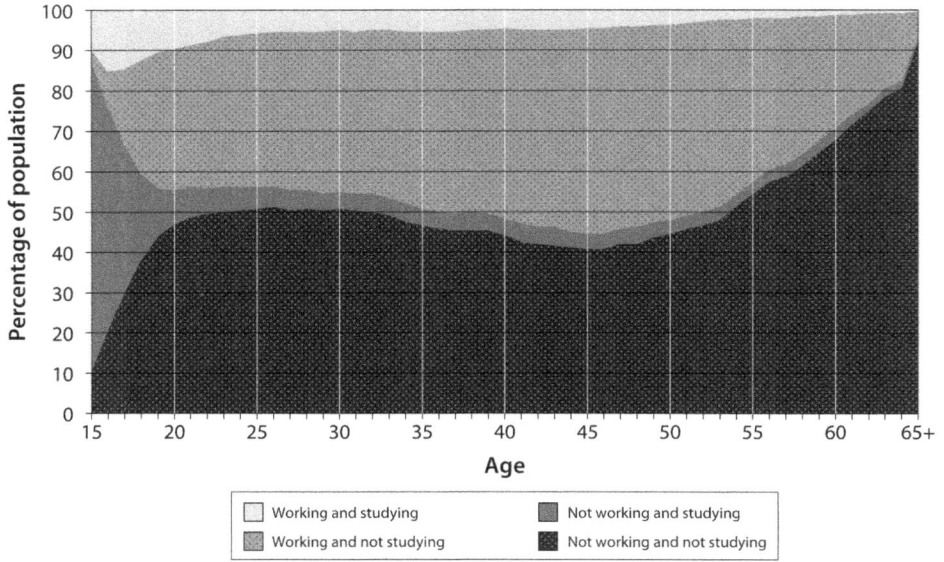

Non-Indigenous females

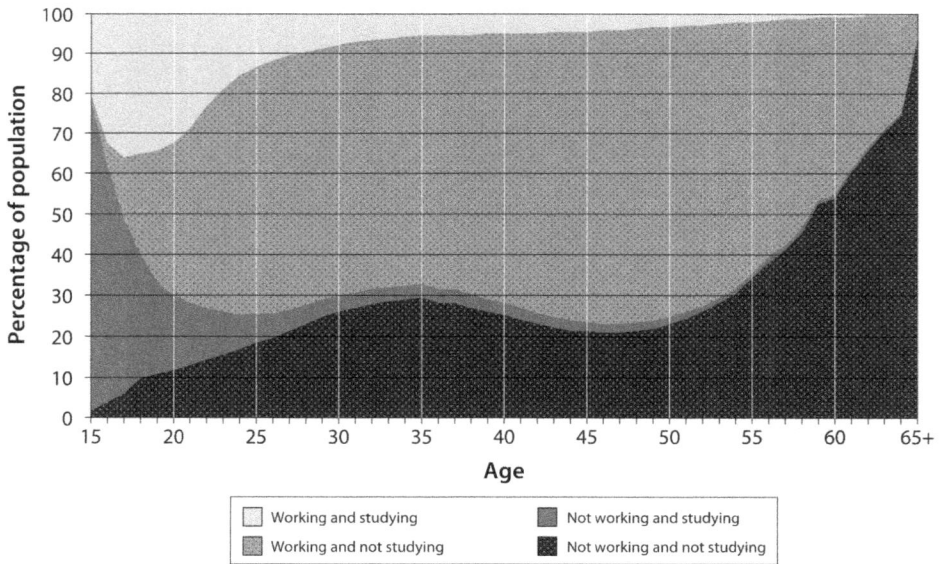

Source: Customised calculations using the 2006 5% CSF, ABS Census of Population and Housing

The results presented in Fig. 10.1 point to a number of key differences between Indigenous and non-Indigenous Australians in the patterns of education participation and employment across the lifecourse. Firstly, and most obviously, Indigenous Australians spend a much higher proportion of their life both not studying and not working. For males between the ages of 18 and 49, this percentage is reasonably flat, averaging around 30–35 per cent for Indigenous males compared to 10–12 per cent for non-Indigenous males. For females, there is a localised peak during the main childbearing years. However, this peak is much higher and occurs earlier for Indigenous compared to non-Indigenous females.

The second major difference between Indigenous and non-Indigenous Australians is the flatter profile by age in terms of education participation. The percentage of the non-Indigenous population who were participating in education either without working or whilst working starts off very high and then declines dramatically. Education participation is also concentrated amongst the relatively young for the Indigenous population. However, participation rates do not fall as dramatically and are even higher than the rates for the non-Indigenous population.

The analysis is repeated in Fig. 10.2 using two key demographic variables from the census – marital status and providing unpaid child care.[2]

The most noticeable difference between Indigenous and non-Indigenous Australians in general, and Indigenous and non-Indigenous females in particular, is the much higher percentage of the population who are not married but are providing unpaid child care. This is most noticeable from the age of 25 years and onwards, and is likely to explain the lower rates of employment during the prime working years and be explained by the lower rates of education participation during youth (both shown in Fig. 10.1).

---

2   The variable for the number of children ever born is more often used as a measure of fertility than provision of unpaid child care. However, it is not available for males, does not capture whether the child is still alive or under the primary care of the individual, and does not take into account the age of the child. Hence the number of children even born does not adequately capture the extent to which the children that a female has had are currently playing a role in her time constraints.

Fig. 10.2 Variation in marital status and unpaid child care across the lifecourse, 2006

Indigenous males

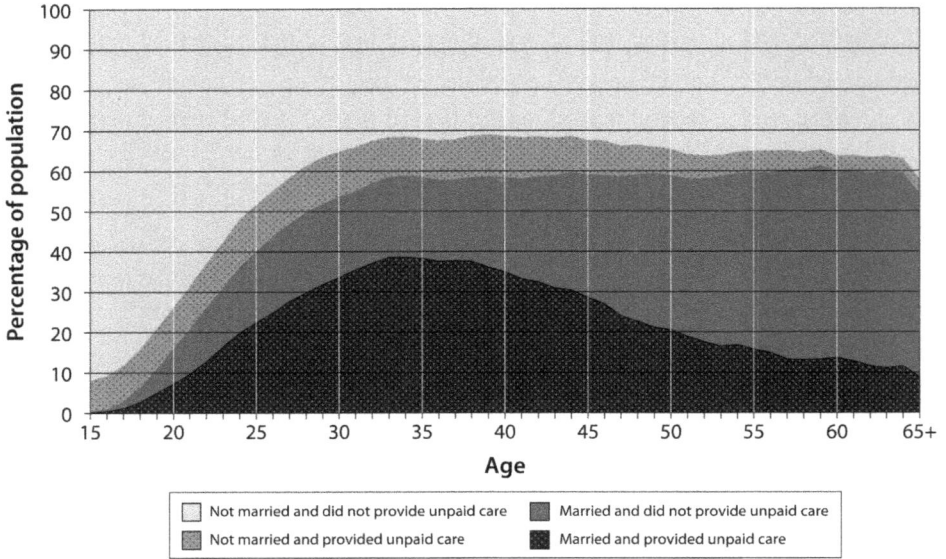

Not married and did not provide unpaid care
Not married and provided unpaid care
Married and did not provide unpaid care
Married and provided unpaid care

Non-Indigenous males

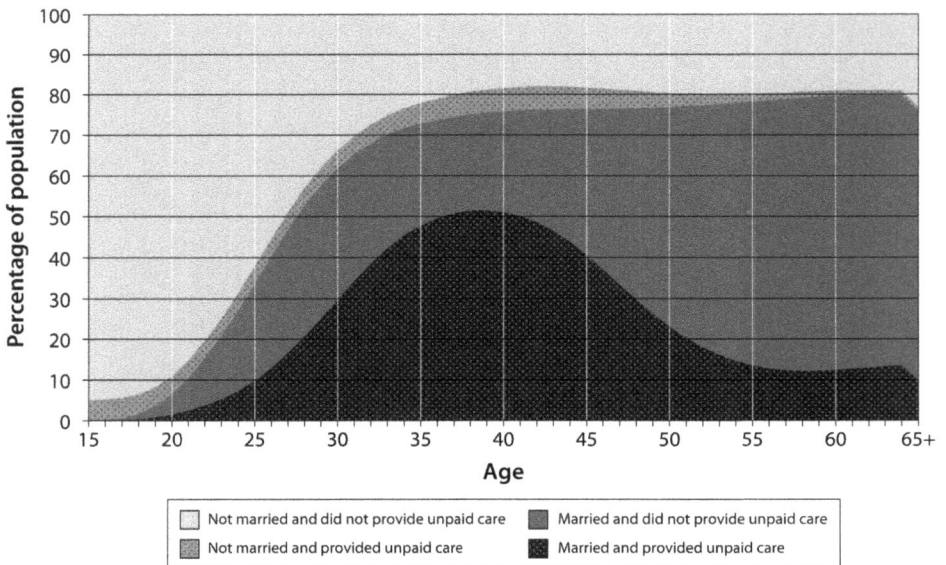

Not married and did not provide unpaid care
Not married and provided unpaid care
Married and did not provide unpaid care
Married and provided unpaid care

Indigenous females

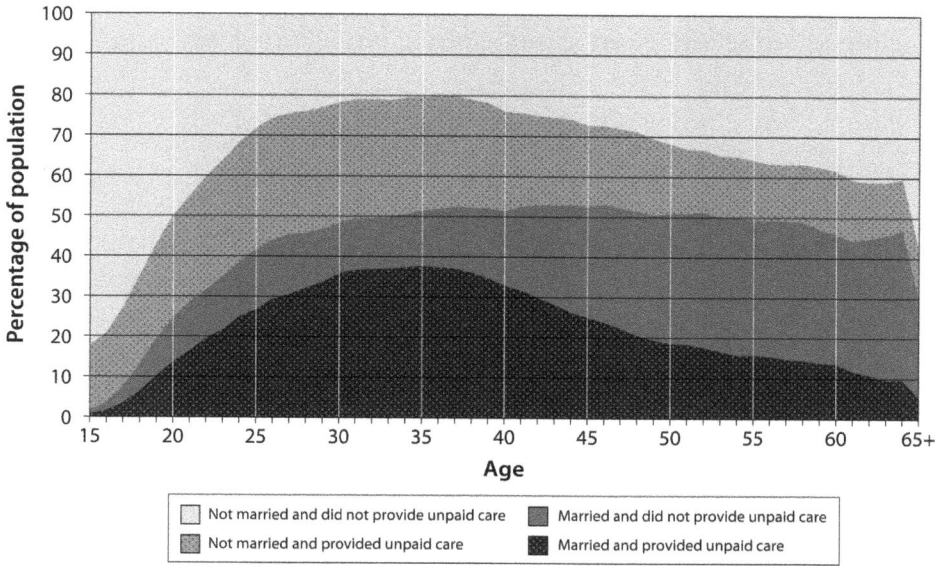

Legend:
- Not married and did not provide unpaid care
- Not married and provided unpaid care
- Married and did not provide unpaid care
- Married and provided unpaid care

Non-Indigenous females

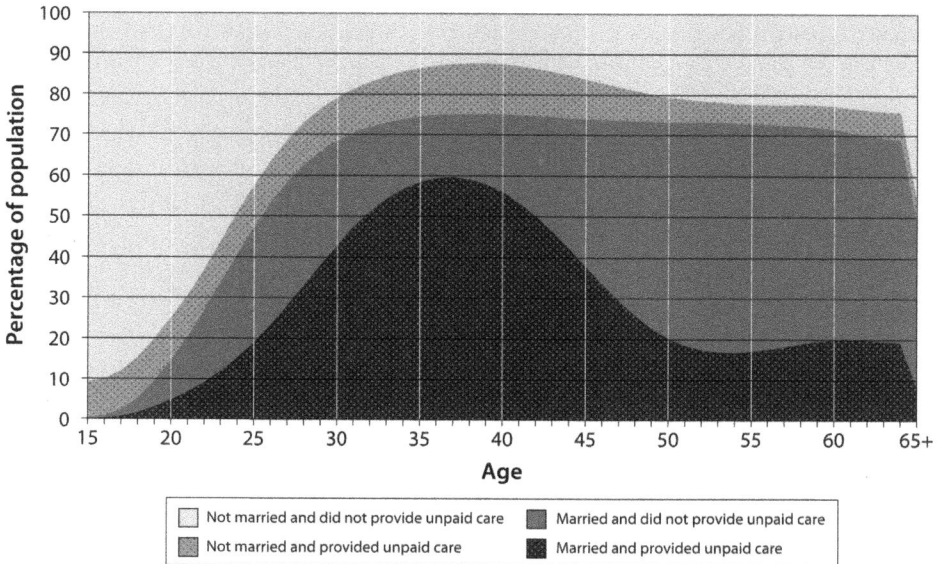

Legend:
- Not married and did not provide unpaid care
- Not married and provided unpaid care
- Married and did not provide unpaid care
- Married and provided unpaid care

Source: Customised calculations using the 2006 5% CSF, ABS Census of Population and Housing

Implications for policy and planning

The differences across the lifecourse summarised in Figures 10.1 and 10.2 are just a few examples of the many variables summarised in this paper. While specific to the individual variables, the research and policy implications of these specific results are reasonably clear and covered in the individual sections. Less clear are the overarching policy implications. What makes it difficult to provide specific policy recommendations are the two major data limitations. As covered in the following section (and in more detail in Chapter 2), it is not possible to track individuals through time, to identify individual life events, or establish causal relationships between the variables.

Despite these limitations, there are a number of points raised by this study that can be used to shape Indigenous policy more generally. Firstly, by bringing together so many demographic and socioeconomic variables, it is clear how significant an influence education attainment has on such a range of outcomes. For example, it was shown that Indigenous Australians with reasonably high levels of education attainment have similar levels of employment to similarly qualified non-Indigenous Australians. It was those with relatively low skills where the difference was greatest.

The relationship between education and employment has been shown in previous research cited in this monograph. However, what this research has shown is that there is a strong association between education and a number of other variables that have not previously been analysed in such a way. This includes volunteer work, marital status and residential mobility. Furthermore, the relationship between completion of high school and education participation when older (especially at university), and the education participation of children in the household, is also highlighted. A proportion of this association is likely to be due to selection effects or unobserved characteristics of the individual, with longitudinal data required to better establish the direction of the relationship.

Another finding from the analysis that has clear policy implications is the relationship between high rates of fertility and high levels of child care provision for young Indigenous females. Much of the difference between Indigenous and non-Indigenous females in terms of education participation and employment is explained by higher fertility rates. Once again, the causal relationship is complex, with individuals who are less likely to work or undertake education for other reasons having lower opportunity costs of having children. Nonetheless, if it were feasible to reduce the high rates of Indigenous fertility amongst the relatively young, the results presented in this paper suggest that this might have flow-on effects throughout the remainder of the lifecourse.

Although variables that are significant and have large marginal effects tend to stand out from analysis such as this, there are often important policy implications from variables that were not significant. One such example is the general lack of significance or small marginal effect for the 'major city' variable in a number of the sets of analysis. For example, there is no significant difference between Indigenous Australians who live in a major city and Indigenous Australians who live in the rest of Australia once other characteristics had been controlled for in terms of residential mobility, education participation for the 25 years and over age group, and employment. While the geographic variable on the 2006 5% CSF is not ideal for undertaking analysis of the Indigenous population, it would appear that at least some of the variation by geography found for these and other variables is caused by other characteristics of the individual. In other words, for some outcomes, it is not that living outside a major city has a direct effect, but rather that the characteristics of Indigenous Australians who do live outside a major city are different.

Although the issue of multiple disadvantage has not been explicitly examined here – with the exception of child outcomes – it is important to keep in mind the multidimensional experience of disadvantage and how the variables are interlinked. Policies aimed at improving the outcomes of one will inevitably have spillover effects. Similarly, the lack of one factor may also lead to experiences of another disadvantage.

Ultimately, the general conclusion that there is significant variation within the Indigenous population across most outcomes is perhaps the most important finding from the analysis. National analysis and even analysis by jurisdiction or region tends to overlook systematic variation across individuals. By looking at averages, one can easily forget that there are many Indigenous Australians who have quite good employment or housing prospects. However, it is clear from this analysis that it is Indigenous Australians with relatively high levels of human capital that are doing well in the contemporary labour market.

Data gaps and future analysis

The title of this monograph highlights one of the main limitations of the analysis, namely the reliance on a single cross-section (the 2006 Census). So, while we are able to show the difference between a 30–34 year old and a 50–54 year old in 2006 (for example), we are not able to show how the characteristics of an individual Indigenous Australian has changed over a 20-year period. This was not an oversight or a poor choice of dataset. Rather, there is no dataset currently available that tracks a sufficient number of Indigenous Australians to make sensible comparisons, either within the population or between Indigenous and non-Indigenous Australians. Nor are there randomized controlled trials available to properly test for causal relationships (Leigh 2010).

There are some datasets that have the potential to be used for limited longitudinal lifecourse analysis. The HILDA survey has a small Indigenous sample (and identifier) and can be used to do crude Indigenous versus non-Indigenous comparisons. However, comparisons within the Indigenous population are limited. The Longitudinal Study of Indigenous Children has the potential to be used to track the outcomes of children through time. However, at the time of publication, only Wave 1 of the data had been released and no assessment had been done of the quality of the longitudinal information or sample attrition. Furthermore, there is no non-Indigenous comparison available.

An alternative data source is administrative data that tracks individuals through time, either with a unique identifier or by matching people based on their name and/or address. Possible examples include schools, hospitals and payments databases. While these datasets give some longitudinal information and are able to identify certain events and transitions, they are limited to the particular population of interest to the data collection and usually only cover a limited period of people's lives. Furthermore, they rarely contain detailed socioeconomic information and the quality of the data is highly contingent on the quality of the Indigenous identifier and the way in which individuals are tracked through time.

A final alternative for obtaining lifecourse information on the Indigenous population is through qualitative surveys. While limited in terms of sample, these surveys or interviews can provide a rich source of data on a range of topics. The major limitation is the lack of ability to make generalisations, and statistical power.

Unfortunately, for now and for many years to come, our view of the Indigenous lifecourse is likely to remain limited by the available data. In terms of large-scale surveys, there are three main sources of data for the Indigenous population: the 2006 5% CSF that was used in this paper; the National Aboriginal and Torres Strait Islander Social Survey (NATSISS); and the National Aboriginal and Torres Strait Islander Health Survey (NATSIHS). The NATSISS was most recently carried out in 2008, with data becoming available for analysis in early 2010. The most recent NATSIHS was carried out in 2004–05, with the next survey scheduled for 2010–11.

In addition to the Labour Force Survey (which is analysed by the ABS but not made available to outside researchers and major administrative collections), the above three surveys will provide the majority of the data that governments use to track progress in meeting the Closing the Gap targets. Because of this, it is important that they are kept as nationally representative as possible. Replacing them with a longitudinal survey that is likely to suffer from significant sample attrition is not a viable alternative. However, the Indigenous population is also one of the most surveyed populations in Australia; adding an additional large-scale survey to the congested schedule may place too onerous a burden on the Indigenous community.

One alternative would be to implement a rolling-panel approach to the collection of national statistical datasets. This would be a similar approach to the Labour Force Survey, where households are retained in the sample for a fixed number of surveys but are eventually dropped out and replaced to keep the data representative of the nation as a whole. A hypothetical structure of a six-year collection cycle beginning with a NATSISS in 2012 (two years ahead of schedule) and 2018 as well as a NATSIHS in 2016 (six years after the next survey) and 2021 is given in Table 10.2. In the intervening years, we propose that a reduced module of questions be asked that allow key lifecourse events to be tracked and COAG's Closing the Gap targets to be analysed. This survey is referred to as the National Closing the Gap Survey (NCGS) in Table 10.2 and, depending on costs, could be carried out on a subset of the original cohort only.

Table 10.2 Proposal for rolling panel to collect longitudinal Indigenous information

Year	Cohort 1	Cohort 2	Cohort 3	Cohort 4
2012	NATSISS			
2013	NCGS			
2014	NCGS			
2015	NATSIHS	NATSIHS		
2016		NCGS		
2017		NCGS		
2018		NATSISS	NATSISS	
2019			NCGS	
2020			NCGS	
2021			NATSIHS	NATSIHS
…				…

In essence, Cohort 1 is given the NATSISS questionnaire in 2012, the NCGS in 2013 and 2014 and the NATSIHS questionnaire in 2015. Cohort 2 would include the NATSIHS questionnaire in 2015, the NCGS in 2016 and 2017 and the NATSISS questionnaire in 2018. National estimates for the 2012 NATSISS would use Cohort 1, while national estimates from the 2015 NATSIHS would use Cohort 2. This would then be repeated using Cohort 3 and Cohort 4.

The benefits of the above structure are threefold. Firstly, it will be possible for the first time to undertake robust longitudinal analysis of a core set of Indigenous outcomes. This would be restricted the questions that are available on the NATSISS, the NATSIHS and the new NCGS. However, this would include the major aspects of the Closing the Gap agenda like employment, education and health, as well as some of their determinants like housing, crime and mobility. Nonetheless, research on these surveys would likely yield vital policy relevant findings.

The second benefit of the above structure (as opposed to a single longitudinal study) would be that the sample for the major surveys would still be nationally representative. That is, Cohort 1 for the 2012 NATSISS, Cohort 2 for the 2015 NATSIHS and so on. The third major benefit is that, by overlapping the cohorts, the representativeness of the longitudinal aspects of the cohorts could be tested against the new cohorts that replace them. For example, the characteristics of Cohort 1 in 2015 could be tested against the characteristics of Cohort 2 in the same year. It may not be possible to maintain a sufficient sample to undertake-robust-through time analysis for all jurisdictions. However, the Closing the Gap targets are set at the national level, and hence it is vital that they be evaluated in these broad terms.

The above structure would clearly require a significant investment from all levels of government. It would not be possible for the ABS to follow such an approach within their existing budget. However, compared to the investment governments have made, and will need to make – in order to substantially reduce Indigenous disadvantage, the investment in adequate data collection is inconsequential.

In addition to properly conducted randomised controlled trials, longitudinal information is the only way to truly analyse the Indigenous lifecourse, the determinants of Indigenous socioeconomic disadvantage and the types of social and economic policies that are likely to result in COAG's Closing the Gap targets being met. Until such datasets are available, robust analysis of individual trajectories and the timing of key events remains elusive.

Appendix 1. Additional model estimates

Table A1 Factors associated with the probability of having at least one child, females aged 15 years and over

Explanatory variables[a]	Total population		Indigenous population	
	Model 1	Model 2	Model 1	Model 2
Indigenous	0.219	0.170		
Aged 15–19	−0.567	−0.524	−0.655	−0.655
Aged 20–24	−0.469	−0.282	−0.317	−0.276
Aged 25–29	−0.271	−0.148	−0.066	−0.050
Aged 35–39	0.189	0.102	n.s.	n.s.
Aged 40–44	0.254	0.124	0.062	0.052
Aged 45–49	0.273	0.120	n.s.	n.s.
Aged 50–54	0.290	0.118	0.088	0.072
Aged 55 +	0.315	0.110	n.s.	n.s.
Victoria		−0.012		n.s.
Queensland		0.015	n.s.	n.s.
South Australia		0.021	n.s.	n.s.
Western Australia		0.022	0.042	n.s.
Tasmania		−0.013*	n.s.	n.s.
Northern Territory		−0.062	−0.087	−0.083
Australian Capital Territory		0.028	n.s.	n.s.
Major city		−0.066	−0.063	−0.044
Secondary school student		−0.447	−0.485	−0.447
Tertiary student		−0.171	−0.173	−0.149
Part-time student		0.091	0.105	0.082
Completed Year 9 or less		0.112	0.122	0.095
Completed Year 10 or 11		0.100	0.109	0.085
Does not have any qualifications		0.104	0.100	0.082
Has a Diploma or Certificate only		0.078	0.056	0.048
Speaks another language and English well		−0.013	−0.050	−0.077
Speaks another language and English not well or not at all		n.s.	−0.263	−0.301
Never married		−0.540	−0.256	−0.257
Divorced, separated or widowed		−0.043	0.061	0.036*
Lives in a mixed Indigenous and non-Indigenous household				−0.084

Probability of the base case[b]	0.578	0.740	0.790	0.839
Pseudo R-Squared	0.3391	0.4705	0.3769	0.3823
Number of observations	374 399	330 181	5 491	5 307

[a]. n.s. = Those variables that were not significant at the 10% level of significance.

* = Those variables that were significant at the 10% level of significance but not the 5% level

[b] The base case for the total population is non-Indigenous. For all estimates, the base case is aged 30–34 years and in addition, for Model 2 (for the total population and for the Indigenous estimates), the base case lives in New South Wales, outside a major city, is not a student, has completed Year 12, has a university degree, speaks English only, and is married. For Model 4, an additional characteristic of the base case is that they are living in an Indigenous-only household.

Source: Customised calculations using the 2006 5% CSF, ABS Census of Population and Housing

References

Australian Bureau of Statistics (ABS) 2004. *National Aboriginal and Torres Strait Islander Social Survey 2002*, cat. no. 4714.0, ABS, Canberra.

—— 2006a. *Schools, Australia*, cat. no. 4221.0, ABS, Canberra.

—— 2006b. *ANZSCO – Australian and New Zealand Standard Classification of Occupations, First Edition*, cat. no. 1220.0, ABS, Canberra.

—— 2006c. *Census Dictionary Australia 2006*, cat. no. 2901.0, ABS, Canberra.

—— 2008a. *Maps and Census Profiles, Australian Indigenous Geographical Classification, 2006*, cat. no. 4706.0.30.001, ABS, Canberra.

—— 2008b. *Experimental Estimates of Aboriginal and Torres Strait Islander Australians, June 2006*, cat. no. 3238.0.55.001, ABS, Canberra.

—— 2009. *Corrective Services, Australia, Sep 2009*, cat. no. 4512.0, ABS, Canberra.

—— and Australian Institute of Health and Welfare (AIHW) 2005. *The Health and Welfare of Australia's Aboriginal and Torres Strait Islander Peoples*, cat. no. 4704.0, ABS, Canberra.

Australian Institute of Health and Welfare (AIHW) 2005. *Indigenous Housing Needs 2005:A Multi-Measure Needs Model*, cat. no. HOU 129, AIHW, Canberra.

—— 2008. *The Health and Welfare of Australia's Aboriginal and Torres Strait Islander Peoples 2008*, cat. no. IHW 21, AIHW, Canberra.

Altman, J. C. 2009. 'Beyond Closing the Gap: Valuing diversity in Indigenous Australia', *CAEPR Working Paper No. 54*, CAEPR, ANU.

Aboriginal and Torres Strait Islander Commission (ATSIC) 2002. *CDEP – What It's All About*, viewed 25 January 2004, <http://www.atsic.gov.au/programs/ Economic/CDEP/Doc/whats_it_all_about_2002.doc>

Bailie, R. S. and Wayte, K. J. 2006. 'Housing and health in Indigenous communities: Key issues for housing and health improvement in remote Aboriginal and Torres Strait Islander communities', *Australian Journal of Rural Health*, 14: 178–83.

Barnett, W.S. 1995. 'Long-term effects of early childhood programs on cognitive and school outcomes', *The Future of Children*, 5 (3): 25–50.

—— 1998. 'Long-term cognitive and academic effects of early childhood education on children in poverty', *Preventive Medicine*, 27: 204–7.

Baxter, J. 2005. 'Mothers' employment transitions following childbirth', *Family Matters*, 71: 11–17.

Bell, M. 2004. 'Measuring temporary mobility: Dimensions and issues', *Discussion Paper 2004/01*, Queensland Centre for Population Research, School of Geography, Planning and Architecture, The University of Queensland, Brisbane.

Biddle, N. 2006a. 'The association between health and education in Australia: Indigenous/non-Indigenous comparisons', *The Economic and Labour Relations Review*, 17 (1): 107–42.

—— 2006b. 'Is it worth going to school? Variation in the predicted benefits of education for Indigenous Australians', *Australian Journal of Labour Economics*, 9 (2): 173–99.

—— 2007. Does It Pay To Go To School? The Benefits of and Participation in Education of Indigenous Australians, PhD Thesis, ANU, Canberra.

—— 2008. 'The scale and composition of Indigenous housing need, 2001–06', *CAEPR Working Paper No. 47*, CAEPR, ANU, Canberra.

—— 2009a. 'Location and segregation: The distribution of the Indigenous population across Australia's urban centres', *CAEPR Working Paper No. 53*, CAEPR, ANU, Canberra.

——2009b. 'The geography and demography of Indigenous migration: Insights for policy and planning', *CAEPR Working Paper No. 58*, CAEPR, ANU, Canberra.

—— 2009c. 'Location or qualifications? Revisiting Indigenous employment through an analysis of census place-of-work data', *CAEPR Working Paper No. 61*, CAEPR, ANU, Canberra.

—— 2010. 'A human capital approach to the educational marginalisation of Indigenous Australians', *CAEPR Working Paper No. 67*, CAEPR, ANU, Canberra.

—— and Hunter, B.H. 2006. 'An analysis of the internal migration of Indigenous and non-Indigenous Australians', *Australian Journal of Labour Economics*, 9 (4): 33–50.

—— and Prout, S. 2009. 'The geography and demography of Indigenous temporary mobility: An analysis of the 2006 Census snapshot', *Journal of Population Research,* 26 (4): 305–26.

—— and Taylor, J. 2009. 'Planning for growth: Indigenous population projections 2006 to 2031', *CAEPR Working Paper No. 56,* CAEPR, ANU, Canberra.

——, Taylor, J. and Yap, M. 2008. 'Indigenous participation in regional labour markets, 2001–06' *CAEPR Discussion Paper No. 288,* CAEPR, ANU, Canberra.

——, ——, and —— 2009. 'Are the gaps closing? Regional trends and forecasts of Indigenous employment', *Australian Journal of Labour Economics,* 12 (3): 263–80.

Birdsall-Jones, C. and Shaw, W. 2008. 'Indigenous homelessness: Place, house and home', *AHURI Positioning Paper No. 107,* Australian Housing and Urban Research Institute, Melbourne.

Birrell, B. and Rapson, V. 2006. *Clearing the Myths Away: Higher Education's Place in Meeting Workforce Demands,* Dusseldorp Skills Forum, viewed 11 May 2010, <http://www.dsf.org.au/resources/detail/?id=71>.

Booth, A. L., Leigh, A. and Varganova, E. 2009. 'Does racial and ethnic discrimination vary across minority groups? Evidence from a field experiment', viewed 11 May 2010, <http://people.anu.edu.au/andrew.leigh/pdf/AuditDiscrimination.pdf>.

Borland, J. 2002. 'New estimates of the private rate of return to university education in Australia', *Melbourne Institute Working Paper No. 14/02,* Melbourne Institute of Applied Economic and Social Research, The University of Melbourne, Melbourne.

Caldas, S. 1993. 'The private and societal economic costs of teenage childbearing: The state of the research', *Population and Environment: A Journal of Interdisciplinary Studies,* 14 (4): 389–99.

Card, D. 2001. 'Estimating the return to schooling: Progress on some persistent econometric problems', *Econometrica,* 69 (5): 1127–60.

Carneiro, P. and Heckman, J. J. 2003. 'Human capital policy', in J. J. Heckman, A. B. Krueger and B. M. Friedman (eds), *Inequality in America: What Role for Human Capital Policies?* MIT Press, Cambridge, Massachusetts.

Cooke, M. and McWhirter, J. 2008. *Aboriginal Inequality and the Life Course, Final Report,* Strategic Policy Research Directorate, Strategic Analysis, Audit and Evaluation Branch, Human Resources and Skills Development Canada.

Commonwealth Treasury 2010. *The 2010 Intergenerational Report,* viewed 11 May 2010, <http://www.treasury.gov.au/igr/igr2010/>.

Daly, A. E. 1995. *Aboriginal and Torres Strait Islander People in the Australian Labour Market: 1986 and 1991*, cat. no. 6253.0, ABS, Canberra.

—— and Hunter, B.H. 1999. 'Incentives to work: Replacement ratios and the cost of job loss among unemployed Indigenous Australians', *Australian Economic Review*, 32 (3): 219–36.

—— and Smith, D.E. 1998. 'The continuing disadvantage of Indigenous sole parents: A preliminary analysis of 1996 Census data', *CAEPR Discussion Paper No. 153*, CAEPR, ANU, Canberra.

—— 2003. 'Reproducing exclusion or inclusion? Implications for the wellbeing of Indigenous Australian children', *CAEPR Discussion Paper No. 253*, CAEPR, ANU, Canberra.

Daly, M. 2000. 'A fine balance: Women's labour market participation in international comparison', in F. W. Scharpf and V. A. Schmidt (eds), *Welfare and Work in the Open Economy, Vol. II: Diverse Responses to Common Challenges*, Oxford University Press, Oxford.

Department of Education, Employment and Workplace Relations (DEEWR) 2008. *National Report to Parliament on Indigenous Education and Training, 2006*, viewed 11 May 2010, <http://www.dest.gov.au/sectors/indigenous_ education/publications_resources/other_publications/National_Report_ Parliament_Indigenous_2006.htm>.

de Vaus, D.A. 2002. 'Fertility decline in Australia: A demographic context', Family Matters, 63: 30–37.

Dempsey, K. and de Vaus, D. 2004. 'Who cohabits in 2001? The significance of age, gender, religion and ethnicity', *The Australian Sociological Association*, 40: 157–78.

Edwards. B. 2005. 'Does it take a village? An investigation of neighbourhood effects on Australian children's development', *Family Matters,* 72: 36–43.

Elder, G. 1994. 'Time, human agency and social change: Perspectives on the life course', *Social Psychology Quarterly*, 57 (1): 4–15

—— 1999. 'The life course and aging: Some reflections', Distinguished Scholar Lecture, 10 August 1999, American Sociological Association, Chicago, viewed .25 August 2010 <http://www.unc.edu/~elder/pdf/asa-99talk.pdf>.

Department of Families, Housing, Community Services and Indigenous Affairs (FaHCSIA) 2009. *Closing the Gap on Indigenous Disadvantage: The Challenge for Australia*, FaHCSIA, Canberra.

Finalyson, J., Daly, A. and Smith, D. 2000. 'The Kuranda community case study', in D.E. Smith (ed), *Indigenous Families and the Welfare System: Two Community Case Studies*, CAEPR Research Monograph No. 17, CAEPR, ANU, Canberra.

Gauldie, E. 1974. *Cruel Habitations: A History of Working Class Housing, 1780–1918*, Allen and Unwin, London.

Giele, J. Z. and Elder, G. H. (eds) 1998. *Methods of Life Course Research: Qualitative and Quantitative Approaches*, Sage Publications, Newbury Park, California.

Greenwood, M.J. 1997. 'Internal migration in developed countries', in M.R. Rosenzweig and O. Stark (eds), *Handbook of Population and Family Economics*, Elsevier Science, Amsterdam.

Heard, G., Birrell, B. and Khoo, S-E. 2009. 'Intermarriage between Indigenous and non-Indigenous Australians', *People and Place*, 17 (1): 1–14.

Heckman, J. J. and Masterov, D. V. 2005. *The Productivity Argument for Investing in Young Children*, viewed 25 March 2010, <http://jenni.uchicago.edu/Invest/>.

Henry, R. and Daly, A. 2001. 'Indigenous families and the welfare system: The Kuranda community case study, Stage Two', *CAEPR Discussion Paper No. 216*, CAEPR, ANU, Canberra.

Hérault, N. and Kalb, G. 2009. 'Intergenerational correlation of labour market outcomes', *Melbourne Institute Working Paper No.14/09*, Melbourne Institute of Applied Economic and Social Research, The University of Melbourne.

Human Rights and Equal Opportunity Commission (HREOC) 1996. 'Housing as a human right', Address by Chris Sidoti, Human Rights Commissioner, at the National Conference on Homeless Council to Homeless People, 4 September 1996, Melbourne.

—— 1997. *Bringing them Home: A Guide to the Findings and Recommendations of the National Inquiry into the Separation of Aboriginal and Torres Strait Islander Children from their Families*, HREOC, Sydney.

Hunter, B. H. 2004. *Indigenous Australians in the Contemporary Labour Market*, cat. no. 2052.0, ABS, Canberra.

————— and Daly, A. E. 2008. 'Interactions between crime and fertility in the labour supply of Indigenous Australian women', *CAEPR Working Paper No. 40*, CAEPR, ANU, Canberra.

————— and Schwab, R. G. 1998. 'The determinants of Indigenous educational outcomes', *CAEPR Discussion Paper No. 160*, CAEPR, ANU, Canberra.

Junankar, P. N. and Liu, J. 2003. 'Estimating the social rate of return to education for Indigenous Australians', *Education Economics,* 11 (2): 169–92.

Keys Young 1998. *Homelessness in the Indigenous and Torres Strait Islander Context and its Possible Implications for the Supported Accommodation Assistance Program (SAAP): Final Report*, prepared for Department of Family and Community Services, Canberra, viewed 23 March 2010, <http://www.homelessnessinfo.net.au/index.php?option=com_content&view=article&id=421:homelessness-in-the-aboriginal-and-torres-strait-islander-context-and-its-possible-implications-for-the-supported-accommodation-assistance-program&catid=133:homelessness&Itemid=111>.

Kohler, H-P., Behrman, J. R. and Skytthe, A. 2005. 'Partner + Children = Happiness? The effects of partnerships and fertility on wellbeing', *Population and Development Review*, 31 (3): 407–45.

Laws, P. J., Grayson, N. and Sullivan, E. A. 2006. *Australia's Mothers and Babies 2004*, cat. no. PER 34 (Perinatal Statistics Series no. 18), AIHW National Perinatal Statistics Unit, Sydney.

Le, A. T. and Miller, P. W. 2003. 'Choice of school in Australia: Determinants and consequences', *Australian Economic Review*, 36 (1): 55–78.

Leigh, A. 2010. 'Evidence-based policy: Summon the randomistas?', in Productivity Commission, *Strengthening Evidence Based Policy in the Australian Federation, Volume 1: Proceedings*, Roundtable Proceedings, Productivity Commission, 17–18 August 2009, Canberra.

Matthews, R., Jagger, C. and Hancock, R. 2006. 'Does socio-economic advantage lead to a longer, healthier old age?', *Social Science and Medicine*, 62 (10): 2489–99.

Memmott, P., Long, S. and Chambers, C. 2003. 'Categories of Indigenous 'homeless' people and good practice responses to their needs', *AHURI Positioning Paper No.53*, Australian Housing and Urban Research Institute, Melbourne.

Memmott, P., Moran, M., Birdsall-Jones, C., Fantin, S., Kreutz, A., Godwin, J., Burgess, A., Thomson, L. and Sheppard, L. 2009. 'Can home ownership work for Indigenous Australians living on communal title land?', *AHURI Research and Policy BulletinIssue 123*, Australian Housing and Urban Research Institute, Melbourne.

Morphy, F. 2006. 'Lost in translation? Remote Indigenous households and definitions of the family', *Family Matters*, 73: 23–31.

—— 2007. *Agency, Contingency and Census Process: Observations of the 2006 Indigenous Enumeration Strategy in Remote Aboriginal Australia*, CAEPR Research Monograph No. 28, ANU E Press, Canberra.

O'Rand, A. 1996. 'The precious and the precocious: Understanding Cumulative disadvantage and cumulative advantage over the life course', *The Gerontologist*, 36.(2,): 230–38

Parker, R. and Alexander, M. 2004. 'Factors influencing men's and women's decisions about having children', *Family Matters*, 69: 24–31.

Pearson, N. 2009. *Up From the Mission: Selected Writings*, Black Inc., Melbourne.

Pech, J. and McCoull, F. 1998. 'Transgenerational poverty and income support dependence in Australia: Work in progress', *Social Security Journal*, 2: 167–82.

Pholeros P., Rainow, S. and Torzillo, P. 1993. *Housing for Health: Towards a Healthy Living Environment for Aboriginal Australia*, Healthabitat, Newport Beach.

Prout, S. 2008. 'On the move? Indigenous temporary mobility practices in Australia', *CAEPR Working Paper No. 48*, CAEPR, ANU, Canberra.

Ryan, C. and Watson, L. 2004. 'The drift to private schools in Australia: Understanding its features', *CEPR Discussion Paper No. 479*, Centre for Ecnomic Policy Research, ANU, Canberra.

Sanders, W. G. 2005. 'Housing tenure and Indigenous Australians in remote and settled areas', *CAEPR Discussion Paper No. 275*, CAEPR, ANU, Canberra.

Schwab, J. and Liddle, L. 1997. 'Principles and implications of Aboriginal sharing', *CAEPR Issue Brief No. 17*, CAEPR, ANU, Canberra.

Schweinhart, L. J., Montie, J., Xiang, Z., Barnett, W. S., Belfield, C. R. and Nores, M. 2005. *Lifetime Effects: The HighScope Perry Preschool Study through Age 40*, HighScope Educational Research Foundation Monograph No. 14, HighScope Press, Ypsilanti, Michigan.

Steering Committee for the Review of Government Service Provision (SCRGSP) 2009. *Overcoming Indigenous Disadvantage: Key Indicators 2009*, Productivity Commission, Canberra.

Shields, M. and Wooden, M. 2003. 'Marriage, children and subjective wellbeing', Paper presented at the 8th Australian Institute of Family Studies Conference, Step Forward for Families: Research, Practice and Policy, 12–14 February 2003, Melbourne Exhibition Centre, viewed 11 May 2010, <http://www.melbourneinstitute.com/hilda/hbiblio-cp.html>.

Smith, D.E. and Roach, L.M. 1996. 'Indigenous voluntary work: NATSIS empirical evidence, policy relevance and future data issues', in J. C. Altman and J. Taylor (eds), *The 1994 National Aboriginal and Torres Strait Islander Survey: Findings and Future Prospects*, , CAEPR Research Monograph No. 11, CAEPR, ANU, Canberra.

Taylor, A. and Steinhauer, E. 2008. 'Factoring that affects the education and work transitions of First Nations youth', *Horizons*, 10 (1): 45–8.

Taylor, J. 2006. 'Population and diversity: Policy implications of emerging Indigenous demographic trends', *CAEPR Discussion Paper No. 283*, CAEPR, ANU, Canberra.

—— 2009. 'Indigenous demography and public policy in Australia: Population or peoples?', *Journal of Population Research*, 26 (2): 115–30.

—— 2010. 'Demography as destiny: Schooling, work and Aboriginal population change at Wadeye', *CAEPR Working Paper No. 64*, CAEPR, ANU, Canberra.

Thoits, P. A. and Hewitt, L.N. 2001. 'Volunteer work and wellbeing', *Journal of Health and Social Behavior*, 42 (2): 115–31.

Thomson, H., Petticrew, M. and Morrison, D. 2001. 'Health effects of housing improvement: Systematic review of intervention studies', *British Medical Journal*, 323: 187–90.

Tobias, J. L. 2003. 'Are returns to schooling concentrated among the most able? A semiparametric analysis of the ability–earnings relationships', *Oxford Bulletin of Economic and Statistics*, 65 (1), 1–29.

United Nations Children's Fund 2006. *The State of the World's Children 2007: Women and children—The double dividend of gender equality*, UNICEF, New York.

Universities Australia 2007. *Australian University Student Finances 2006: A Summary of Findings from a National Survey of Students in Public Universities*, viewed 11 May 2010, <http://www.universitiesaustralia.edu.au/documents/ publications/policy/survey/AUSF-Final-Report-2006.pdf>.

Wei, H. 2004. *Measuring the Stock of Human Capital for Australia*, cat. no. 1351.0.55.001, ABS, Canberra.

Weiss, Y. 1997. 'The formation and dissolution of families: Why marry? Who marries whom? And what happens upon divorce?', in M. R. Rosenzweig and O. Stark (eds), *Handbook of Population and Family Economics*, Elsevier Science, Amsterdam.

Wilkinson, R. and Marmot, M. 2003. *Social Determinants of Health: The Solid Facts*, 2nd edition, World Health Organization, Copenhagen.

Wolfe, B. and Haveman R. 2001. 'Accounting for the social and non-market benefits of education', in J. Helliwell (ed.), *The Contribution of Human and Social Capital to Sustained Economic Growth and Wellbeing*, University of British Columbia Press, Vancouver.

World Health Organization 1948. *Constitution of the World Health Organization*, viewed 11 May 2009, <www.searo.who.int/LinkFiles/About_SEARO_const. pdf>.

Yinger, J. 1986. 'Measuring racial discrimination with fair housing audits: Caught in the act', *The American Economic Review*, 76 (5): 881–93.

Zubrick, S. R., Silburn, S. R., de Maio, J. A., Shepherd, C., Griffin, J. A., Dalby, R. B., Mitrou, F. G., Lawrence, D. M., Hayward, C., Pearson, G., Milroy, H., Milroy, J. and Cox, A. 2006. *The Western Australian Aboriginal Child Health Survey: Improving the Educational Experiences of Aboriginal Children and Young People*, Curtin University of Technology and Telethon Institute for Child Health Research, Perth.

CAEPR Research Monograph Series

1. *Aborigines in the Economy: A Select Annotated Bibliography of Policy Relevant Research 1985–90*, L. M. Allen, J. C. Altman, and E. Owen (with assistance from W. S. Arthur), 1991.

2. *Aboriginal Employment Equity by the Year 2000*, J. C. Altman (ed.), published for the Academy of Social Sciences in Australia, 1991.

3. *A National Survey of Indigenous Australians: Options and Implications*, J. C. Altman (ed.), 1992.

4. *Indigenous Australians in the Economy: Abstracts of Research, 1991–92*, L. M. Roach and K. A. Probst, 1993.

5. *The Relative Economic Status of Indigenous Australians, 1986–91*, J. Taylor, 1993.

6. *Regional Change in the Economic Status of Indigenous Australians, 1986–91*, J. Taylor, 1993.

7. *Mabo and Native Title: Origins and Institutional Implications*, W. Sanders (ed.), 1994.

8. *The Housing Need of Indigenous Australians, 1991*, R. Jones, 1994.

9. *Indigenous Australians in the Economy: Abstracts of Research, 1993–94*, L. M. Roach and H. J. Bek, 1995.

10. *The Native Title Era: Emerging Issues for Research, Policy, and Practice*, J. Finlayson and D. E. Smith (eds), 1995.

11. *The 1994 National Aboriginal and Torres Strait Islander Survey: Findings and Future Prospects*, J. C. Altman and J. Taylor (eds), 1996.

12. *Fighting Over Country: Anthropological Perspectives*, D. E. Smith and J. Finlayson (eds), 1997.

13. *Connections in Native Title: Genealogies, Kinship, and Groups*, J. D. Finlayson, B. Rigsby, and H. J. Bek (eds), 1999.

14. *Land Rights at Risk? Evaluations of the Reeves Report*, J. C. Altman, F. Morphy, and T. Rowse (eds), 1999.

15. *Unemployment Payments, the Activity Test, and Indigenous Australians: Understanding Breach Rates*, W. Sanders, 1999.

16. *Why Only One in Three? The Complex Reasons for Low Indigenous School Retention*, R. G. Schwab, 1999.

17. *Indigenous Families and the Welfare System: Two Community Case Studies*, D. E. Smith (ed.), 2000.

18. *Ngukurr at the Millennium: A Baseline Profile for Social Impact Planning in South-East Arnhem Land*, J. Taylor, J. Bern, and K. A. Senior, 2000.

19. *Aboriginal Nutrition and the Nyirranggulung Health Strategy in Jawoyn Country*, J. Taylor and N. Westbury, 2000.

20. *The Indigenous Welfare Economy and the CDEP Scheme*, F. Morphy and W. Sanders (eds), 2001.

21. *Health Expenditure, Income and Health Status among Indigenous and Other Australians*, M. C. Gray, B. H. Hunter, and J. Taylor, 2002.

22. *Making Sense of the Census:Observations of the 2001 Enumeration in Remote Aboriginal Australia*, D. F. Martin, F. Morphy, W. G. Sanders and J. Taylor, 2002.

23. *Aboriginal Population Profiles for Development Planning in the Northern East Kimberley*, J. Taylor, 2003.

24. *Social Indicators for Aboriginal Governance: Insights from the Thamarrurr Region, Northern Territory*, J. Taylor, 2004.

25. *Indigenous People and the Pilbara Mining Boom: A Baseline for Regional Participation*, J. Taylor and B. Scambary, 2005.

26. *Assessing the Evidence on Indigenous Socioeconomic Outcomes: A Focus on the 2002 NATSISS*, B. H. Hunter (ed.), 2006.

27. *The Social Effects of Native Title: Recognition, Translation, Coexistence*, B. R. Smith and F. Morphy (eds), 2007.

28. *Agency, Contingency and Census Process: Observations of the 2006 Indigenous Enumeration Strategy in remote Aboriginal Australia*, F. Morphy (ed.), 2008.

29. *Contested Governance: Culture, Power and Institutions in Indigenous Australia*, Janet Hunt, Diane Smith, Stephanie Garling and Will Sanders (eds), 2008.

30. *Power, Culture, Economy: Indigenous Australians and Mining*, Jon Altman and David Martin (eds), 2009.

For information on CAEPR Discussion Papers, Working Papers and Research Monographs (Nos 1-19) please contact:

> Publication Sales, Centre for Aboriginal Economic Policy Research,
> College of Arts and Social Sciences,
> The Australian National University, Canberra, ACT, 0200
>
> Telephone: 02–6125 8211
> Facsimile: 02–6125 2789

Information on CAEPR abstracts and summaries of all CAEPR print publications and those published electronically can be found at the following WWW address: http://caepr.anu.edu.au

www.ingramcontent.com/pod-product-compliance
Lightning Source LLC
Chambersburg PA
CBHW061245270326
41928CB00041B/3433